BRITAIN IN OLD PHOTOGRAPHS

SHREWSBURY
REVISITED

DAVID TRUMPER & DAVID WOODHOUSE

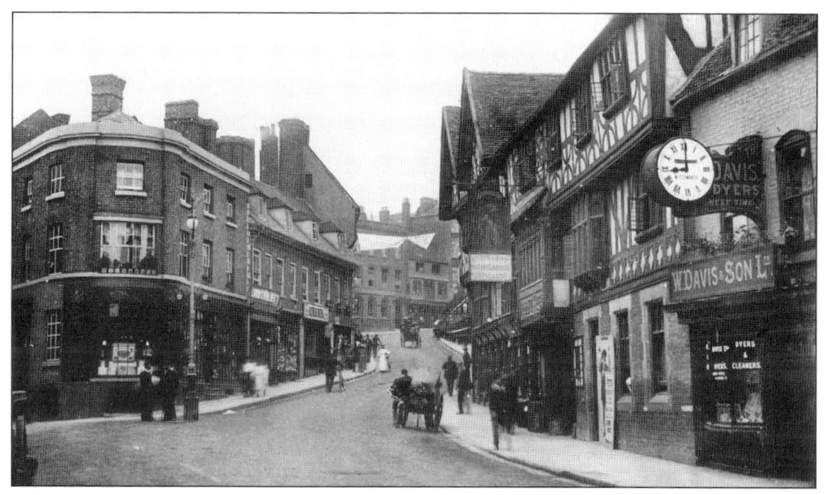

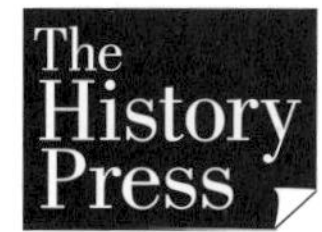

To Jean
For forty-eight years

For my grandchildren Sam and Alice Radford
For all the pleasure they give their Nanny and Grandad

Title page: Wyle Cop, *c.* 1910. W. Davis & Son Ltd were dyers and cleaners who were eventually taken over by Johnson Brothers. The shop once housed a watch and clockmakers business occupied first by Andrew Gottlieb (whose name has been blacked out on the clock over the door) and then by Herbert Henry Powell. The Unicorn Hotel to the left was first licensed in the eighteenth century. Opposite, on the corner of Beeches Lane and the Cop, is the confectionery shop belonging to Thomas Pidduck Deakin. He moved there from Market Street in the 1870s, selling the business to Morris & Co. in 1910.

Opposite, below Contents: Smithfield Road, *c.* 1938. The road, which was laid out in about 1835, follows the line of the river and links Mardol Quay to Chester Street. During the construction, part of the town wall known as Roushill Walls had to be demolished but a section remains in Meadow Place. The cattle market was opened in Raven Meadow in November 1850 and Smithfield Road appears as a name for the first time in 1856. At that time it was the first and only road within the loop of the river. In about 1938 the road was widened by building an extension on concrete piers over the river. The whole road surface was then relaid. Here we see council workers breaking up the old surface before the days of the pneumatic drill. The man on the right is Wallace Steventon, a well-known Frankwell character, known locally as 'Gudgeon'.

First published 2011

The History Press
The Mill, Brimscombe Port
Stroud, Gloucestershire, GL5 2QG
www.thehistorypress.co.uk

British Library Cataloguing in Publication Data.
A catalogue record for this book is available from the British Library.

ISBN 978 0 7524 5293 7

Typesetting and origination by The History Press
Printed in Great Britain

Manufacturing managed by Jellyfish Print Solutions Ltd

CONTENTS

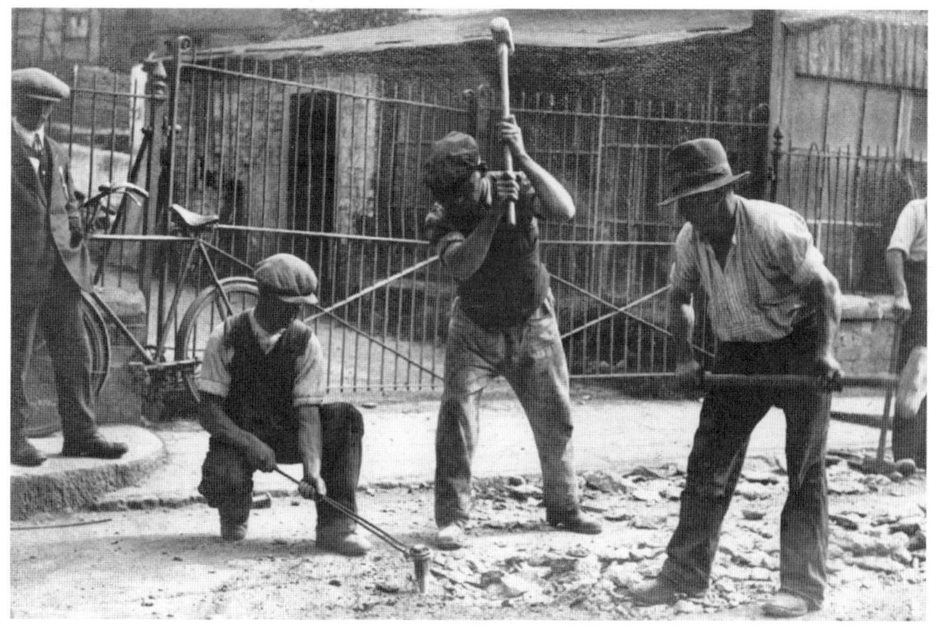

INTRODUCTION

Shrewsbury Revisited features over 200 postcards from the vast collection of David Woodhouse, depicting the town from late Victorian times to the middle of the twentieth century. The postcard was once the e-mail of its time, taking messages across town in just a few hours. In 1900 there were four postal deliveries in Shrewsbury – at 7 a.m., 11.10 a.m., 1.45 p.m. and 6.30 p.m. – and constant collections from forty-four post-boxes, which meant rapid communication with family and friends within the boundaries of the town. Thousands of postcards were published by a number of companies showing the gems of the town such as The Square and the wealth of timber-framed buildings; but it was the local firms such as Wilding & Son, Chic Studios, James Mallinson and Richard Mansell who published the most obscure and interesting scenes.

Local family businesses also published trade cards showing their shop fronts, giving us an insight into the trade and commerce taking place at this time. Until the 1930s Shrewsbury was confined within a much smaller area with Harlescott and Meole Village outside the town's boundary. The

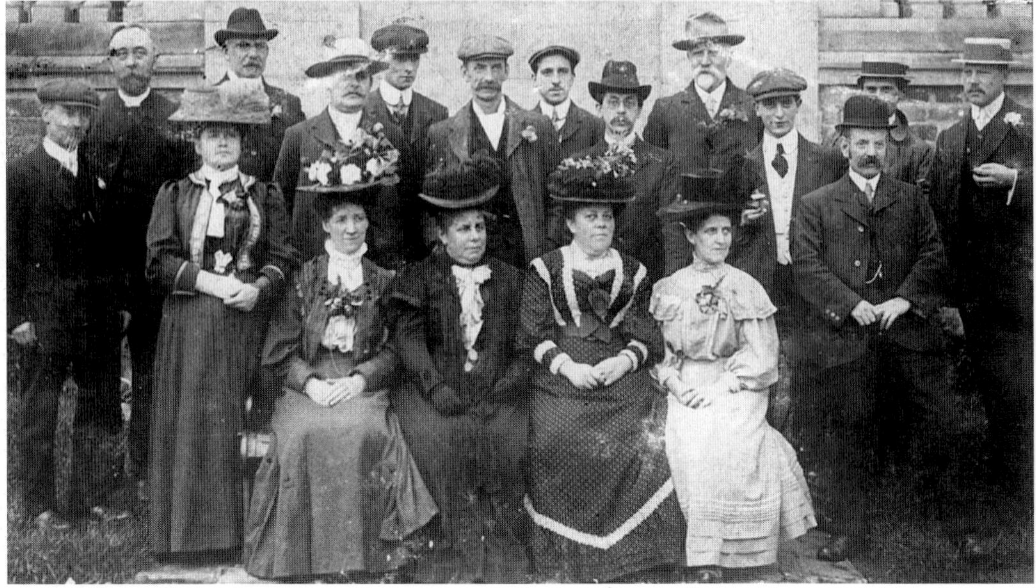

St Chad's Terrace, summer 1906. A group of dignitaries pose in front of the new wall. In the Flower Show edition of the *Chronicle* in August 1906 the paper praises the Shropshire Horticultural Society for their generosity to the town. They write, 'Another of the Society's works, newly completed and not yet formally dedicated is the substitution of handsome stonework for the unlovely brick wall which formally bounded the Quarry from St Chad's Terrace.' A simple inscription carved on both sides of the wall reads, 'This Balustrade Was Erected By The Shropshire Horticultural Society 1906'.

1891 Census lists the number of people living in Shrewsbury as 26,967 but by 1931 the population had grown to 36,732 – a rise of nearly 10,000. In *Shrewsbury Illustrated*, the official guide of the Shrewsbury Corporation printed by Wilding & Son in 1921, modern Shrewsbury was described as:

> Charming in its environment, undisturbed by the turmoil which characterises industrial centres, and unpolluted by the smoke of manufactories, Shrewsbury is naturally a desirable place of residence and in this connection it appeals to distinct classes of the community: to retired people of means seeking quietude and pleasant surroundings; to those who require special educational facilities for their children and wish to be in residence with them; and to professional and business men to whom a convenient railway centre is an indispensable condition. These requirements Shrewsbury fulfils, possessing as it does fine healthy suburbs south, east and west of the town; numerous beautifully situated and well managed schools, both public and private; and a quick train service. Shrewsbury is the centre of a thriving community, chiefly concerned in agriculture, and although attractive to strangers principally on account of its proud history and antiquities, it must by no means be concluded that its inhabitants are unprogressive. On the contrary, its public buildings and institutions are adequate to the requirements of the town, and proof of the enterprise of the trading community is forthcoming in the numerous handsome shops in the principal streets. Of late years many business premises have been improved and enlarged, and fine modern fronts substituted for the narrow windows previously in vogue, the former contrasting somewhat curiously with the hoary half-timbered buildings beloved by Salopians and universally admired. With regard to modern improvements those responsible for local government have shown foresight and enterprise. The Corporation own the Water Works, and

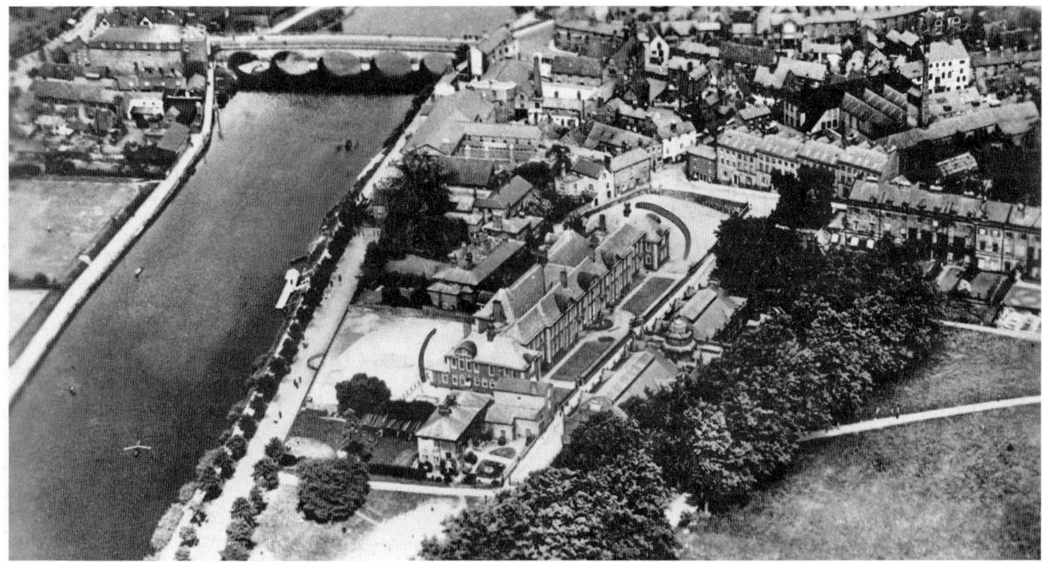

The River Severn, *c.* 1918. The Welsh Bridge straddles the Severn between Frankwell on the left and the town on the right. The bridge was built by John Carline and John Tilley in 1795 and cost £8,000. The builders were also responsible for Claremont Buildings on the far right, which date from 1794. The large building in the centre is the Priory Grammar School, built in the Queen Anne Revival style and opened in 1911. It catered for boys and girls, who were closely segregated, until the girls moved to a new school on Longden Road in 1939. Across the road and partially hidden by the old lime trees in The Quarry are the Jubilee Baths, opened in 1893 to commemorate Queen Victoria's Golden Jubilee in 1887.

> also the Electric Light Works, from which the town is thoroughly well illuminated; a comprehensive and costly sewage scheme has been completed within comparatively recent years, the undertaking involving the laying of an entirely new system of mains, the construction of a pumping station, and the establishment of a large sewage farm some distance from the town. The present supply of pure, clear and palatable drinking water has recently been improved.

At this period Shrewsbury was the largest town in Shropshire, a thriving market town and the hub of a large hinterland of trade and commerce that stretched into Mid-Wales. On market days the town was crowded with shoppers and the sound of the Welsh language was common. The town had two large departmental stores – Maddox and Della Porta – and the main streets of the town were packed with a variety of shops selling an array of items. On Pride Hill in 1921 there were forty-six businesses ranging from banking to basket-making and groceries to ironmongery. As well as the Lion Hotel there was also the Raven, the Crown and the George hotels to cater for the visitor and commercial traveller. In Barker Street there was a large tannery belonging to John Cock. In the 1920s their advert summed up the town at this time: 'Shrewsbury is a fine old town, No matter what the weather, But should the rain come pouring down, Be sure to wear Cock's leather.'

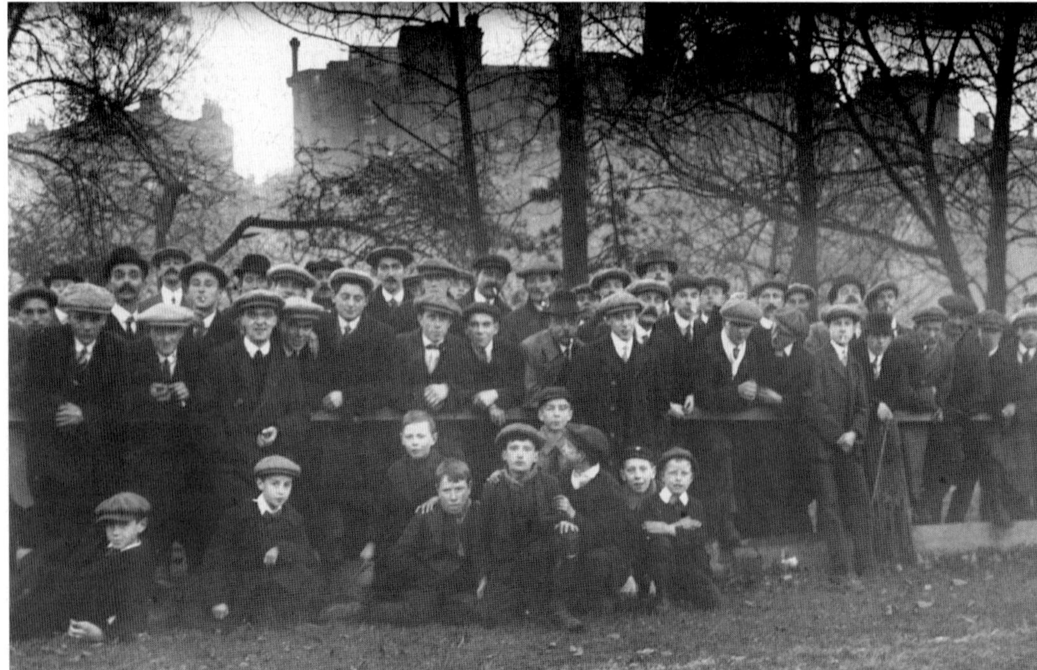

Abbey Foregate, *c.* 1914. Shrewsbury Town Football Club moved to this site in the autumn of 1910 from a pitch opposite the Barracks in Copthorne. The crowd are standing on the river side of the pitch before the stand was built. The large building in the background is the Royal Salop Infirmary. The 'Royal' part of the title was conferred on the hospital during King George V's visit to the town in 1914. Although many people welcomed the football club's move from Copthorne, the hospital authorities objected as they thought the cheering from the crowd would disturb some of their sick patients. However, many of the male patients enjoyed the Saturday afternoon matches although after the riverside stand was completed they could only see the far side of the pitch from the balcony.

1

WITHIN THE LOOP OF THE SEVERN

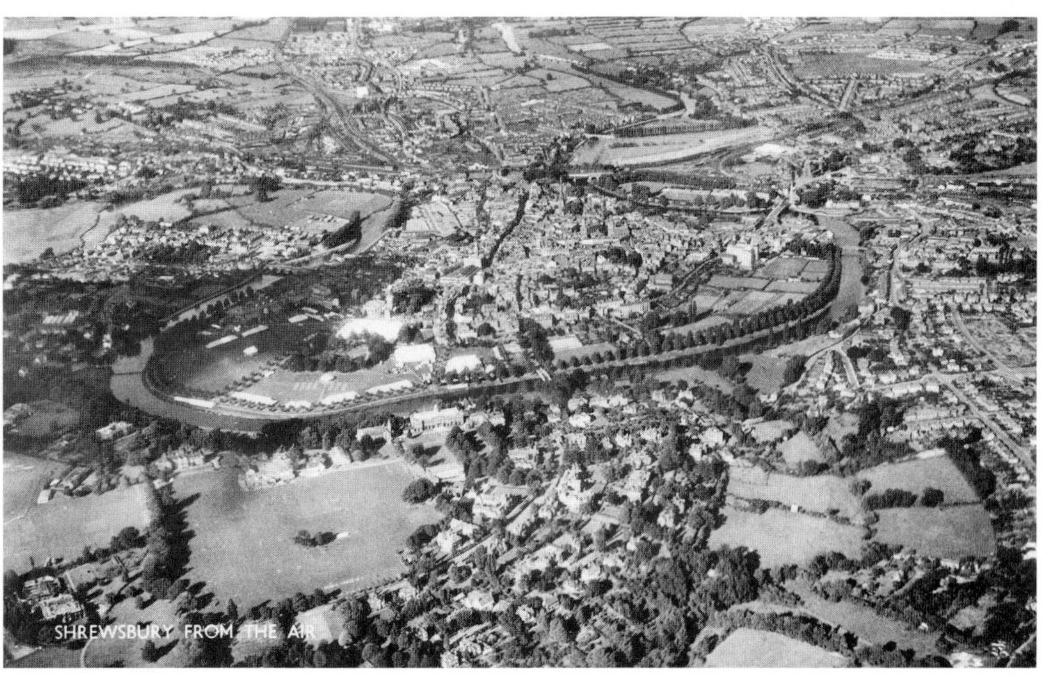

Shrewsbury, *c.* 1950. This view was taken from the south and shows the town centre almost completely encircled by the River Severn. The suburbs are clustered on the opposite bank of the river except for Castle Foregate and Coton Hill that were built on the only land route into Shrewsbury. The leafy suburb of Kingsland with Shrewsbury School is in the foreground; Frankwell lies to the west on the left; Coton Hill and Castle Foregate leading north to Harlescott are at the top and Abbey Foregate and Monkmoor lie to the east (top right) and Coleham and Belle Vue to the south (bottom right).

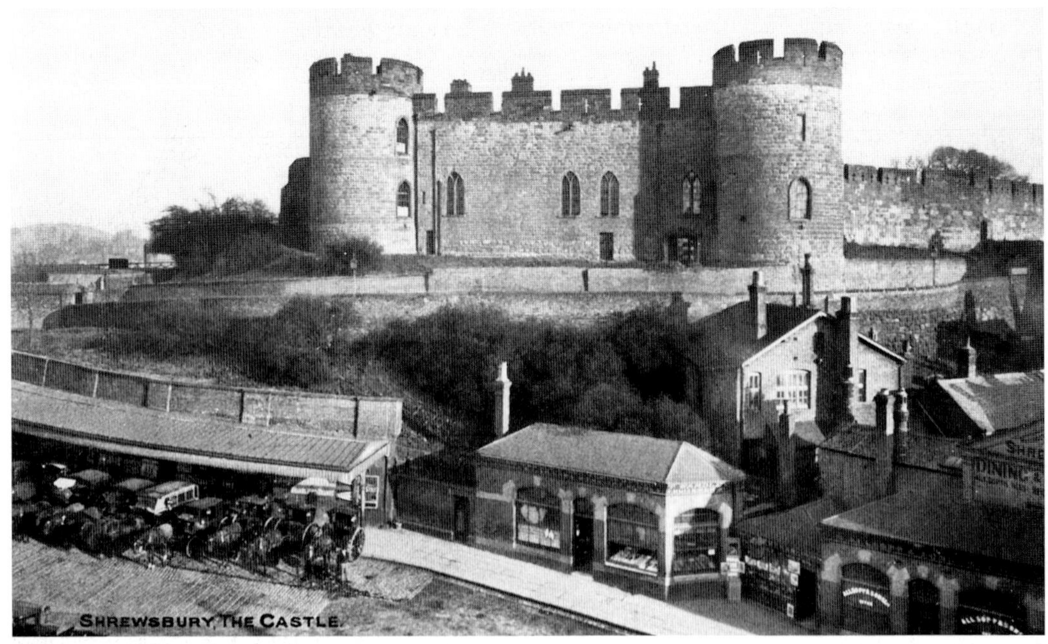

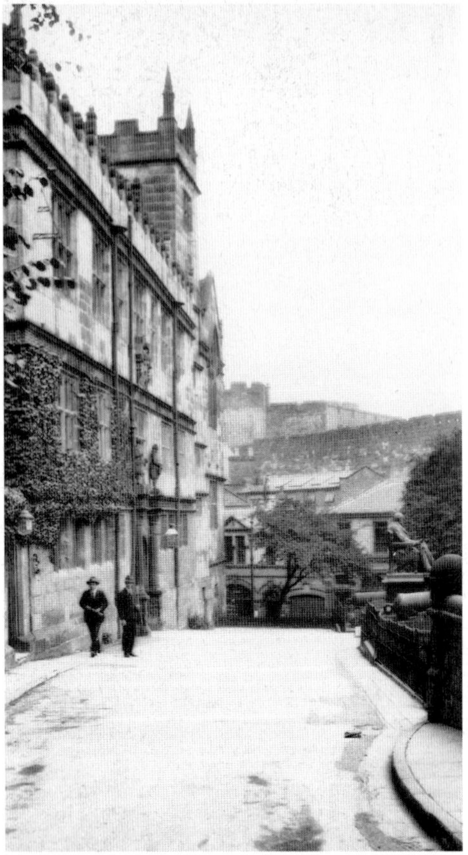

Shrewsbury Castle, Castle Gates, *c.* 1899. The castle was built to protect the only land route into the town. Thomas Telford converted it into a home for William Pulteney and it was occupied until 1926 when it was changed into a council chamber. In 1985 it became the home of a museum dedicated to the Shropshire Regiments, brought together by Geoffrey Archer Parfitt. The hansom cabs and horse-drawn omnibuses wait on the forecourt of the railway station. Soon after this view was taken, the forecourt was lowered leaving the buildings to the right on a narrow pathway. The building on the left was occupied by Thomas Wardle, a fish and game dealer, in the middle was William Tudman a tobacconist who also had a shop on Wyle Cop and to the right were brewers Allsop & Sons.

The Library, Castle Street, *c.* 1930. Shrewsbury School was founded on this site in 1552. The present building built out of Grinshill stone was erected between 1595 and 1630. The school moved to new premises on Kingsland in 1882. The buildings were purchased by the borough in 1884 for £4,000 and converted into a public lending library, reading room, reference library and museum. The bronze statue seated on the plinth represents the school's most famous pupil, Charles Darwin. It was presented to the town by the Shropshire Horticultural Society in 1897 and cost £1,086 9*s* 3*d*. Note the cannon on either side of the statue.

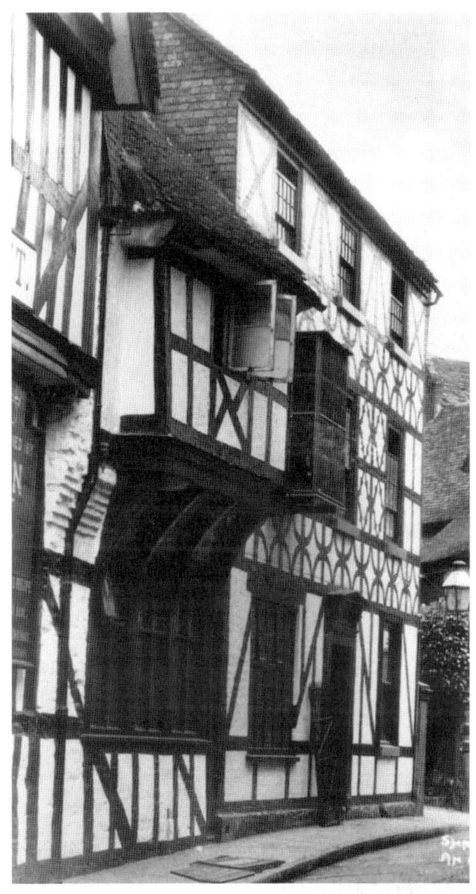

School Gardens, *c.* 1935. Until the sixteenth century this thoroughfare was known as Rotten Row or Lane that led from Castle Street to Castle Gates. After the founding of Shrewsbury School in 1552 the name was changed first to School House Lane, then to School Lane in 1752 and finally to School Gardens in 1936. The lane was turned into a cul-de-sac in about 1825 when the Castle Gates entrance was closed. The timber-framed building is the side of Plimmer's shop and restaurant. Some of the timber-framing is authentic but some has been painted on a brick surface. The gateway on the right by the gas lamp leads into Sidney Court, named after Sir Philip Sidney, a former pupil at the school. It was once known as Gaol Yard from the old county gaol that stood close by.

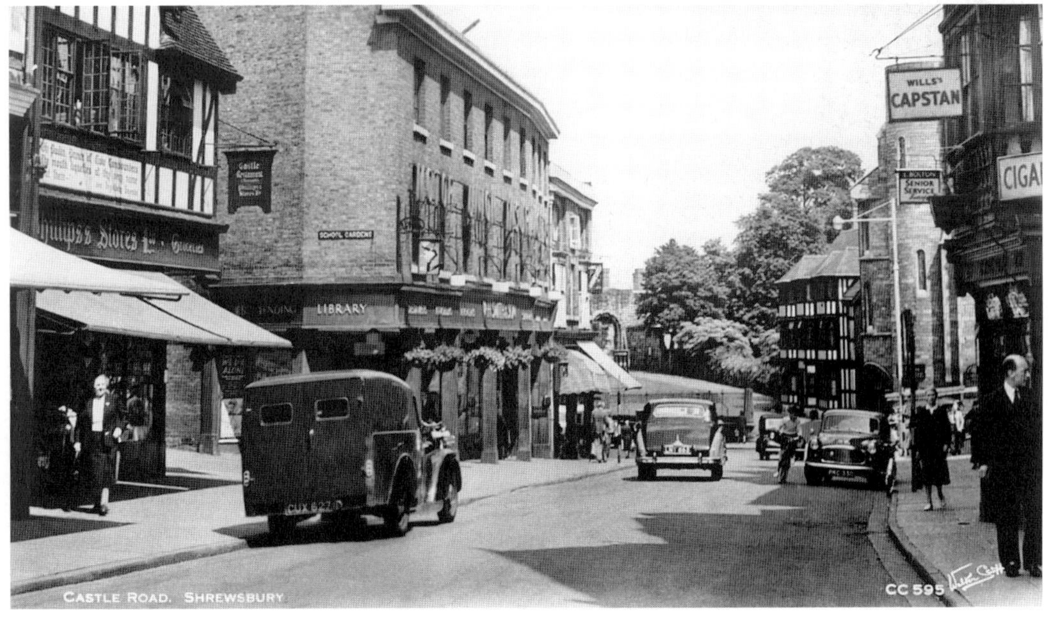

Castle Street, *c.* 1950. The shop on the left housed one of Phillip's stores. It was once Palin's cake shop, where the famous Shrewsbury cake was made. The legend under the window reads, 'Oh Palin, Prince of Cake Compounders. The Mouth Liquefies at thy very name'. It was later occupied by Thomas Plimmer as a cake shop and restaurant. W.H. Smith opened a stall at the railway station in 1866 but it was another forty years before they moved into these premises. In 1938 they purchased the shop next door and were able to put in the arcaded frontage. On the right is Eric Bolton's tobacconist's shop, St Nicholas' Presbyterian Church and Castle Gates House that stood on the site of the present Newport House on Dogpole until about 1700.

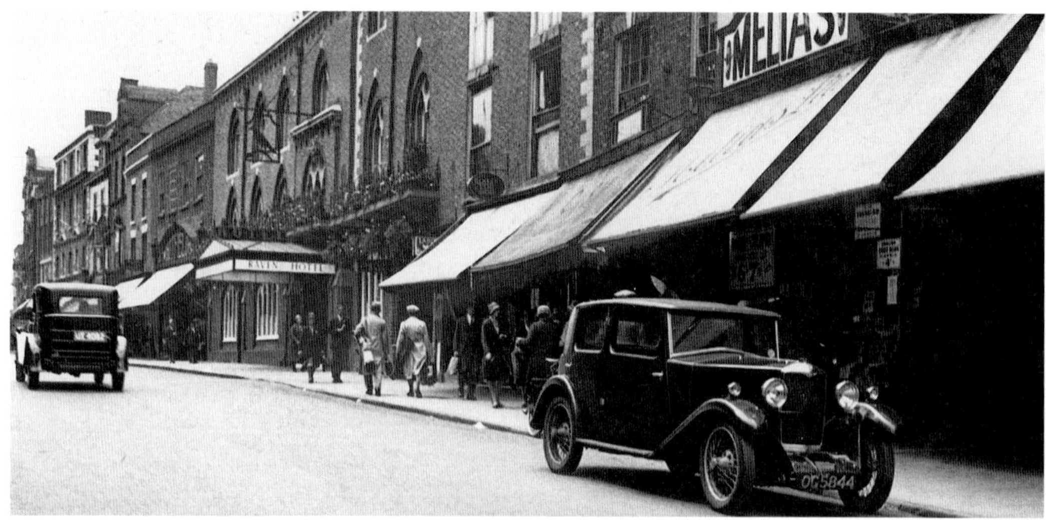

Castle Street, *c.* 1935. Just left of centre is the Raven Hotel with its marvellous canopy stretching out over the pavement. The hotel was there for about 400 years until the site was redeveloped as a Woolworths store. The car on the right is parked outside Melias, one of several grocery shops in the town centre. To the left is the shop belonging to V.C. Smith who was a hunting, saddlery and horse-clothing manufacturer, who made a lot of goods on the premises. He also repaired and restrung tennis racquets. Between Smith's and the Raven was John Cleland & Son, the boot and shoe shop. Above the hotel is Whitfield's ladies shop and Frank Newton's men's shop with their large top hat just visible between the first and second floor.

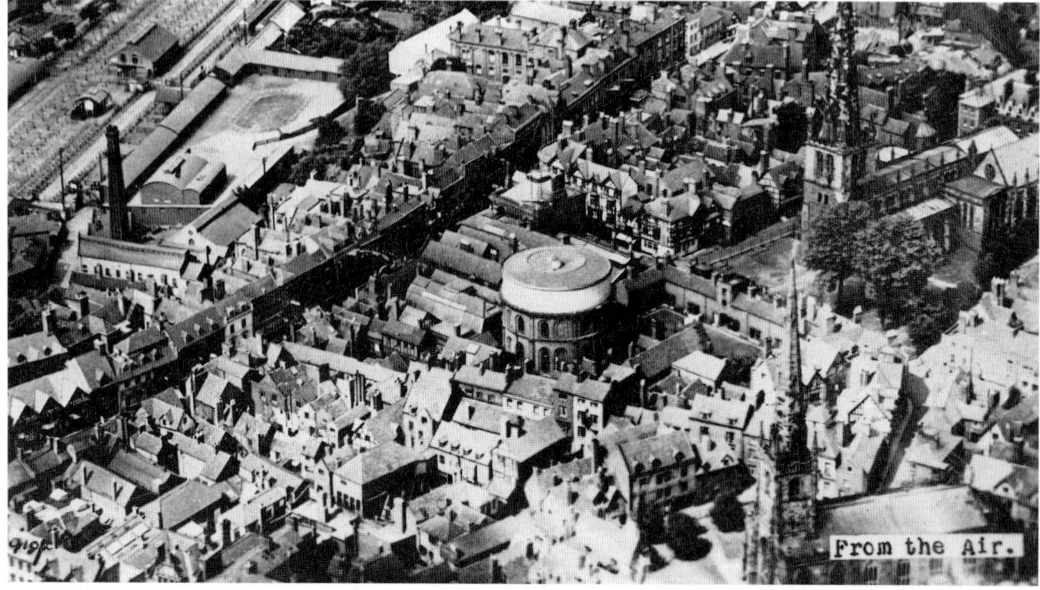

Shrewsbury, 1918. The photograph may have been taken by the Observer School of Reconnaissance and Aerial Photography based at Monkmoor aerodrome. The round building is the water tower that supplied the town until July 1935 when the new water works was opened at Shelton. To the right are the rear of the Draper's Almshouses on St Mary's Street and the spires of St Mary's and St Alkmund's churches. On the left are Pride Hill and Castle Street, the cattle market and horse ring and the Raven Hotel is at the top, centre.

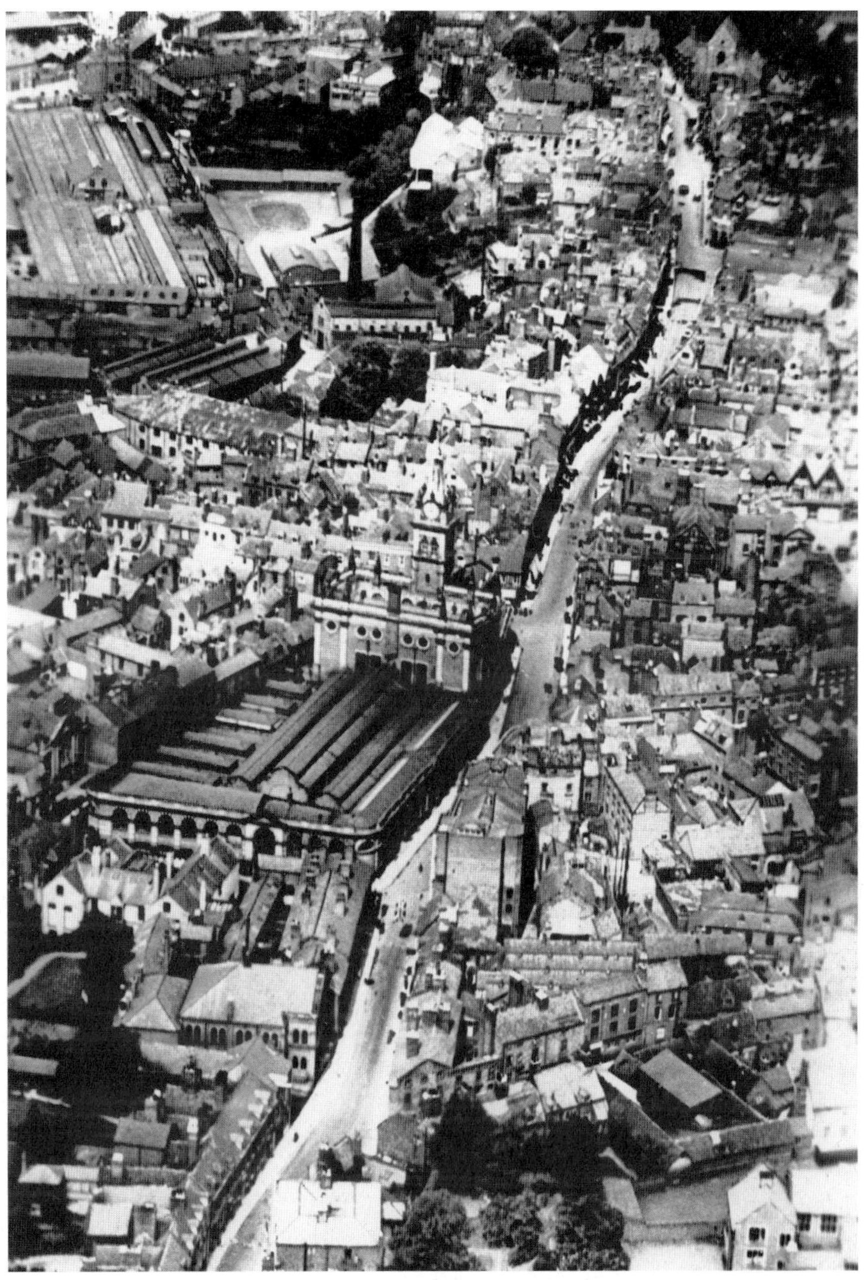

Shrewsbury *c.* 1918. The long road that cuts through the town centre is made up of several streets. The bottom section is St John's Hill, once known as Swine Market Hill as pigs were sold there in the eighteenth century. The Methodist Church is just above the cottages on the left and the site was first developed in 1805 and the church rebuilt in 1879. The whole of the left side of Shoplatch is taken up by the Market Hall. The name is derived from the place where the Schutte family lived. Next is Mardol Head leading on to Pride Hill, named after the family who owned a house and shops there. Beyond is Castle Street, which has also been known as High Pavement and Raven Street.

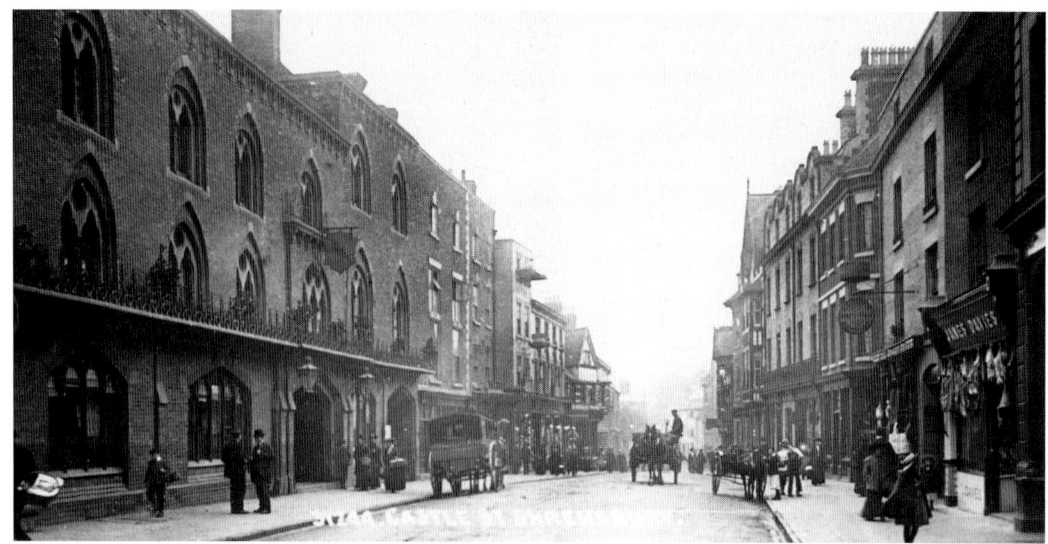

Castle Street, *c.* 1910. In 1894 the Raven on the left was described as 'a fine old fashioned country and family hotel. It contains every accommodation for families and tourists, and there is a table d'hote daily at 7 o'clock, at separate tables. There is also a fine billiard room in the hotel, and the Raven stables will be found to afford all the facilities of a 1st class posting establishment.' Note there is no canopy over the front door. Opposite, meat can be seen hanging outside James Davies' butcher's shop and just beyond is the sign for a provisions shop belonging to John Goodwin.

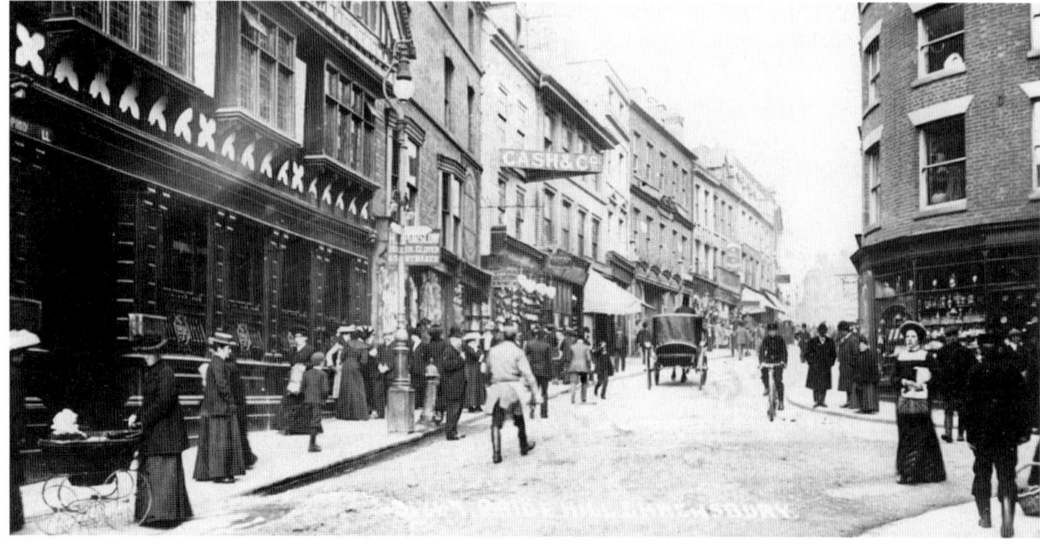

Pride Hill, *c.* 1900. This is a late Victorian view of Shrewsbury's main shopping thoroughfare; note the carriage, the telegraph boy on his bicycle and the farmer striding purposely about his business. On the left is Lloyd's Bank which moved to these premises in about 1876. Moving up the hill there is Purslow's hosiery and boot store, Noblett's sweet shop and Leopard's Shut, named after a public house that stood on the corner until 1883. Then there is Cash and Co. (a boot and shoe manufacturer) and Bythell's Passage, the Home & Colonial grocery store, a hosiery shop run by Jonathan Colman, W.F. Watkins (a tailor) and Martin, Ballinger & Co. (drapers). Within a few years Martin and Ballinger's shop would be transformed into a new Boots store.

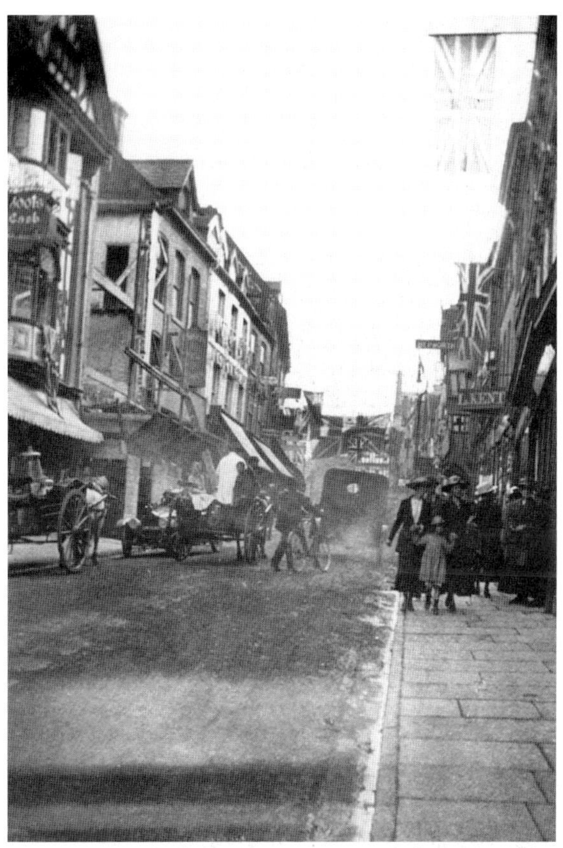

Pride Hill, *c.* 1920. This view, taken soon after the First World War, shows two cars and the new Boots Cash Store on the left. The site under construction next door was once occupied by Lipton's grocery store until about 1920 when Boots added an extension to their shop. Just above is the Beaconsfield Club and Hunters the Teamen Ltd. Opposite are the signs for Hepworth the tailor and Leonard Kent's jewellery shop. The ladies and the little girl are walking past Maddox's store that extended round into High Street.

Pride Hill, *c.* 1935. The sun blinds are all extended in front of the shops on the sunny south side of Pride Hill. The magnificent market clock tower dominates the skyline. William Joyce of Whitchurch provided the clock and one of its four faces was always visible wherever you were in town. Note there are no double yellow lines or any other parking restrictions on the road and the street is open to two-way traffic at this time. The first two shops on the right belong to Masters & Co. and E.F. Afford who were both gentlemen's outfitters. Further down the bank are signs for hairdresser Percy Shaw and opticians Hudson Verity.

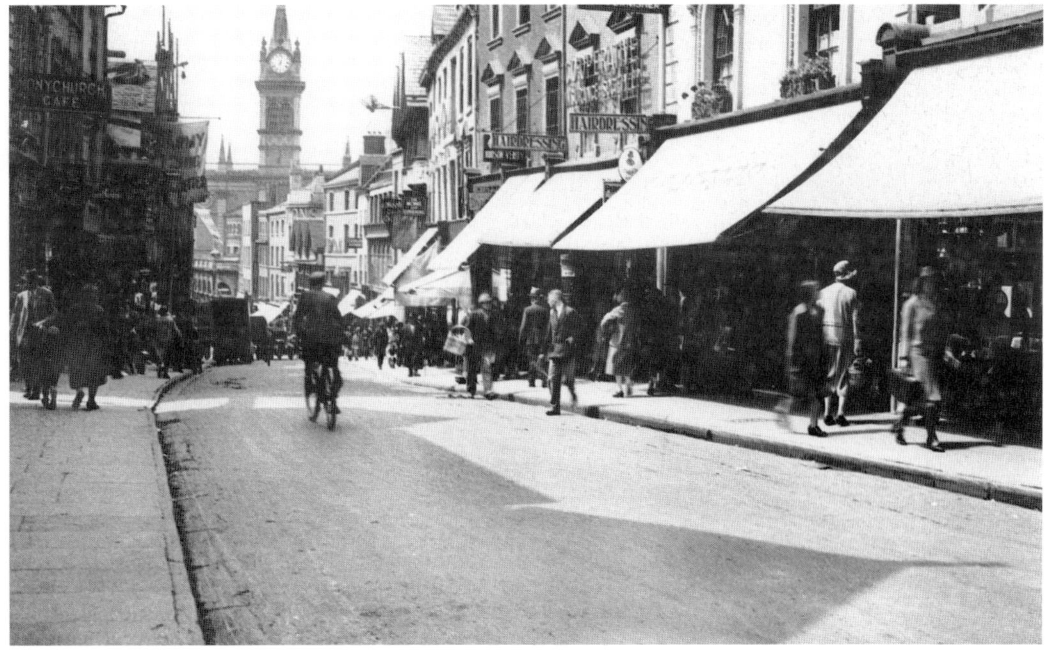

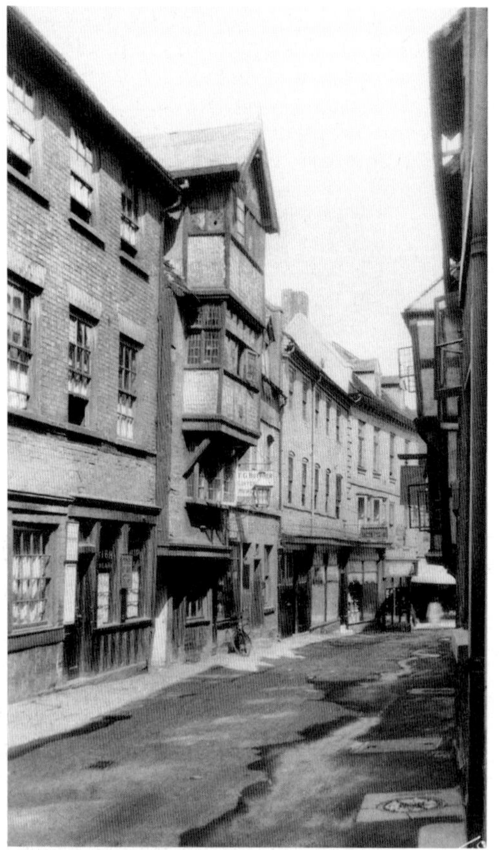

Butcher Row, *c.* 1935. This view is looking down towards Pride Hill. Note the timber-framed building on the left, which was demolished before 1939, with some adjoining property below, to form a goods entrance and warehouse for Maddox's store. The first business on the left was a fish and chip shop belonging to Mrs Annie Evans. As well as fish and chips, she also sold peas and eels. In between the windows is a poster advertising *Jack's the Boy*, a film starring Jack Hulbert and Cicely Courtneidge, being shown at the King's Hall at the bottom of the Wyle Cop. The bicycle is outside a tea and coffee shop belonging to Thomas Butcher, while on the corner of Pride Hill is Harold Honeychurch's café.

Butcher Row, *c.* 1910. The building on the left with its medieval shop fronts is the Abbott's House, built in the fifteenth century. It part housed the business of Jones and Son, builders, who were established in 1837. They were also listed as joiners, coffin-makers and undertakers. Just below is the sign of Sidney Leigh Squires, a house agent who lived in West Hermitage, Belle Vue. On the right is the Bull Inn which was owned and run by George Edwards from about 1880 until 1930. The inn is mentioned in St Alkmund's parish register in 1624. The timber-framed building on the right is known as Greyhound Chambers, named after the Greyhound Inn that stood on the corner of Pride Hill.

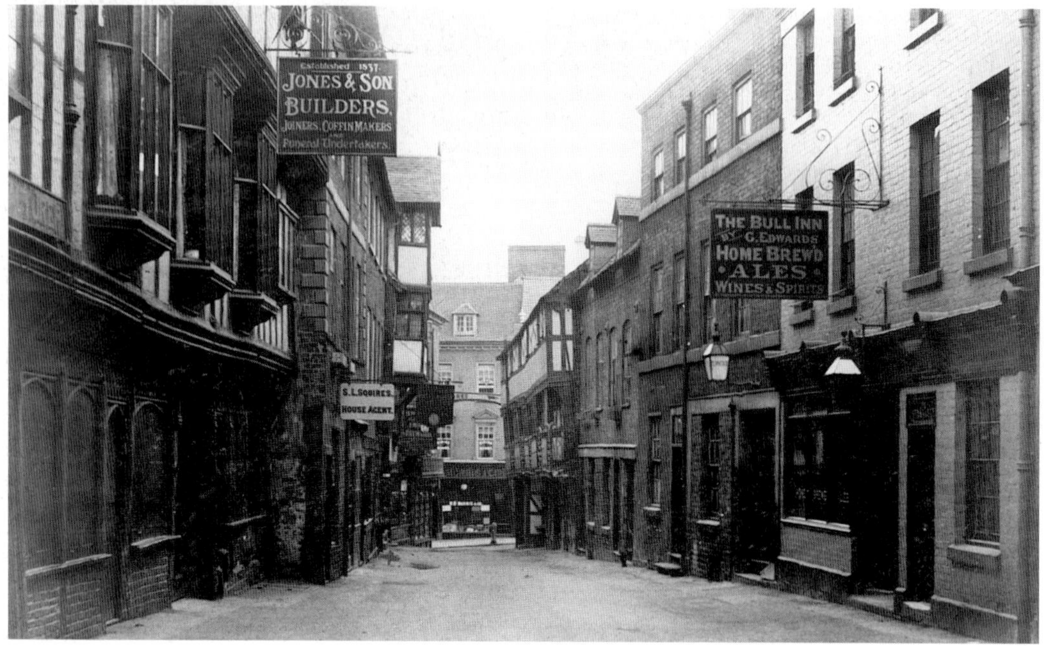

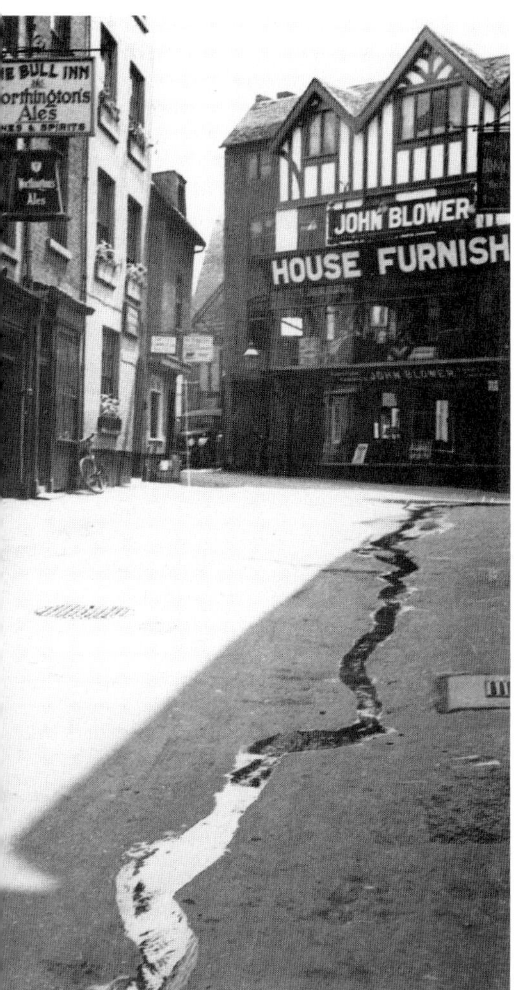

Left: Butcher Row, *c.* 1935. George Edwards had left the Bull and Worthington's ales were sold there instead of the home-brewed beer by the time this photograph was taken. Shortly after this image was captured, John Blower closed his shop and the buildings were later demolished leaving a large hole there for several years. The buildings above the Bull were Mansfield's butcher's shop, Smith's Commercial Hotel and a dairy run by John Barton. The Commercial Hotel was once an inn known as the Cock and was licensed from the early seventeenth century until the middle of the nineteenth century.

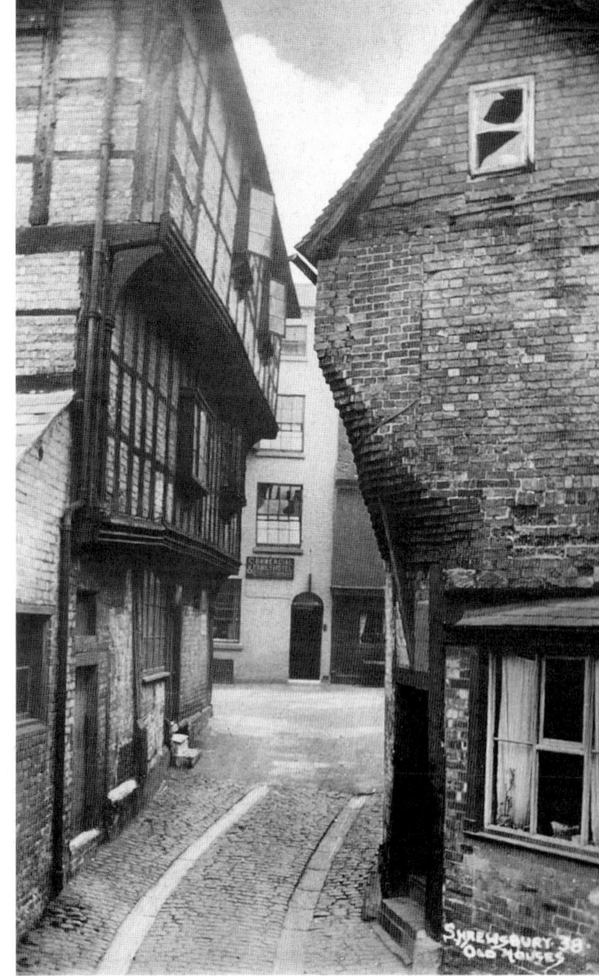

Right: Fish Street, *c.* 1925. This was the view out of Fish Street to the top of Butcher Row. The timber-framed building is the side of the Abbot's House, said to have been built as a residence for the Abbot of Lilleshall but more likely as a commercial enterprise. The sign under the window of the house in Butcher Row reads, 'Commercial & Family Hotel. Cyclist's House'. It was once an inn and was sold at an auction at the Raven and Bell in February 1806. It was advertised as 'All that well accustomed public house known by the sign of the Cock situated in Butcher Row, now in the occupation of Mr Tristram also a dwelling house adjoining and a malt house near to.' Note the fancy brickwork that covers up a timber-framed building and the door and window of a tiny cottage.

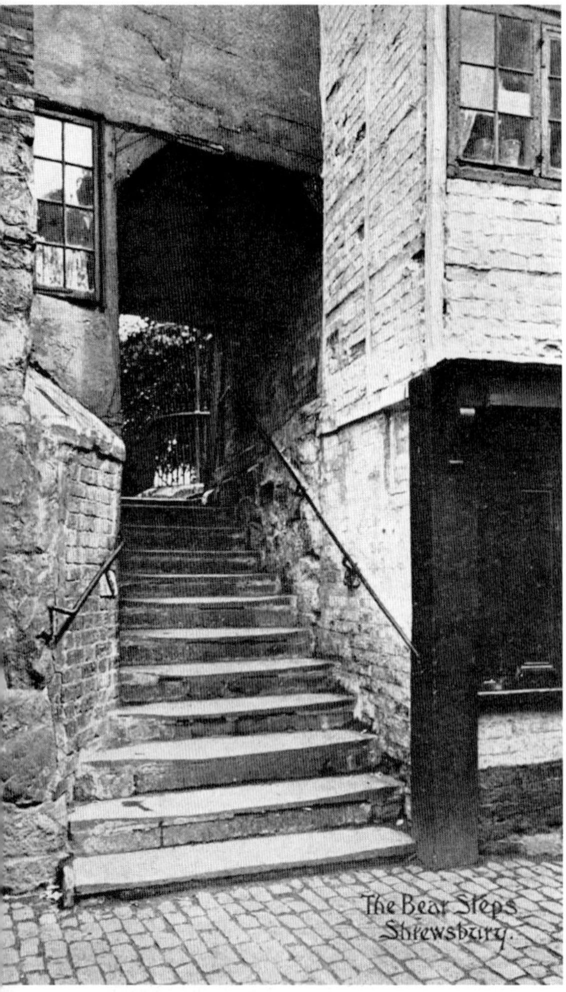

Left: Fish Street, *c.* 1920. The Bear Steps lead up from Fish Street into St Alkmund's churchyard and lie at the very heart of medieval Shrewsbury. The steps take their name from the Bear Inn that stood opposite on the corner of Fish Street and Grope Lane between 1780 and 1910 and has nothing to do with bear-baiting as is often assumed. The steps run through an ancient complex of buildings that are also known as the Bear Steps. The buildings to the left date from the late sixteenth century while the building to the right called the 'Orrel' is early seventeenth-century. Note the timber-framing on the right has been filled in with brick and by the 1960s the whole complex had become very dilapidated and was in danger of demolition. It was rescued and restored in 1968 by the Civic Society.

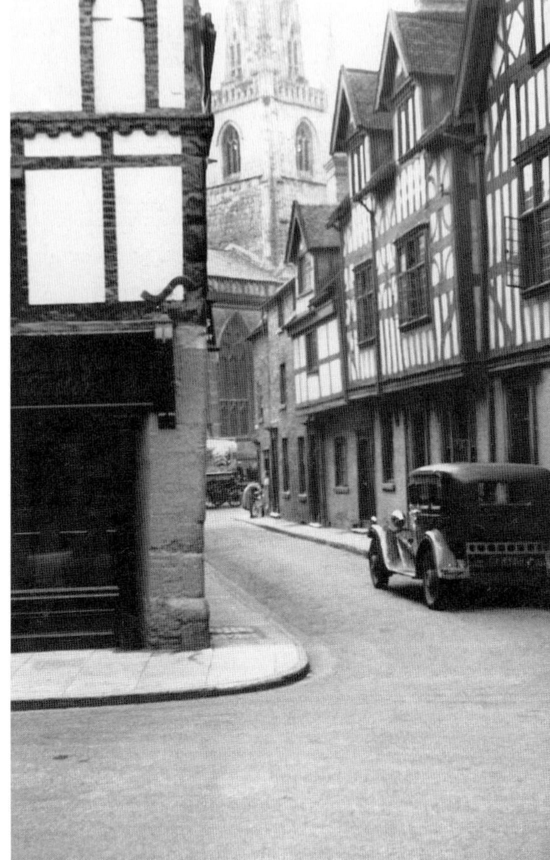

Right: Church Street, *c.* 1935. The street takes its name from St Alkmund's Church seen at the bottom. The origins of the church are Saxon but it was completely rebuilt with the exception of the tower and spire between 1794 and 1795. The timber-framed building is part of Jones' Mansion built by Thomas Jones, a draper, in the seventeenth century. He was bailiff of the town on six separate occasions and he became Shrewsbury's first mayor in 1638. By the end of the nineteenth century the mansion had been divided into five houses. The old building had a new lease of life in the 1950s when it became a hotel, named after Prince Rupert, a nephew of Charles I who lodged there during the Civil War.

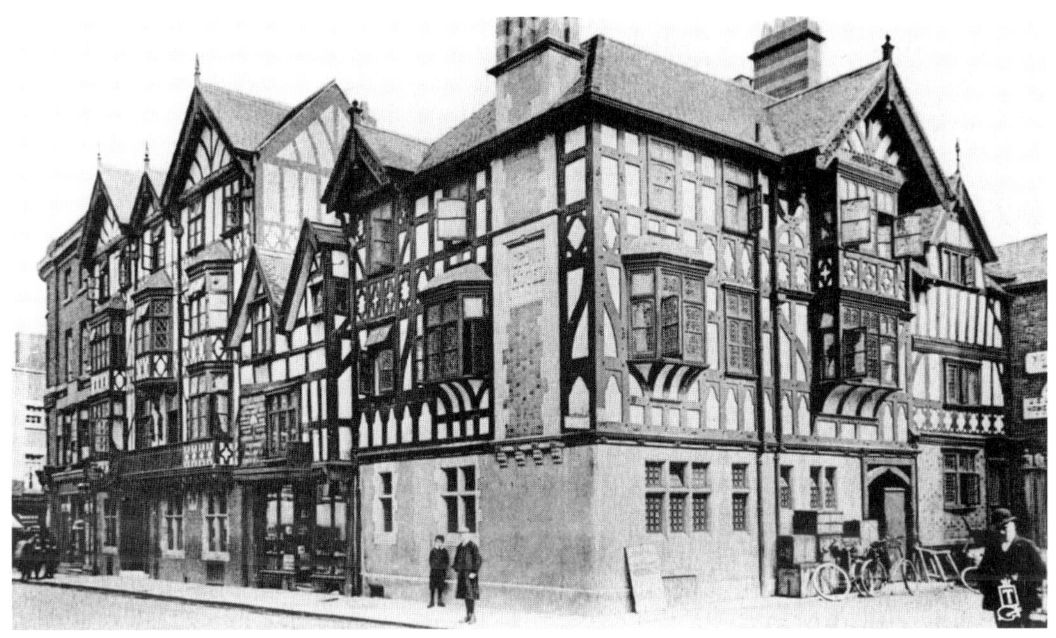

St Mary's Street, *c.* 1901. The Crown Hotel was erected on the site of another hotel that was housed in an old Georgian building. It was built in a U-shape around an original timber-framed building by the Church Stretton Hotel Co. and was opened in August 1901. On the left between the bank and the hotel was a confectionery shop run by Vincent Crump. It was bought by the hotel owners who erected a timber-framed extension there. The new extension contained a billiard room with two tables, which was opened by Mayor Thomas Corbett on 1 July 1907. For many years the small timber-framed building was the home of J.W. Roberts, a fishing tackle- and umbrella-maker who established the business in 1864. He also sold balloons and fireworks. The business was taken over by Harold Hammond until about 1926 when the building was demolished and the site incorporated into the hotel.

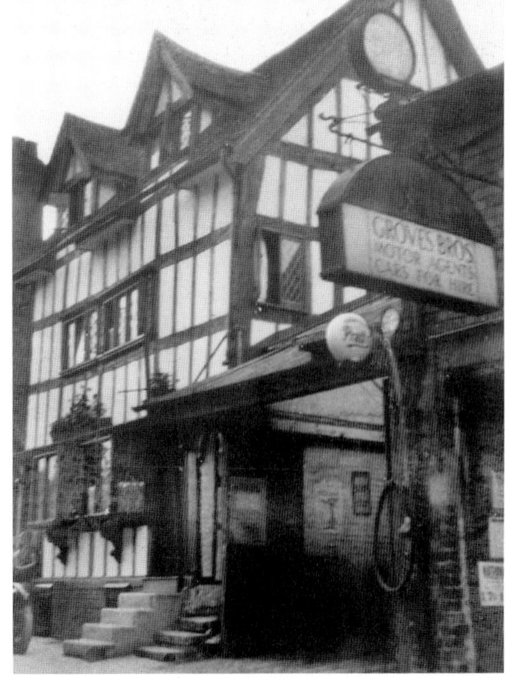

St Mary's Place, *c.* 1925. St Mary's Place was once known as St Mary's Church Yard. The timber-framed cottage, built in the seventeenth century, was split into two dwellings called St Mary's Cottage and the Verger's House. For thirty-seven years until his death in January 1946, the verger was William Hordley. Running to the right of the cottage is St Mary's Shut, which takes pedestrians through to Castle Street. At the beginning of the nineteenth century it was known as Little Shut due to the narrow entrance through the side of the cottage. Next door was the Crown Garage run by Frederick Groves, a motor engineer. In 1916 he sold petrol, charged accumulaters, hired out cars and had another garage on the West Parade at Rhyl.

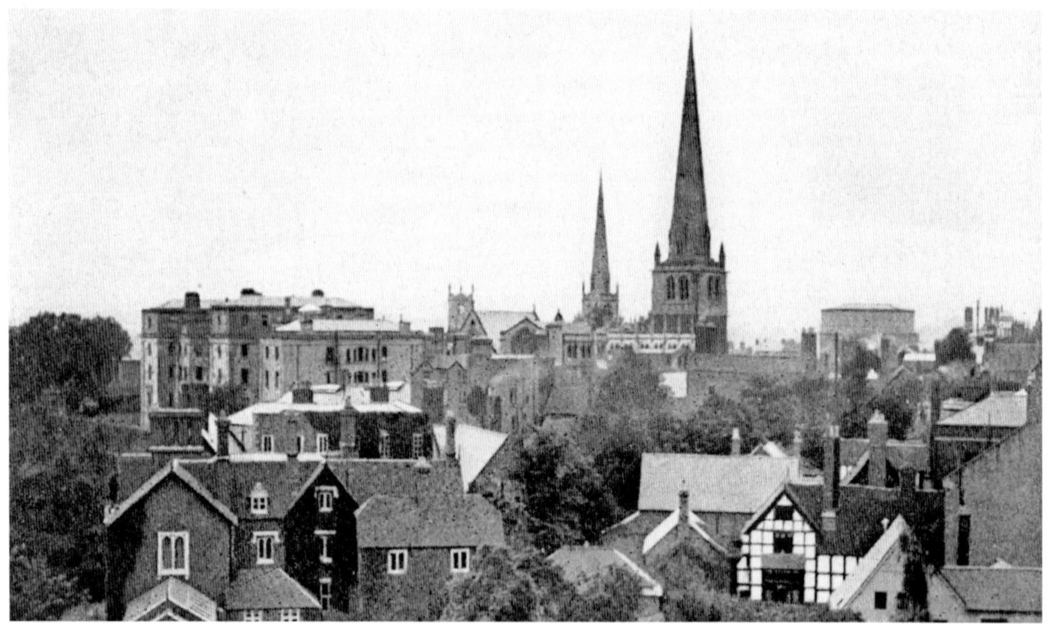

Rooftops from the castle, *c.* 1910. On the skyline are the towers and spires of St Julian's (left), St Alkmund's (middle) and St Mary's (right). On 11 February 1894 the top 50ft of St Mary's tower was blown down in a gale. After rebuilding, the total height of the tower and spire was 222ft 6in, reputedly the third highest in England. To the right is the water tower which serviced the town until 1935. Left of centre is the Salop Infirmary, built in 1830.

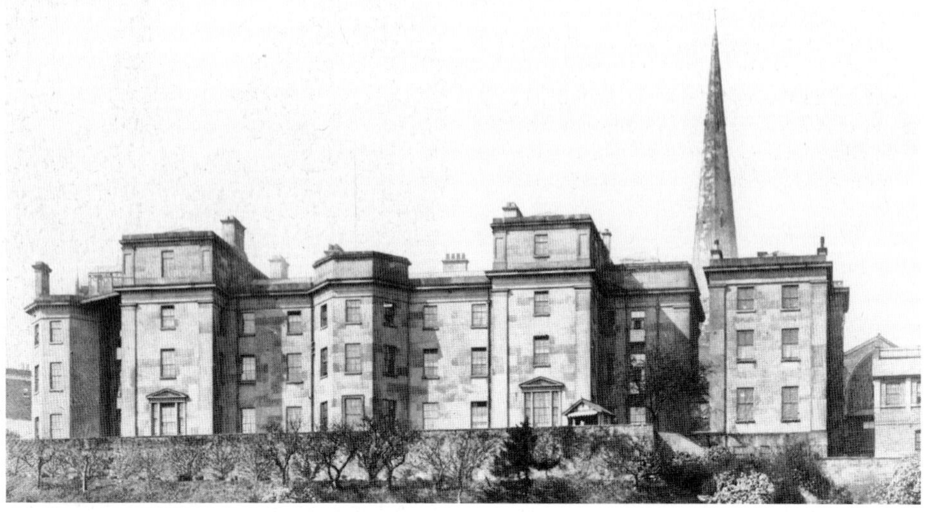

A rear view of the Salop Infirmary before the verandas were built between the bays, *c.* 1905. It occupies the site of Broom Hall built by Corbet Kynaston in 1740, which was converted into a hospital seven years later. This building was designed by Edward Haycock who built it in the classical style between 1828 and 1830 using Grinshill stone. The hospital closed in November 1977. Note St Mary's spire at the rear and Stone House on the right on the site of the nurses' home.

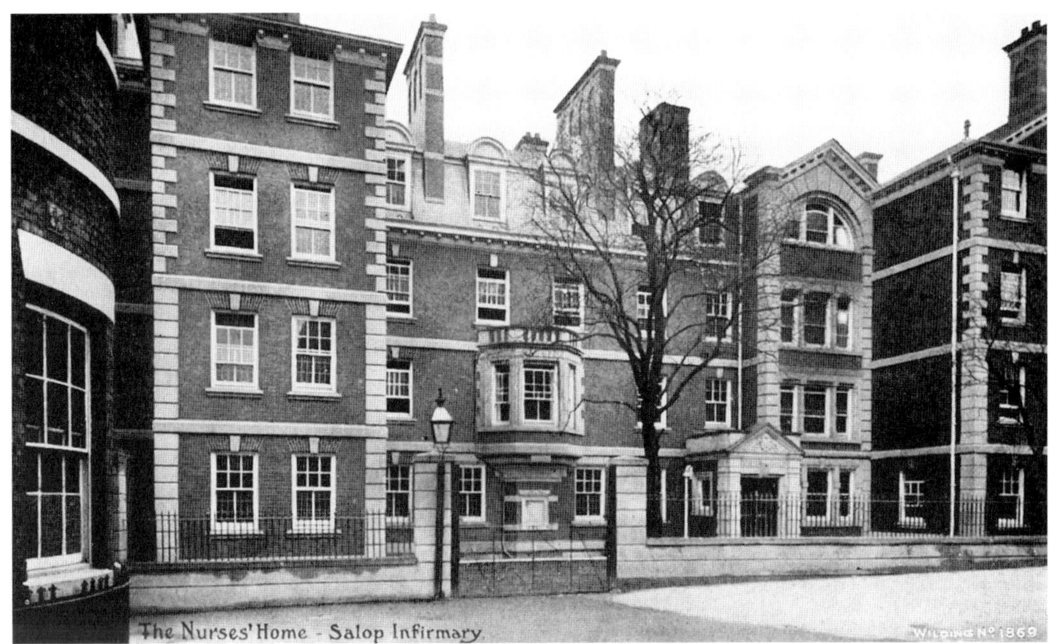

St Mary's Place, *c.* 1912. The Salop Infirmary Nurses' Home was erected on the site of Stone House, next to the hospital. The foundation stone was laid on 5 November 1908 and it was formally opened on 10 November 1910 by the Hon. Mrs Hayward-Lonsdale. It was built out of brick and Grinshill stone at a cost of £9,000. The architect was Mr Lloyd-Oswell and the builder Henry Price of Frankwell. The building contained several large sitting rooms, a writing room and a bicycle room. Scull Brothers carried out the plumbing and there were several bathrooms on each floor. The *Chronicle* commented that the new accommodation was much better for the occupants as, '[Formerly] nurses had to pass the mortuary to reach their quarters.'

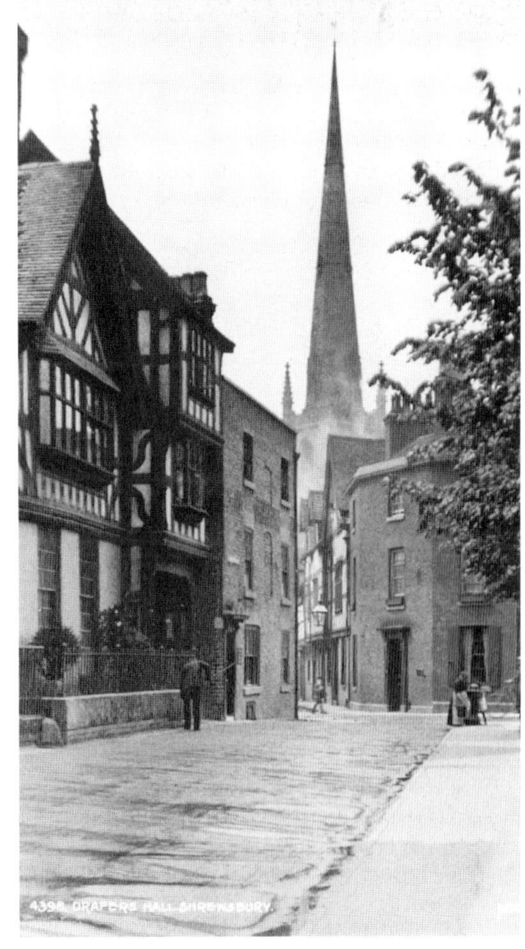

St Mary's Place, *c.* 1910. The timber-framed house on the left is the Draper's Hall. The guild was founded in 1460 and most of the building dates from the second half of the sixteenth century. The beautiful timber-framing is reputed to be the work of Welsh carpenter Roger Smyth. The hall still contains a great deal of its original furniture, including a large oak table made by Francis Bowyer in 1632 for £2 15*s*. The brick building on the right was built in the eighteenth century on the forecourt of Jones' Mansion seen at the rear in Church Street. Note the old lady and little girl drawing drinking water from the conduit on the corner of St Mary's Street.

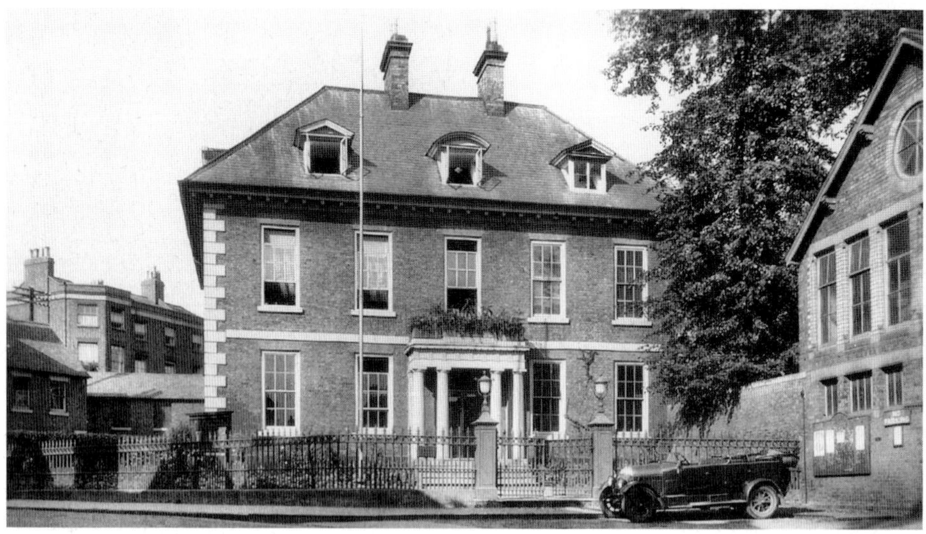

Dogpole, *c.* 1930. Newport House was built in 1696 for Francis Newport, two years after he had been created Earl of Bradford. The porch, which is made of iron, was added in the early nineteenth century. Until about 1920 it was the home of Dr Edward Burd before becoming the Guildhall. The building below was also acquired by the council for offices. Before that it had been a carriage works and a garage belonging to Mountford & Co. who sold it to Mark Davies, a motor engineer, before it was taken over during the First World War by Vincent Greenhous.

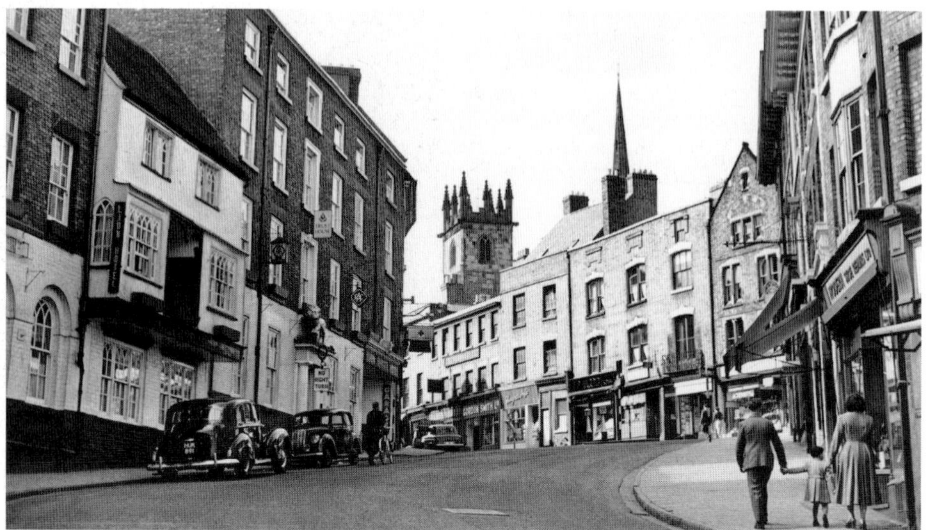

Wyle Cop, *c.* 1950. The Lion Hotel dominates the left-hand side of the hill. The oldest section juts out from the centre and is timber framed under the plaster. It dates from the fifteenth century and was described by Charles Dickens, who stayed there in the nineteenth century as, 'like the stern of a ship'. The top section dates from the eighteenth century. The doorway and the magnificent carved lion are the work of a local sculptor John Nelson and were added in 1777. Inside the Adam-style ballroom has been graced with performances by Dickens and Paganini, but during the First World War it was commandeered by the Territorial Branch Army Pay Office.

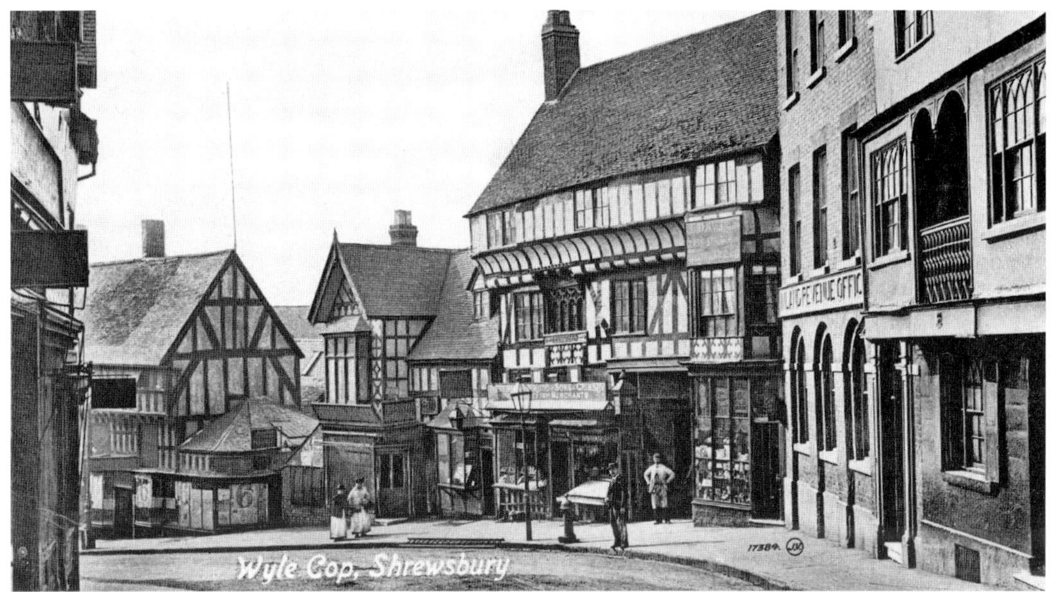

Wyle Cop, *c.* 1900. The oldest part of the Lion Hotel with its open gallery is on the right and just below the Inland Revenue Office. The timber-framed building with the curved overhang of the top storey dates from about 1430 and is known as Henry Tudor House. It's reputed that Henry Tudor lodged there on 22 August 1485 while en route to Castle Bosworth where he defeated Richard III to become Henry VII, the first Tudor king. The man is standing in front of Barrack's Passage. To the left of the passage is the fish, game and poultry shop belonging to Harry Mudd of Grimsby; to the left a fancy repository and glass staining business run by Mr and Mrs J. Davies.

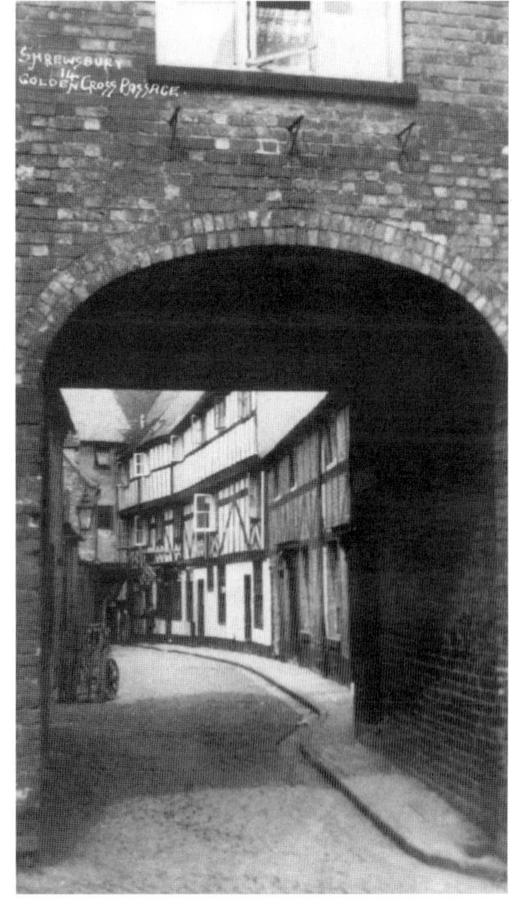

Barracks Passage, *c.* 1915. This postcard was wrongly captioned Golden Cross Passage. The view is taken from Belmont Bank, which was once known as Back Lane, looking towards Wyle Cop. The building at the far end is the rear of Henry Tudor House. In the eighteenth century it was occupied by the Elisha family and for many years the passage was known as Elisha's Shut. No one knows the origin of the name Barracks Passage but H.E. Forrest, in his book *Old Houses of Shrewsbury*, believed that soldiers were once billeted there and that the whole of the right-hand side of the passage 'is said to have been used by the patrol.' At the far end is the Lion Tap, a beerhouse connected to the Lion Hotel and for a short period the shut was called Lion Tap Passage. The Tap, which has also been called the Trotting Horse, is housed in a building dating from the fifteenth century.

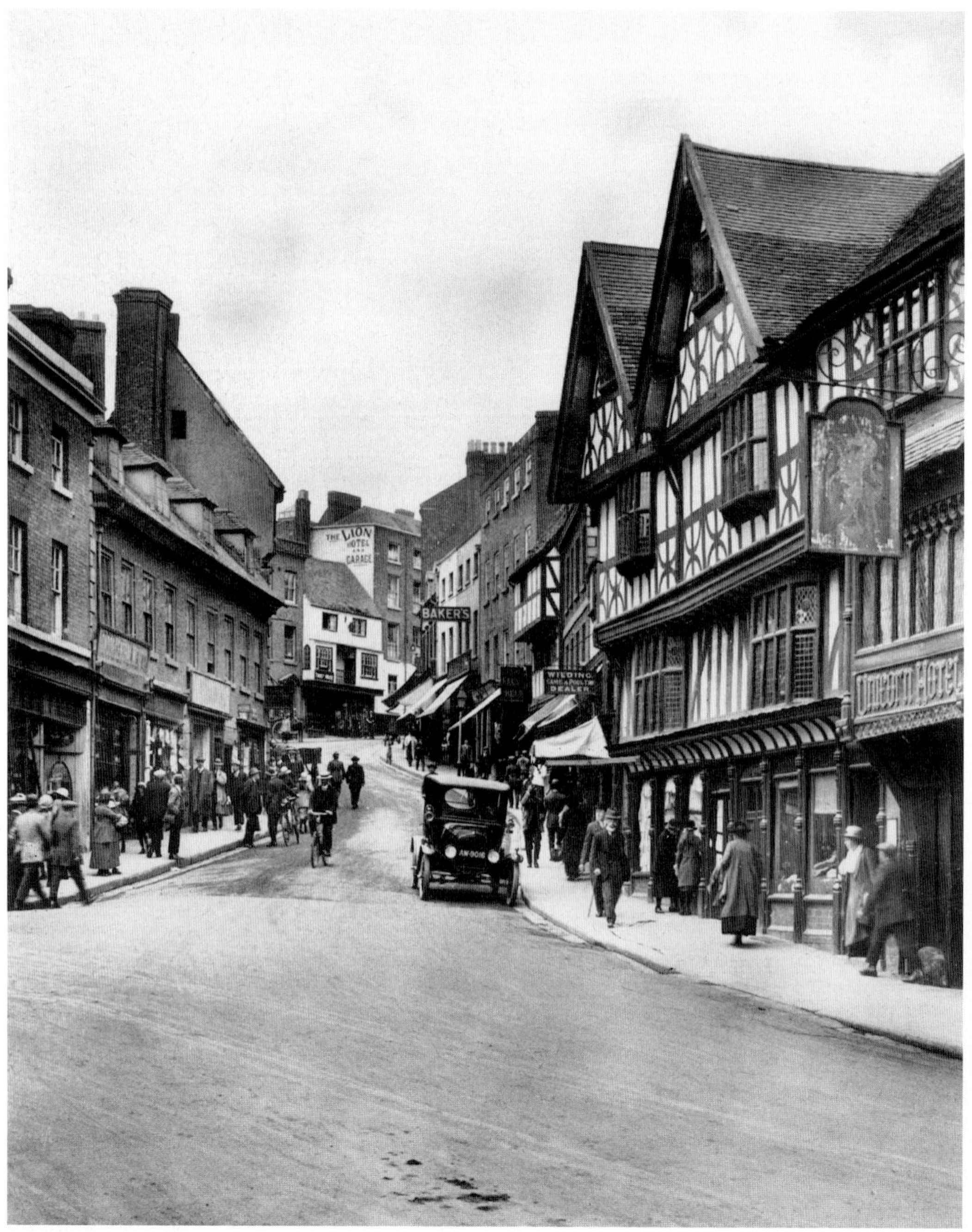

Wyle Cop, *c.* 1913. Originally the street was split into three sections. From the English Bridge to the foot of the hill was called Under the Wyle and the bank was known as the Wyle, while from the top of the hill to the High Street was the Cop. On the right is the sign of the Unicorn Hotel with the name carved into the timber under the oriel window. Unfortunately the window was destroyed a few years later when the passage beneath was made higher to accommodate larger vehicles. To the left are two shops belonging to H. Williams, a saddler, and the Misses Tibbetts who ran a fancy needlework depot.

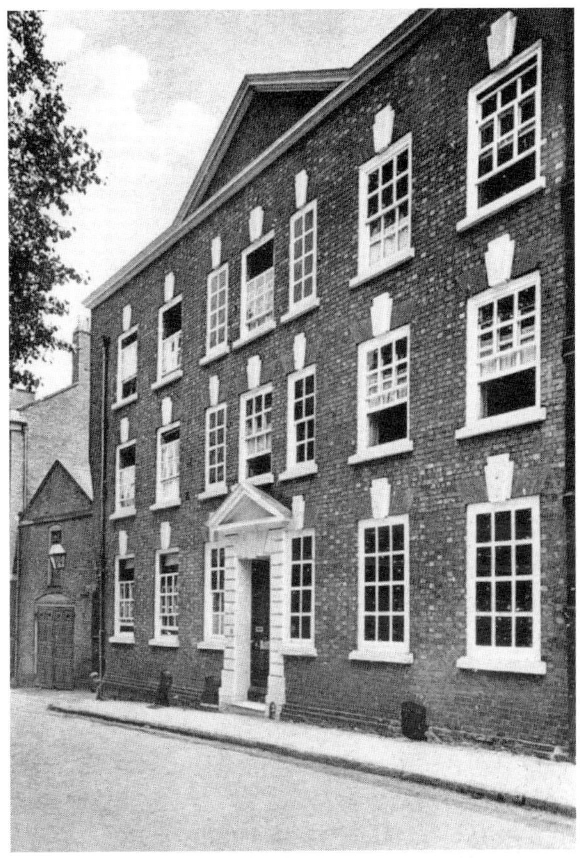

Belmont, *c.* 1913. Belmont House was built as the townhouse for the Tayleur family in the sixteenth century. It's a timber-framed building with a brick frontage added about 200 years later when timber-framing went out of fashion. It was once the home of William Hall of the auctioneers Hall, Wateridge & Owen but at the beginning of the twentieth century it was occupied by Mrs Wateridge. From about 1908 until just after the First World War the house was transformed into a girls' school by Miss Helen McGaffin. The McGaffins were very involved in education at the start of the twentieth century as Miss Gertrude McGaffin, assisted by Sidney McGaffin, ran a preparatory school for boys known as Sycamore House School on Town Walls. By 1922 Belmont House had become the Granville Club, attached to the Shrewsbury Liberal Association. The large building to the left was the Dispensary where 'the poorer classes' could get medical attention and medicine, while the smaller one has been used as a garage by Arthur Greenhous & Son and R.H. Cureton, a motor engineer, until 1935 when the building was replaced by the new St David's Presbyterian Church.

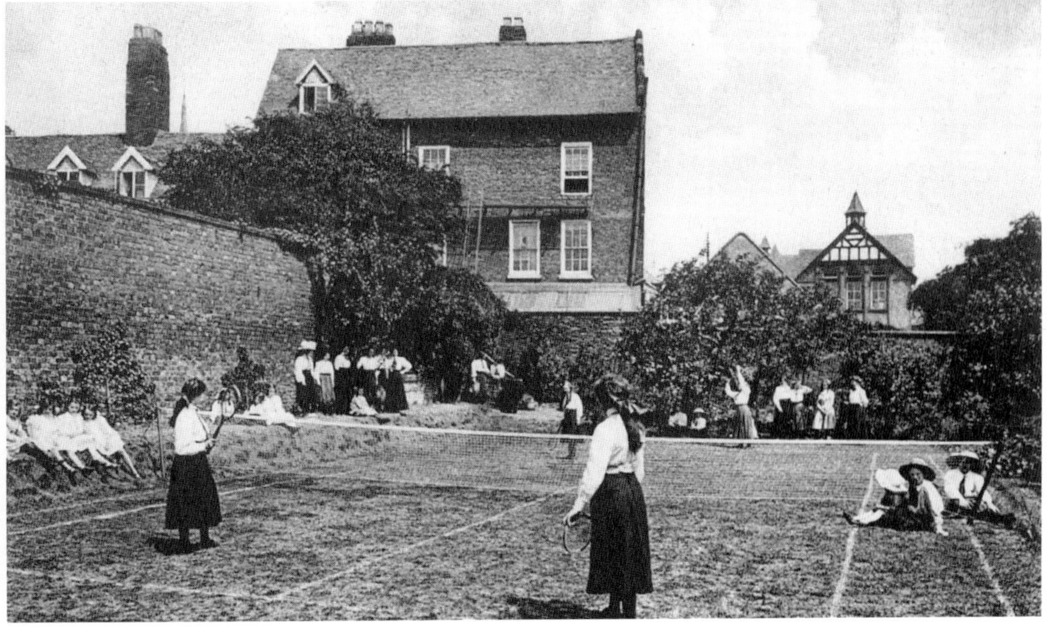

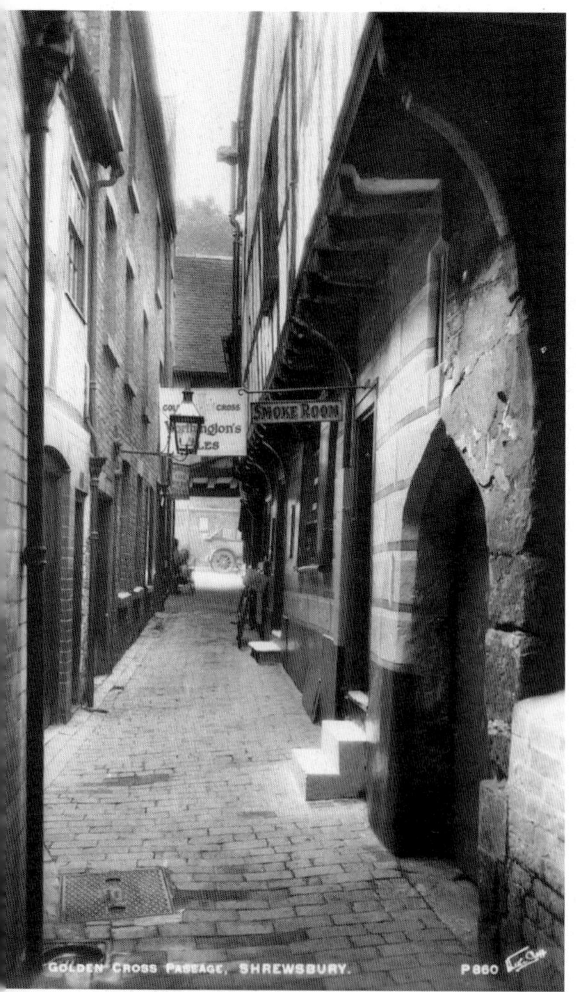

Left: Golden Cross Passage, *c.* 1935. The photographer is looking from High Street towards Princess Street. The car at the top is in front of the retaining wall of old St Chad's Church. The original name for the passage is Sextry Shut, which is derived from sacristy, the place where St Chad's Church would keep its most valuable possessions. The timber-framed building on the right is the Golden Cross Inn which was originally called the Sextry and was connected to the church by a covered passage that went over Princess Street. The inn dates from the fifteenth century but the interesting doorway on the right probably dates from an earlier building. The sign just on the left below the inn sign advertises the Dorothy Café run by Mrs Newns, a confectioner.

Right: Princess Street, *c.* 1900. This view is looking towards The Square and the back of the old Market Hall. The timber-framed house is Lloyd's Mansion, built by David Lloyd in 1570. He was a bailiff of the town and a member of the wealthy Draper's Company. Joseph Della Porta, an Italian immigrant, came to England in 1848 and set up a shop in Princess Street in 1857. Later he extended his business into Lloyds Mansion, adding new departments to his business including ironmongery, hardware and boots and shoes. The property was later acquired by the council who used it as offices until it was demolished in 1930.

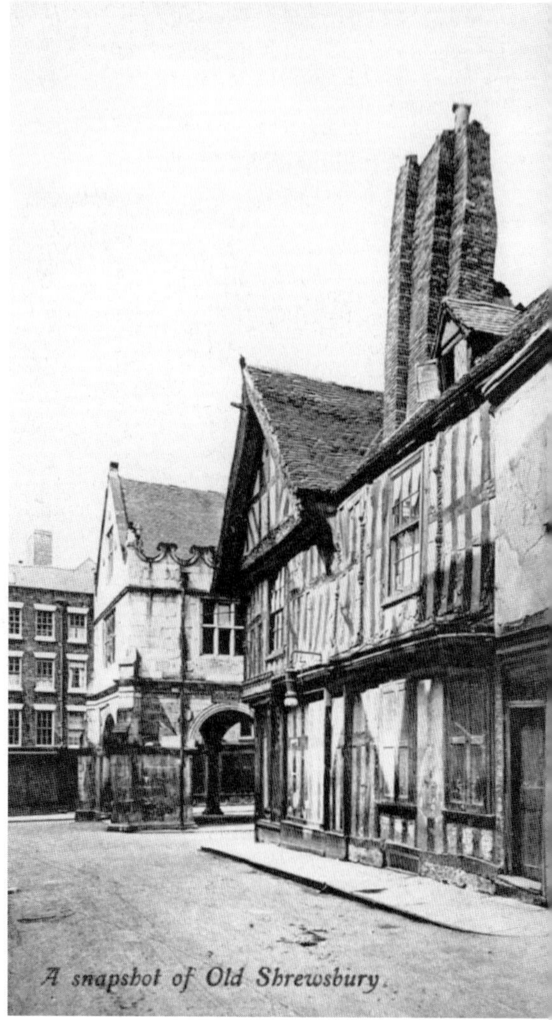

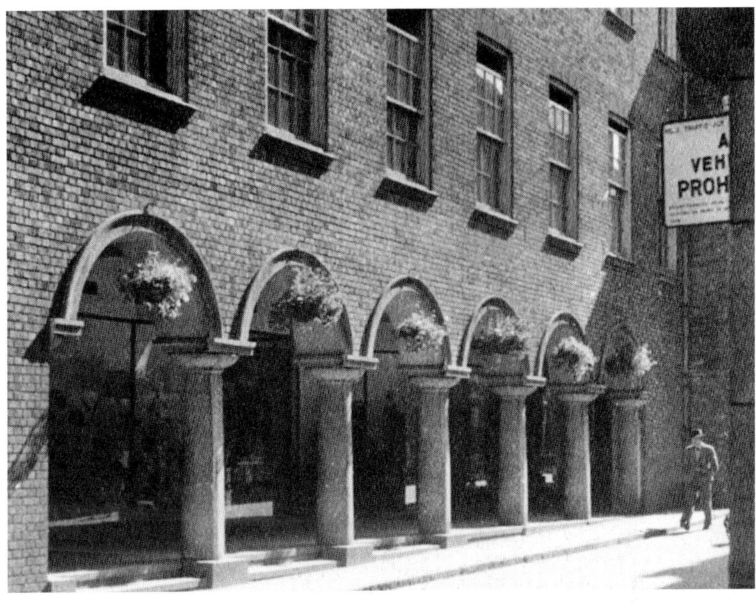

Princess Street, *c.* 1940. After Lloyd's Mansion was taken down, the timber frame was stored in a builder's yard, ready to be re-erected on another site. Unfortunately this never happened and the timbers were lost. The council also bought property in Princess Street, High Street and Peacock's Passage for £45,700 for the building of a third extension to the Shirehall. This section was completed in 1939 and the whole site was officially opened in 1940. Della Porta's did well in the deal as they were able to build a new departmental store extending from Princess Street through to High Street. Note their display windows under the colonnaded arcade, ideal for window shopping on a wet Sunday afternoon.

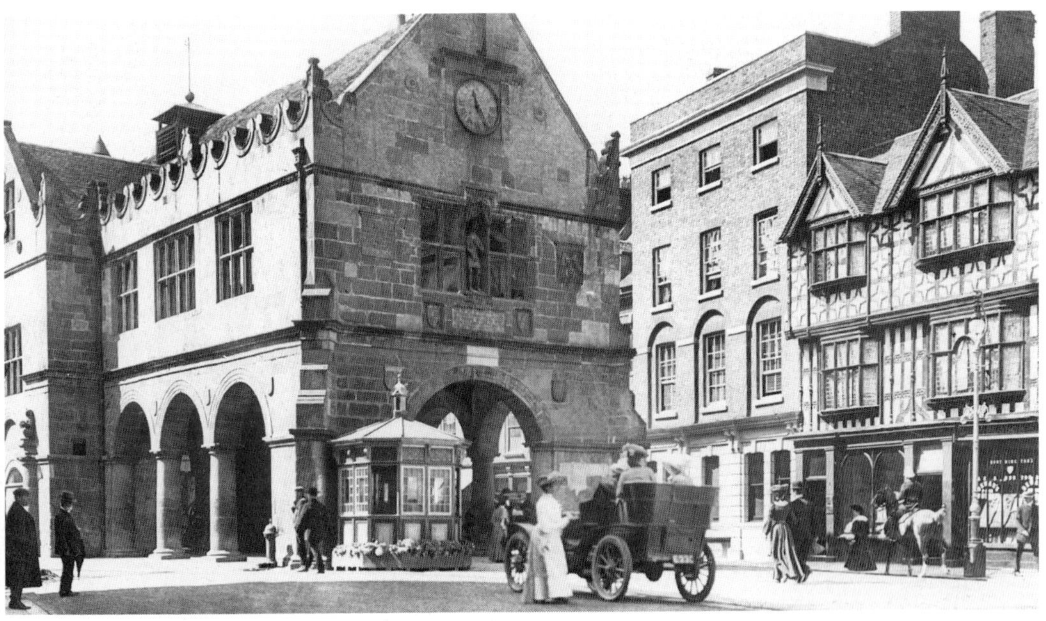

The Square, *c.* 1905. The old Market Hall was erected in 1596 so that a corn market could be held under the arches of the ground floor, while the drapers could hold their sales on the first floor. The statue between the windows once stood on the gateway of the old Welsh Bridge until 1791; it represents Richard, Duke of York. The upper floor was later used as a magistrate's court and is now a café and cinema. Only the first floor of the timber-framed building is genuine – the second storey was added in 1898 but looks authentic as the architects A.B. & W. Scott-Deakin used the same designs as their Elizabethan counterparts. The right-hand section is occupied by the Plough Inn while the left-hand side houses William Toye & Co., coal factors.

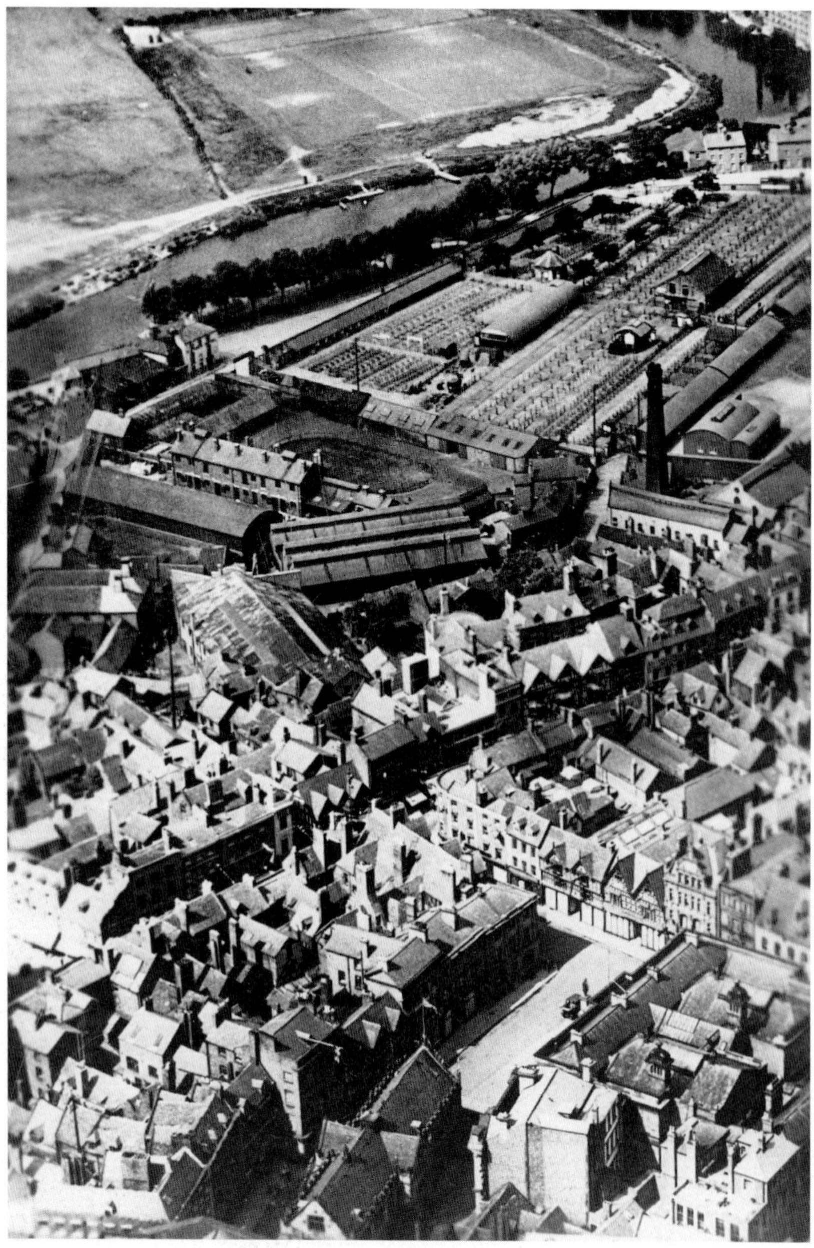

This view shows The Square and old Market Hall looking across High Street and Pride Hill to the cattle market, river and the County Ground in Frankwell, *c.* 1918. The cattle market was formally opened on 19 November 1850 by the Mayor Councillor and followed by a public dinner at the Britannia Hotel. A week earlier it was reported, 'At this, the first market held in the new Smithfield, there was a large attendance of buyers, and all kinds of stock made more money, except pigs. Best beef sold a shade over 5*d.* per lb., sheep made 5*d.* per lb., bacon pigs and porkers, 4*d.* per lb.' The building with the large chimney is the Shrewsbury Electricity Works at the bottom of the Seventy Steps. In the centre is the abattoir, opened in 1911, and to the left is the large roof of Shuker's garage.

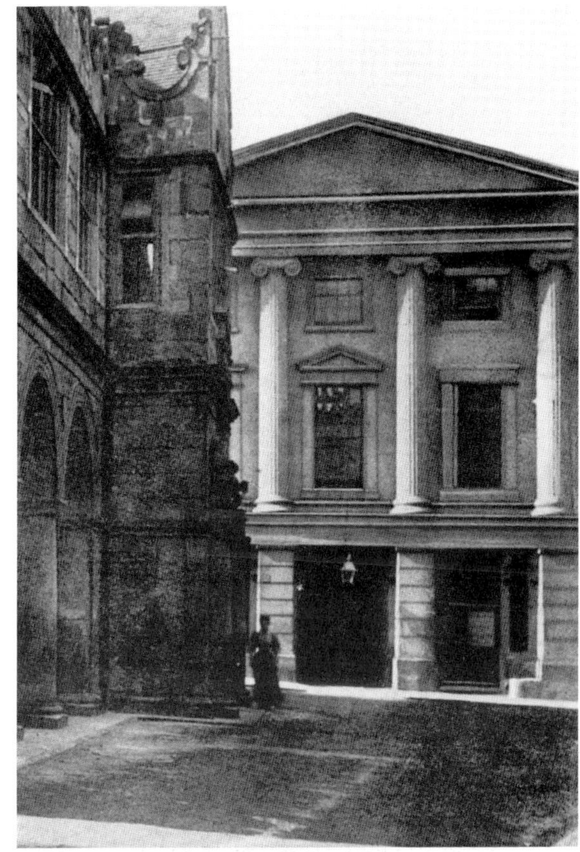

The Square. *c.* 1905. The Music Hall occupies the southern side of The Square at the rear of the old Market Hall on the left. It was erected between 1839 and 1840 costing upwards of £12,000. It was designed in the neoclassical style by Edward Haycock and built by Joseph Stant, both Shrewsbury men. The ground floor was once occupied by a post office, while on the first floor was a public news room and part of the top floor was used for billiards. The main hall was described in 1886 as the only room in town 'of sufficient size and convenience for concerts, entertainments and public meetings.' It was well lit, could seat 1,000 and its acoustics were considered 'unsurpassed for musical effect'. The hall was refurbished in the 1980s and is now being converted into the town's new museum. The opening on the ground floor was known as Fire Office Passage as the Salop Fire Office and station were once situated there.

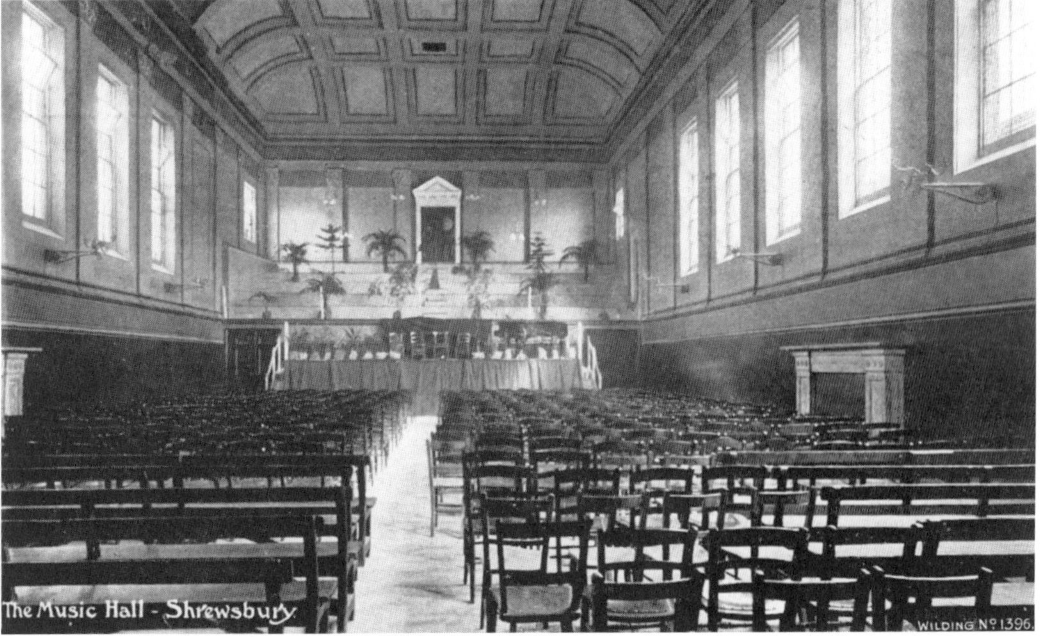

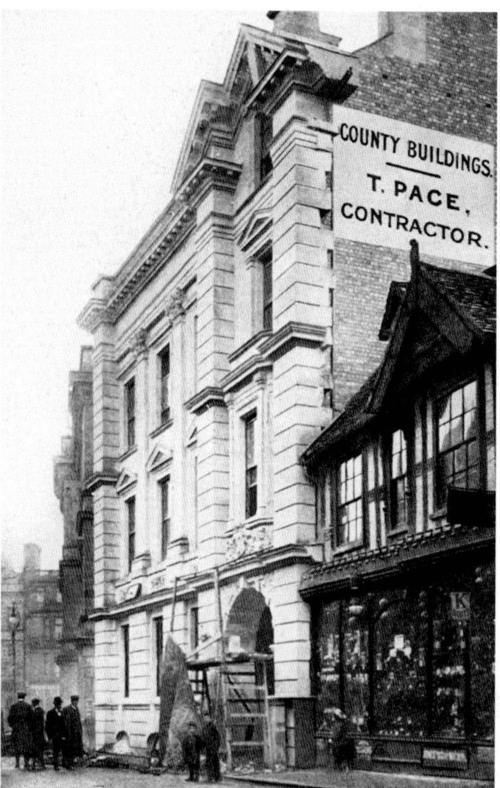

Left: The Square, *c.* 1907. The new County Buildings were built on the site of the County Police Headquarters and a grocery shop belonging to Henry Lee. In 1900 the council purchased Lee's shop for £2,750 when the grocery firm moved into new premises at the back of The Square. By 1903 the police headquarters had moved into a new station on Swan Hill leaving the site next to the Shirehall ready for redevelopment. The new building consisted of two blocks built in the Renaissance style, linked to the Shirehall and to each other. The new complex provided offices for councillors and various departments and also committee rooms and laboratories. Thomas Pace, the contractor, was a local man whose head office was on the Berwick Road. He was Mayor of Shrewsbury in 1922.

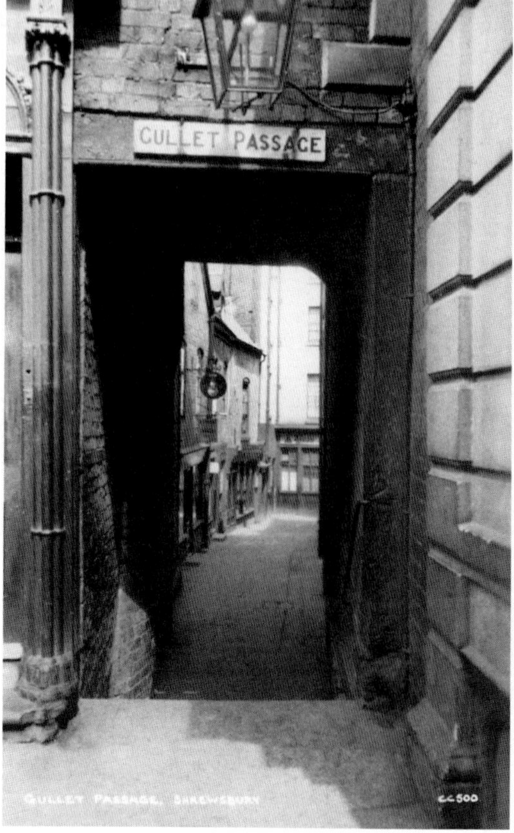

Right: Gullet Passage, *c.* 1940. This is another of the town's ancient shuts or passageways that allows pedestrians to take a shortcut from one street to another. This is the entrance from The Square connecting it with Mardol Head. One explanation for the unusual name is that it was taken from the Gullet Inn that stood at the Mardol end of the passageway in the sixteenth century. Another derivation is that the pool in The Square was once emptied by a stream that ran down the passage towards the Severn and the old English word for such a channel was 'golate'. The building at the bottom is the Market Vaults which is now called the Hole in the Wall. The shops on the left from the top are Richard Young an electrical engineer, Ethel Ward a confectioner and Bertram Sheffield a hairdresser who had another barber shop under the market in Shoplatch.

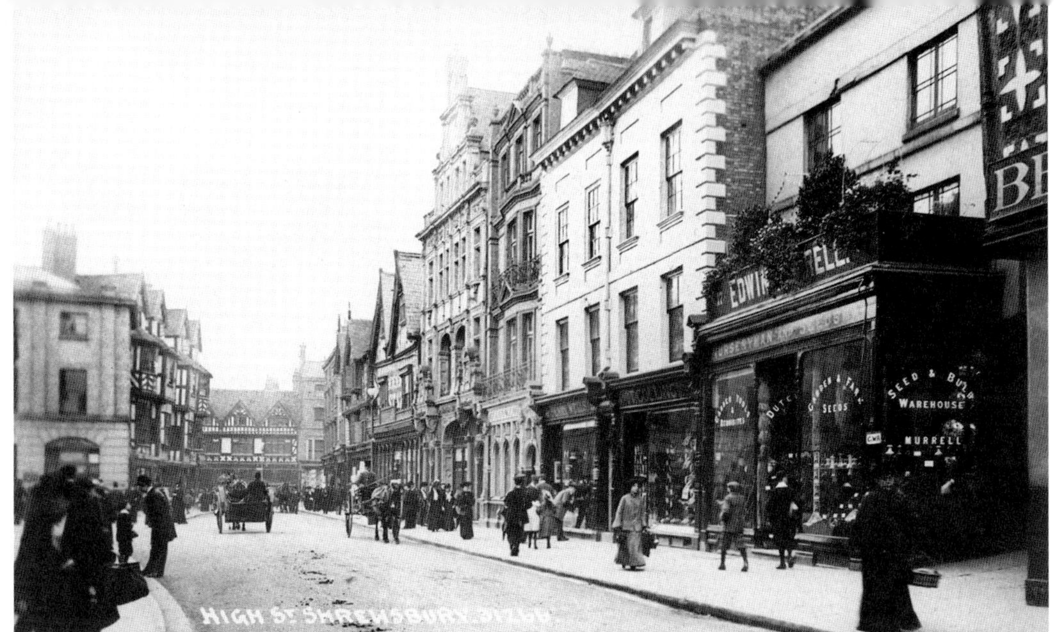

High Street, *c.* 1905. The building on the right at the corner of Grope Lane belonged to Edwin Murrell who had just moved there from a shop further up the High Street. He was a nurseryman, seedsman and florist who had a large garden centre near the Column. The house dates from the sixteenth century but its timber frame has been hidden under plaster. The company of Mercers once met there and in 1841 Benjamin Disraeli made a speech from the balcony before he was elected MP for the town. The shop to the left belonged to Thomas Golling who was listed as a hatter and hosier. Later he expanded his business into a building on the other corner of Grope Lane where he sold the largest collection of ties of any private dealer in the country.

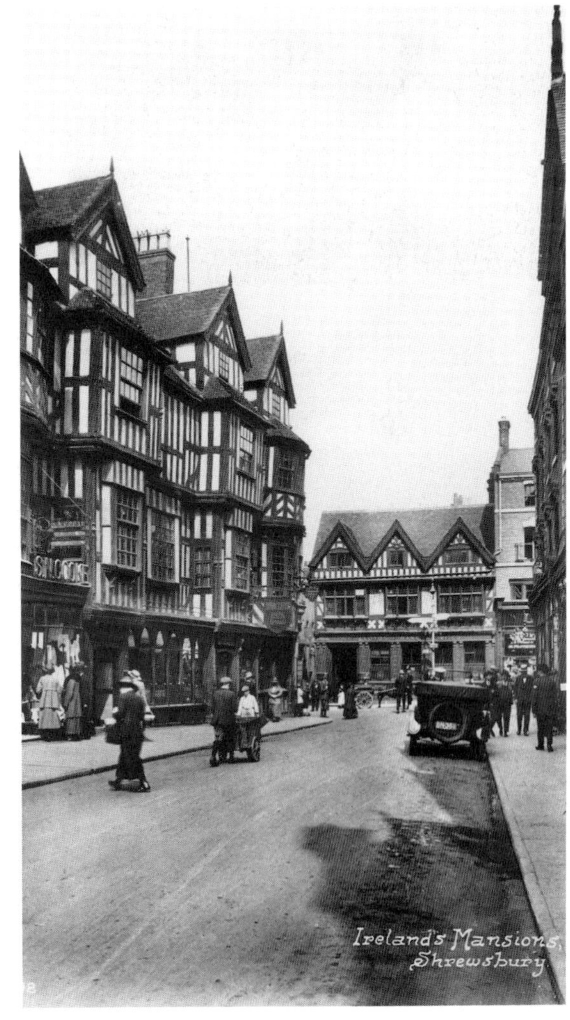

High Street, *c.* 1920. The large timber-framed building on the left is Ireland's Mansion, built for Robert Ireland in 1575. He was a wealthy wool merchant who came from Oswestry. It was such a big rambling building that it was known locally as 'Ireland's Folly'. It was later split into four sections that by 1922 were occupied from the left by S. & N. Cooke ladies' outfitters, Adams & Son chemist and Barclay's Bank. Barclay's also had another branch on the corner of Castle Street and St Mary's Street. Earlier the London & Provincial Bank was located at the end but by 1929 the Westminster Bank was housed there. Facing High Street is Lloyd's Bank who moved there in 1876. Unfortunately the timber-framed frontage has been replaced by a piece of 1960s architecture.

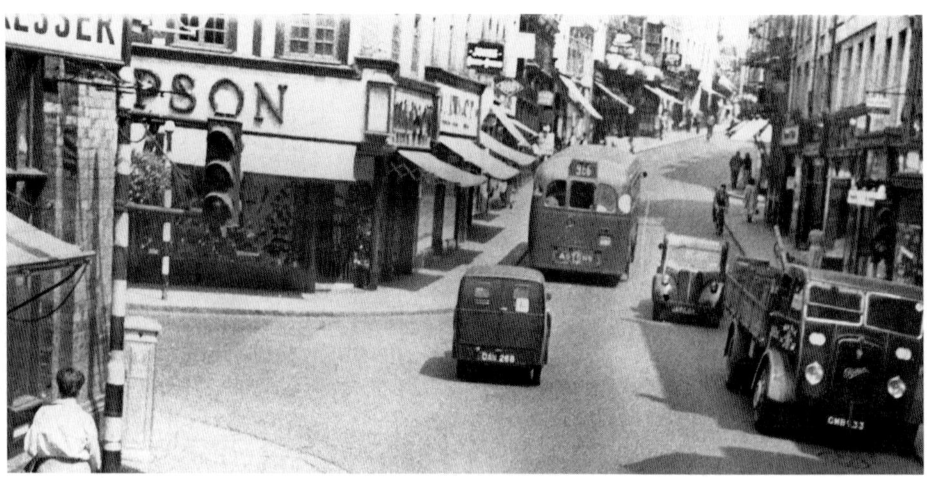

A Midland Red bus makes its way towards Pride Hill while a Southam's Brewery lorry delivers beer to the Market Vaults, *c.* 1955. On the left is Mardol while further up on the right is the entrance to High Street. Mardol Head was once known as Lee Stalls and was the centre for booksellers and stationers in the eighteenth and early nineteenth centuries. Timpson's shoe shop was there for well over half a century. Before that it was Henry Thomas's toy shop, known throughout the town as 'The Penny Bazaar'. Just above is the sign for W.J. Jones, the dispensing chemist. He also sold photographic accessories and had shops on Pride Hill and Wyle Cop.

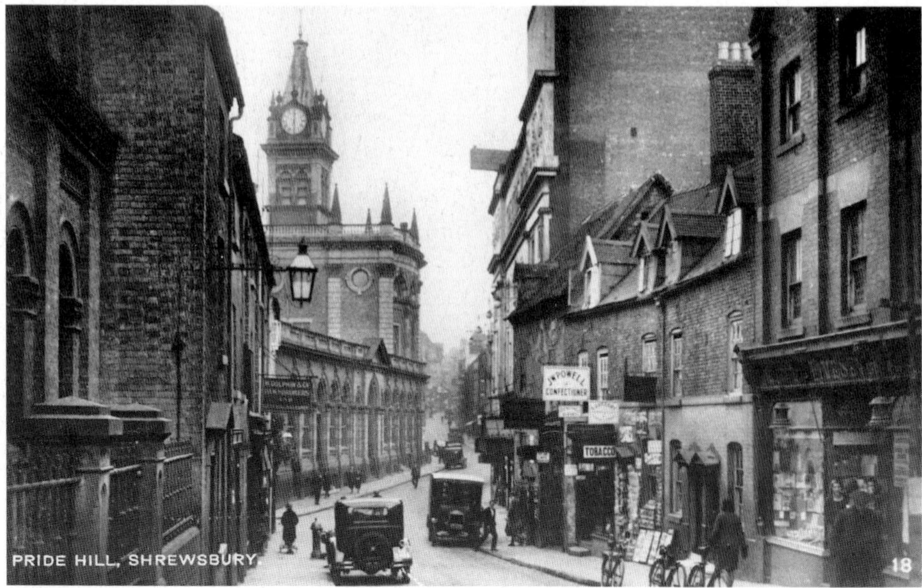

St John's Hill, looking along Shoplatch to Mardol Head and Pride Hill, *c.* 1930. The Methodist Church on the left was built in 1879 on the site of an earlier chapel of 1805. The left side of Shoplatch is dominated by the Victorian Market Hall, which opened in 1869. The large building on the right is the County Theatre or Theatre Royal. Until the interior was destroyed by fire in June 1945 it was the grandest theatre in Shropshire. Moving back up the hill are signs for John Powell's confectionery shop and Edwin Gregory's newsagents and tobacconists. On the right is the Livesey Ltd printers, established by William Wardle on Pride Hill in 1843.

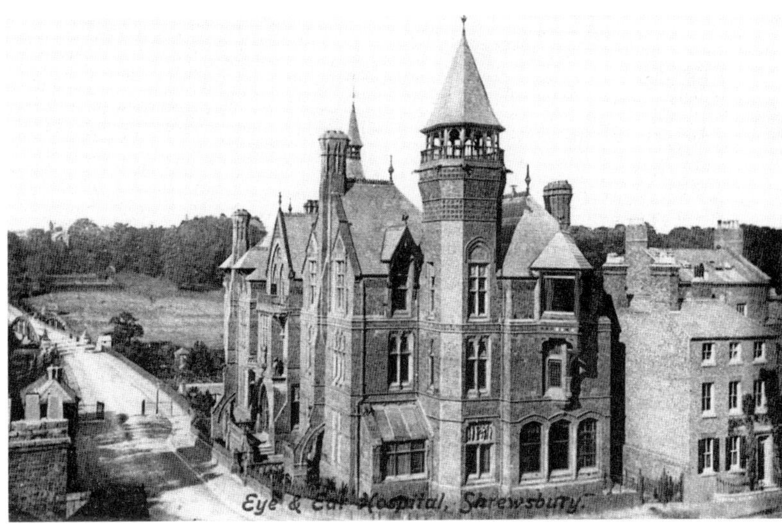

Murivance, *c.* 1905. The Eye, Ear & Throat Hospital was established in 1818. This building, constructed from Ruabon brick with terracotta dressings, was opened in 1881 and cost over £12,000. The hospital contained forty-five beds, several private wards and an operating theatre. In 1909 a new drainage system was installed and in 1921 new kitchens and a lift were fitted. In about 1924 St John's Villa to the right was demolished and an extension was added, which included the remodelling of the outpatients department. The new extension was opened by Princess Mary in 1926. To the left is the entrance to the Kingsland Bridge, which was opened in 1882.

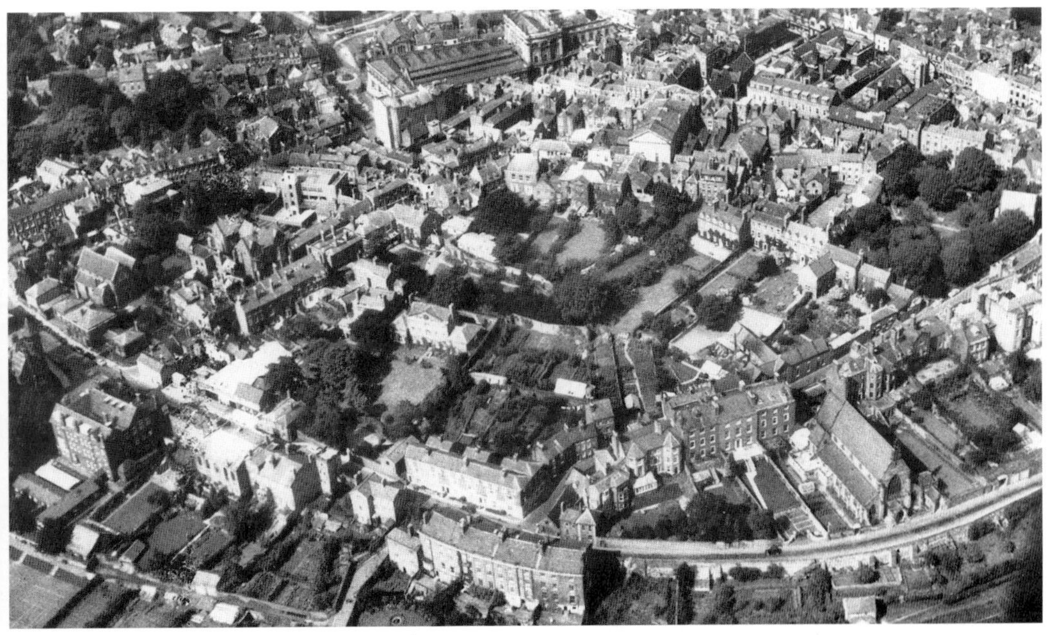

Town Walls, *c.* 1950. Note the large gardens belonging to the fine houses that were built in the eighteenth century along Belmont, College Hill and Town Walls. In the bottom right-hand corner is a large section of the old town wall above which is the Catholic Cathedral built in 1856. To the left of Town Walls is The Crescent (built in 1795) and just beyond is the last remaining tower of the town's defences. Just above the tower is Swan Hill Court House built in the 1760s for Sir William Pulteney, the first Earl of Bath. The group of trees in the top right corner surround the remains of old St Chad's Church that collapsed in 1788.

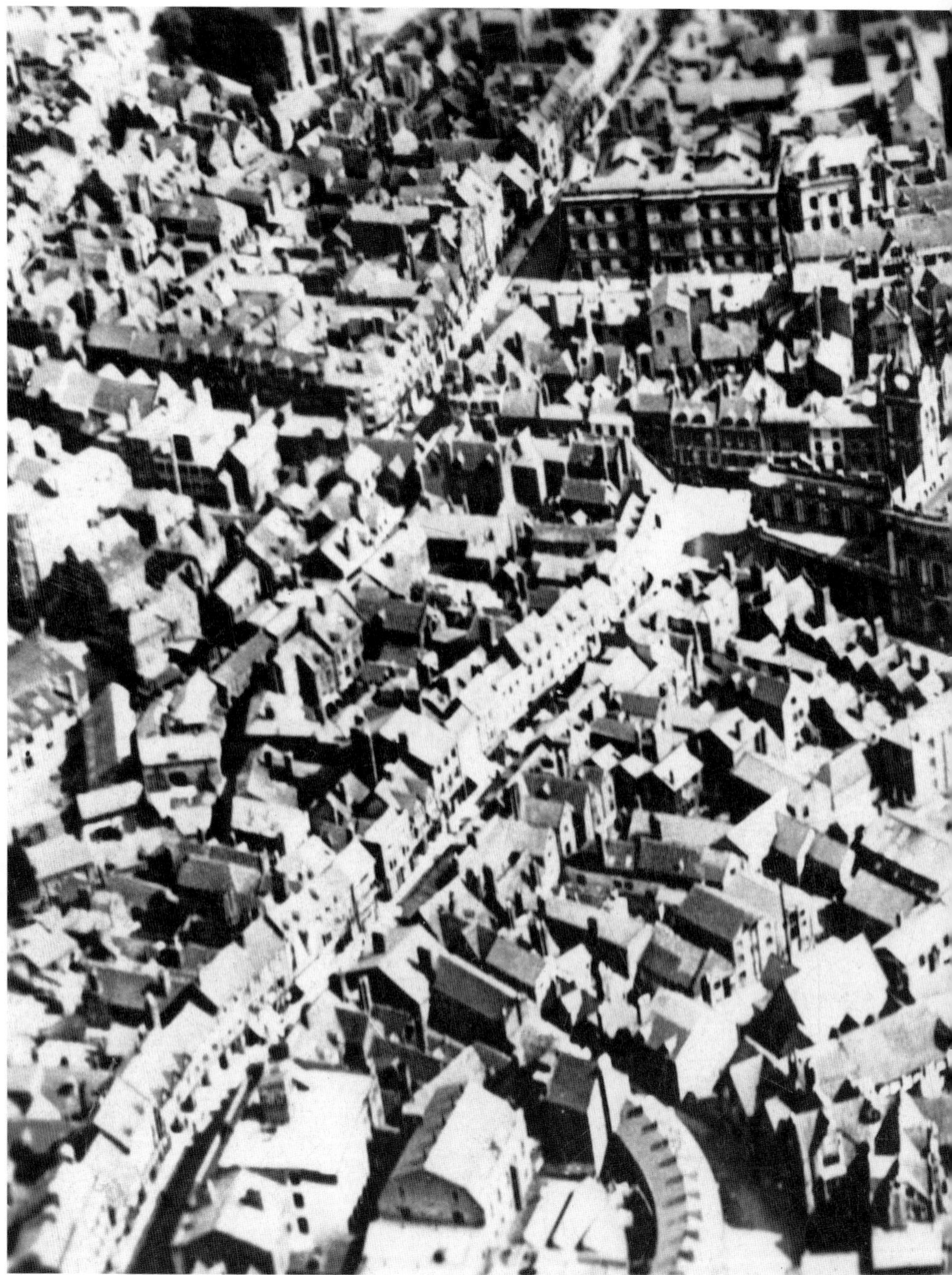

Shrewsbury, 1918. The large building in the centre is the old Market Hall that was opened in November 1869. The road to the left of the market is Mardol, while to the right is Belstone leading to Barker Street. Note how the houses completely hide Rowley's House whose gables and roofline are visible at the bottom centre. The dark building just left of centre at the top is the Shirehall in The Square. The white building above the right-hand corner of the market is the Theatre Royal, complete with its statues of Shakespeare and the comic and tragic muses.

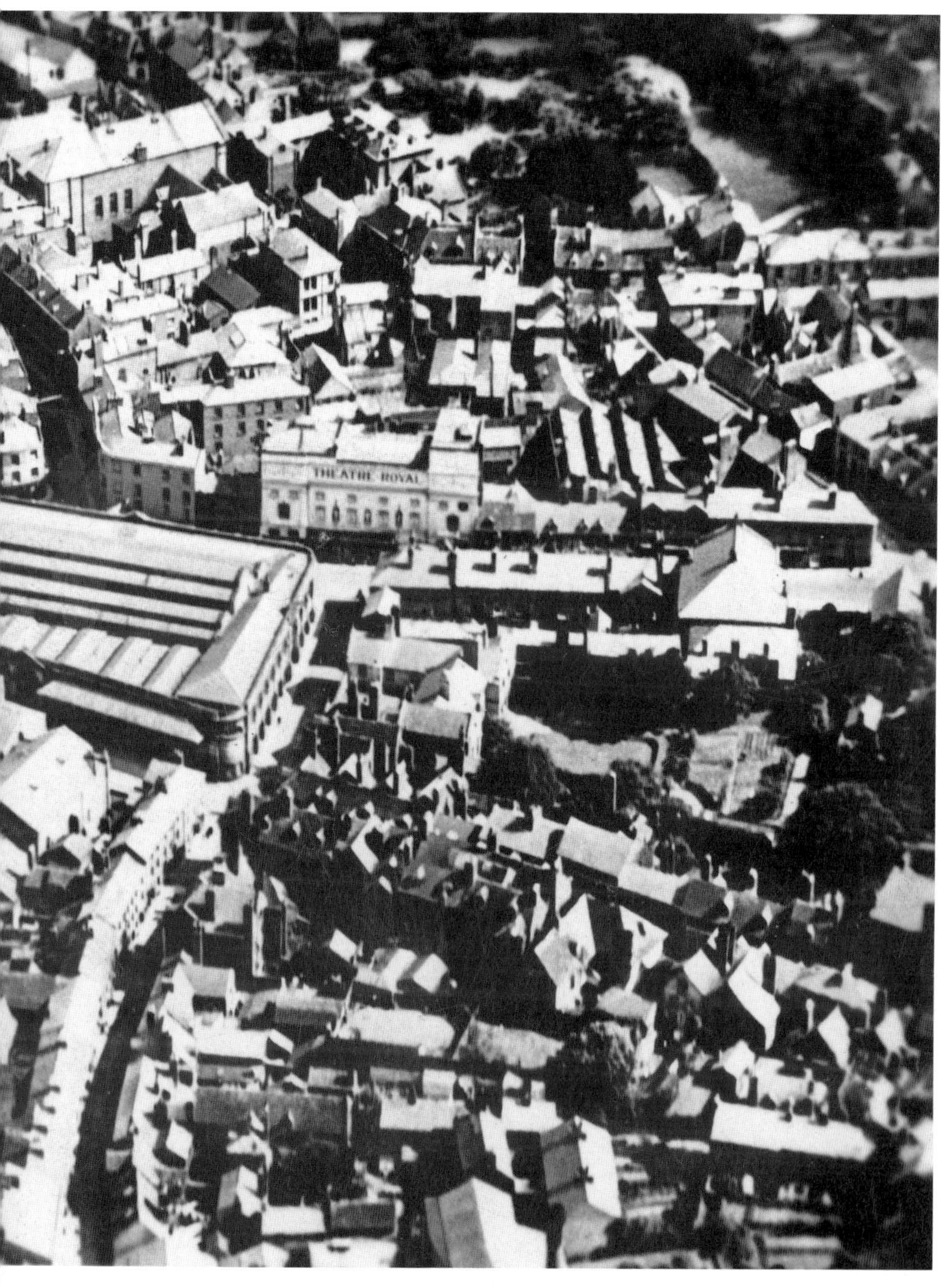
THEATRE ROYAL

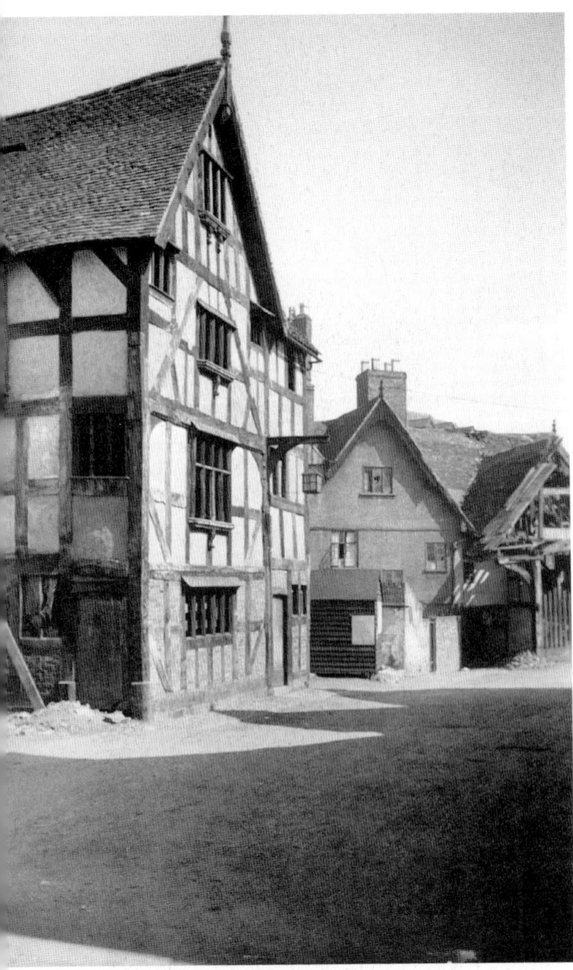

Left: Barker Street, *c.* 1935. In the 1930s a great many dilapidated properties in the Barker Street, Bridge Street and Hill's Lane area were removed to provide an inner loop road and car parking spaces. During the demolition and hidden by other structures, Rowley's House, on the left, was discovered. It was said to be 'terribly dilapidated; almost ruinous', but Arthur Ward the Borough Surveyor believed it was worth saving. The house was built by William Rowley a draper, brewer and maltster who came from Worfield. Note the inverted V on the timbers of the second storey. They are the eaves of the New Ship Inn that was butted right up against the house. The property at the bottom was in the process of demolition.

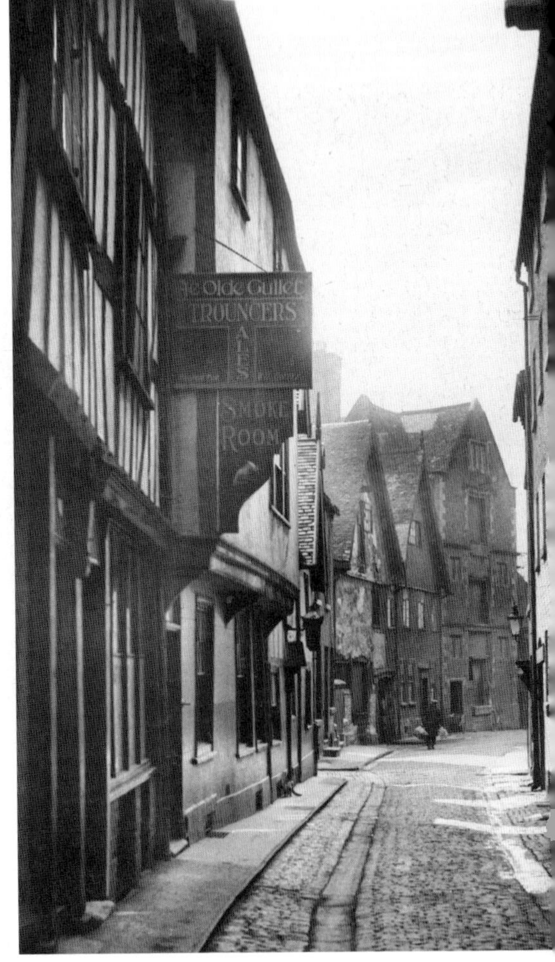

Right: Hill's Lane. The man is just passing the building being demolished on the last photograph. The passage in the centre led to the New Ship Inn. To the right is part of Rowley's Mansion, built in 1618 and reputed to be the first brick building in Shrewsbury. By 1808 it was being used as a woollen factory before becoming a warehouse. It was restored in 1983 and used as the town museum. On the left is the sign of the Olde Gullet Inn, selling Trouncer's ales. In January 1898 the landlord David Horkey revived an old custom of the house by inviting 150 friends and customers to a New Year dinner. The meal contained 'old fashioned fare' that included a boar's head and a round of beef.

Bridge Street, *c.* 1905. The photographer is looking towards the Welsh Bridge situated just around the corner. St Austin's Friars is to the left and Barker Street to the right. The large timber-framed building in the centre is the Old Ship Inn. In about 1900 it belonged to George Birch who had just sold the Bricklayer's Arms, the building on the right in Barker Street, to Bates' Brewery of Wrexham. It was sold for a premium on the assurance that Birch would stop brewing beer. Soon after he moved into the Old Ship he began brewing again. When the brewery took him to court he told magistrates he thought the brewery meant he should stop brewing at the Bricklayer's Arms, which he no longer owned. As it was a verbal agreement, the case was dropped.

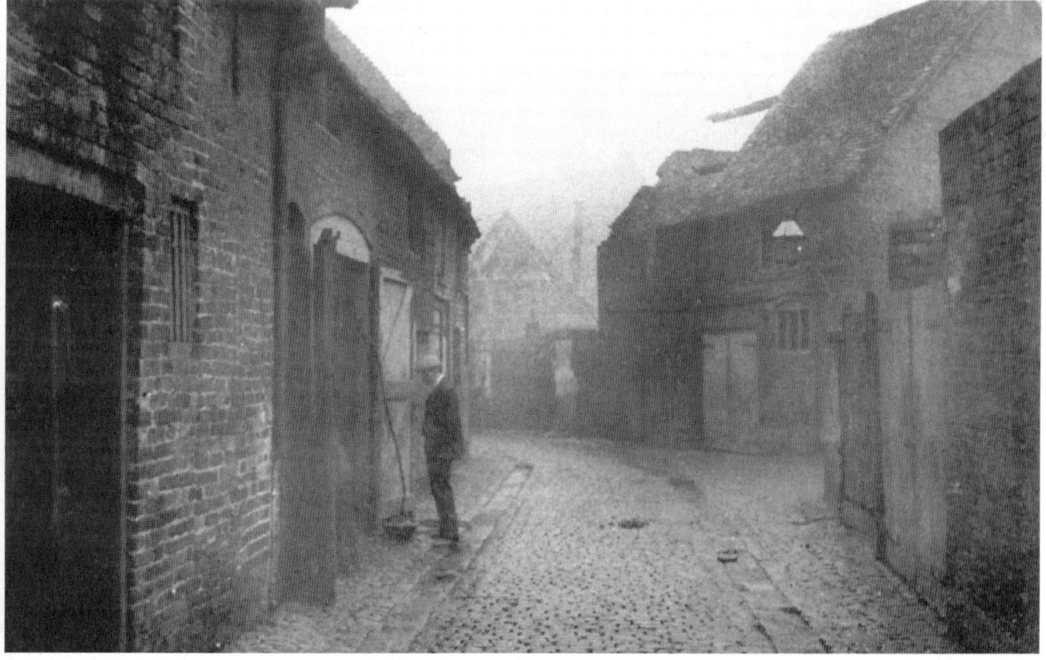

Roushill, *c.* 1900. This road follows a similar line to the modern road leading to the bus station with the Riverside shopping arcade and multi-storey car park on the left and the Pride Hill and Darwin Centres on the right. In this view the slaughterhouses are on the left while the buildings on the right lead to Smithfield Square and beyond to Eagle Foundry Square and Smithfield Buildings. The old slaughterhouses were replaced by the council in 1911 by a new abattoir, which they proclaimed had 'up-to-date equipment comparable with any in the country.' Note that some of the buildings in the centre are being removed to make way for the new 'Electric Generating Station' that was situated at the bottom of the Seventy Steps.

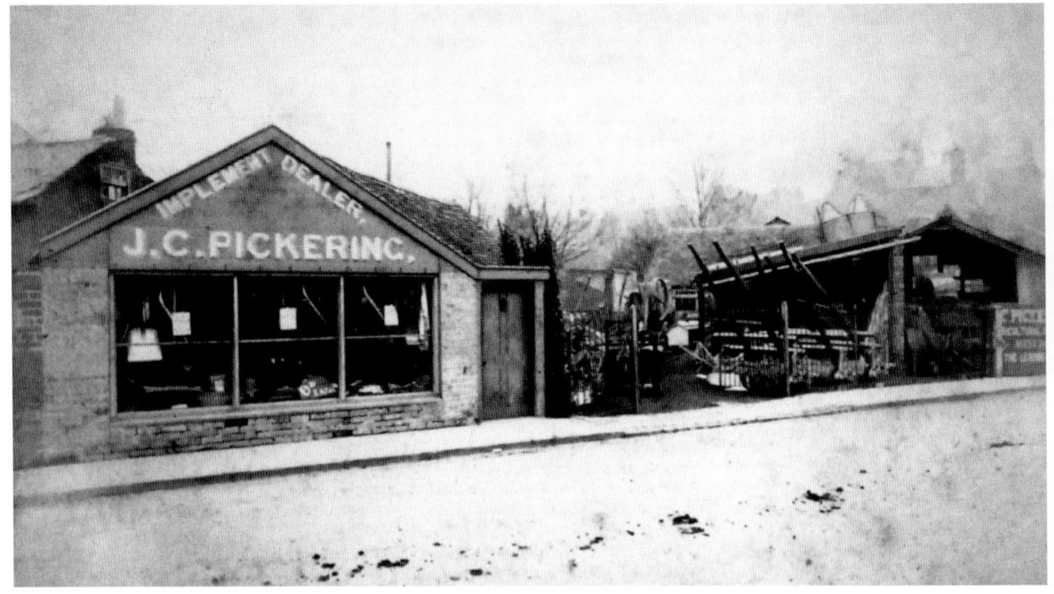

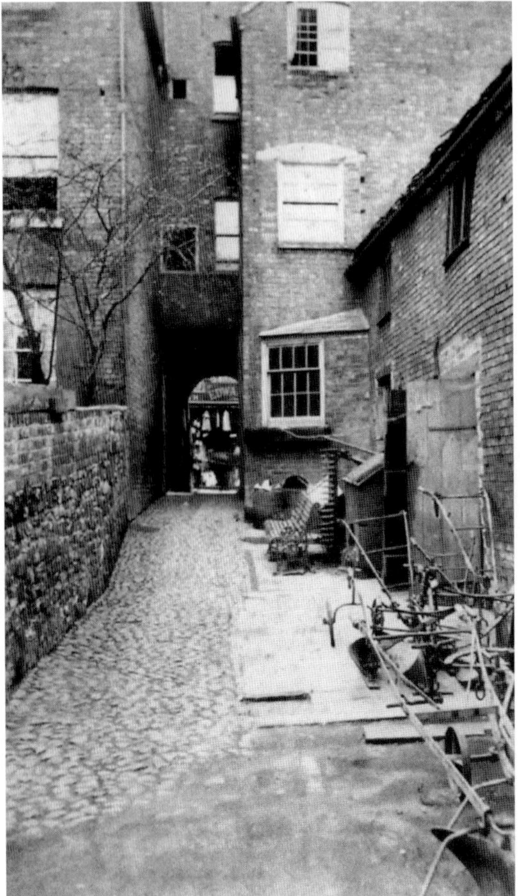

Smithfield Road, *c.* 1895. Since the beginning of the 1890s there have been three generations of the Pickering family, each with the Christian names William Corbet. The family established a business in this area of the town and the first Mr Pickering was listed as an engineer and an agricultural implement maker. In 1895 he had these premises and another further up the road near the Victoria Hotel and a shop at 49 Mardol where he was listed as an ironmonger. The family owned land, which followed a burgage plot that curved round from Mardol to Smithfield Road. By 1916 the family had become motorcycle and cycle agents with their main shop in Mardol, a cycle storage depot in Smithfield Road and workshops in between, accessed by a narrow lane.

Mardol, *c.* 1895. This is the Mardol end of the lane that ran to the side of Mr Pickering's shop to the workshops and storage depot in Smithfield Road. The rear of the Mardol property is on the right, note all the agricultural implements and ironmongery stored outside. Looking through the arch is no. 25 Mardol, the shop of Edward Roberts, a cabinetmaker and furniture dealer. In about 1980 the third Mr J.C. Pickering moved across the road to 26 Mardol, where he continued in business selling mainly toys and bicycle accessories.

2

ABBEY FOREGATE TO THE EAST

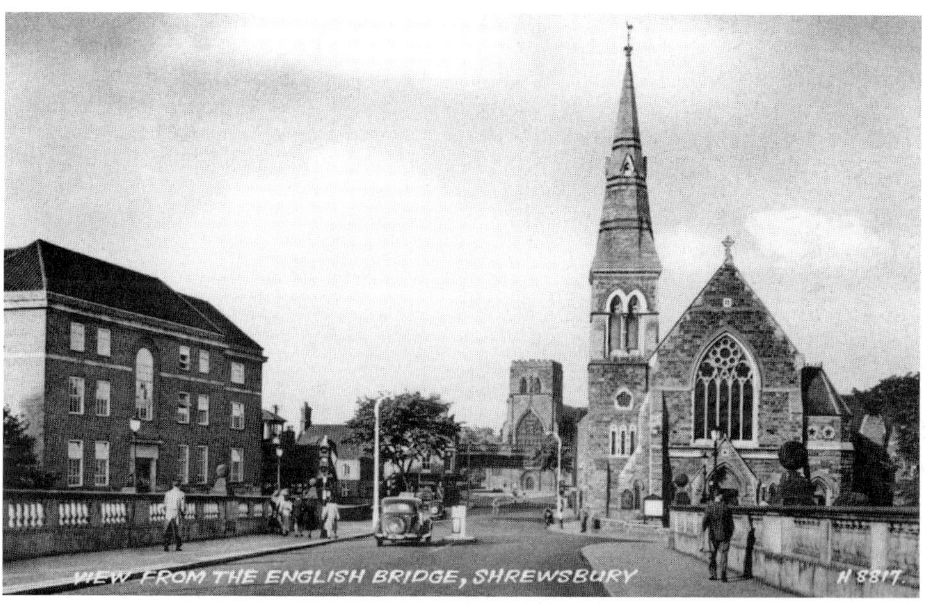

Abbey Foregate, *c.* 1950. A car waits at traffic lights before turning right into Coleham Head in the days before the gyratory system was even thought of. The building on the left is Shrewsbury Technical College that was built on the site of a former college, demolished in 1932. The foundation stone was laid in 1936 and the new college opened in 1938. During this period students were taught mainly at Abbeydale House. The Congregational Church was built in the Gothic style by George Bidlake of Wolverhampton and was opened on 31 May 1864. With its spacious school room, lecture hall, caretaker's house and two tennis courts, it cost in the region of £8,500.

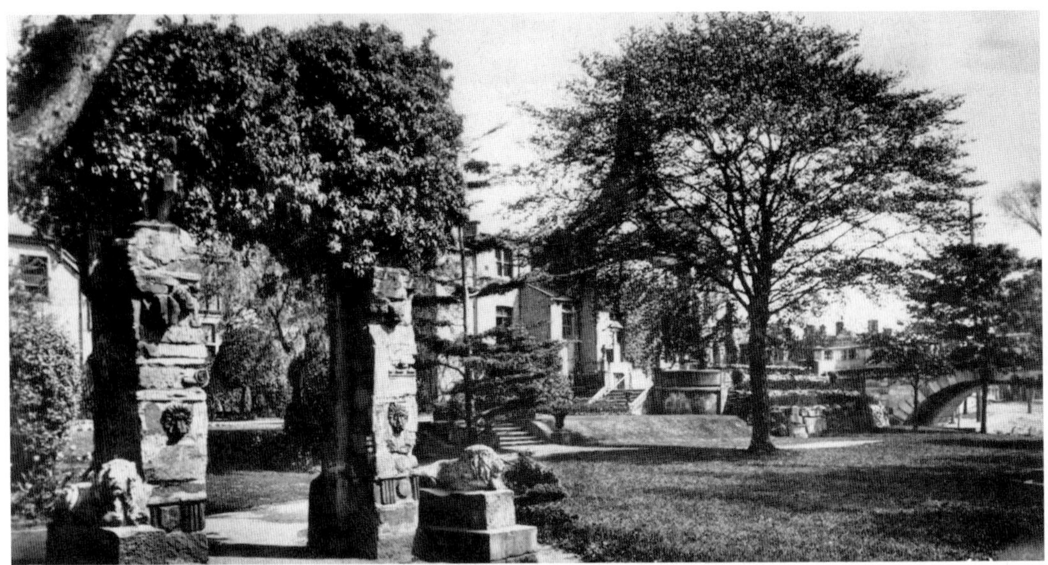

Abbey Foregate, *c.* 1910. The large building to the rear is Abbey House, home to the Carline family of stonemasons until 1862 when it was sold to Richard Palin, a solicitor and agent for the Crown Life & Female Provident Assurance Company. In about 1890 William Tutton turned the house into a school for boys and in 1899 the council opened a technical college there. The open area between the house and the river was known as Mr Palin's Pleasure Ground and was called Abbey Gardens. In 1902 the land was developed into a public park by landscape gardener John Barron. Several interesting features were used including the Rowley portal, seen here covered in ivy and the two lions, which were test pieces for the ones around the base of the Column. The portal was returned to the entrance of Rowley's Mansion in 1983.

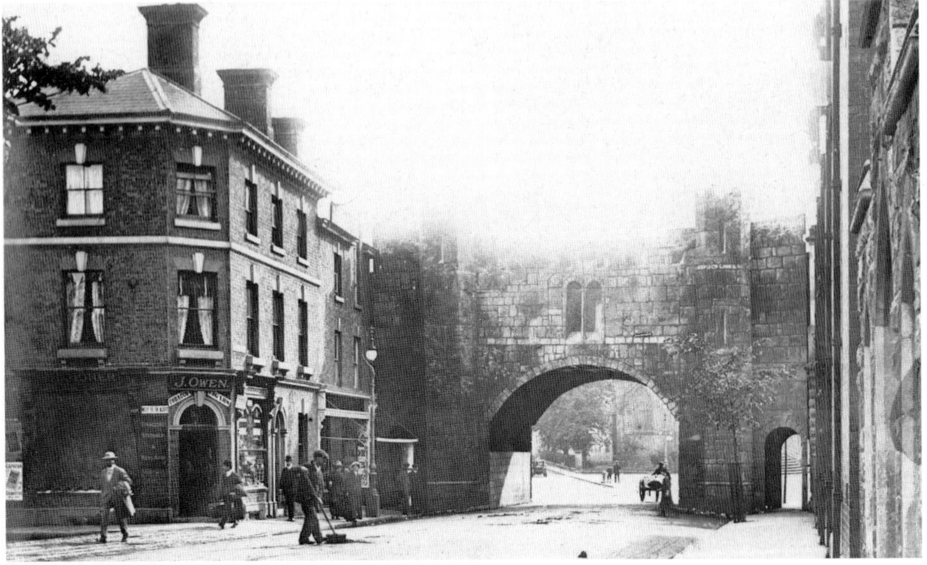

Abbey Foregate, July 1914. The message on the reverse of this card reads, 'Arch erected for Royal Show to hide the old Railway Bridge Aug. 1914. From the windows we had a fine view as the King passed . . . and when he returned.' The large building on the corner was built about the end of the nineteenth century on the site of a timber-framed building known as the Old Court House.

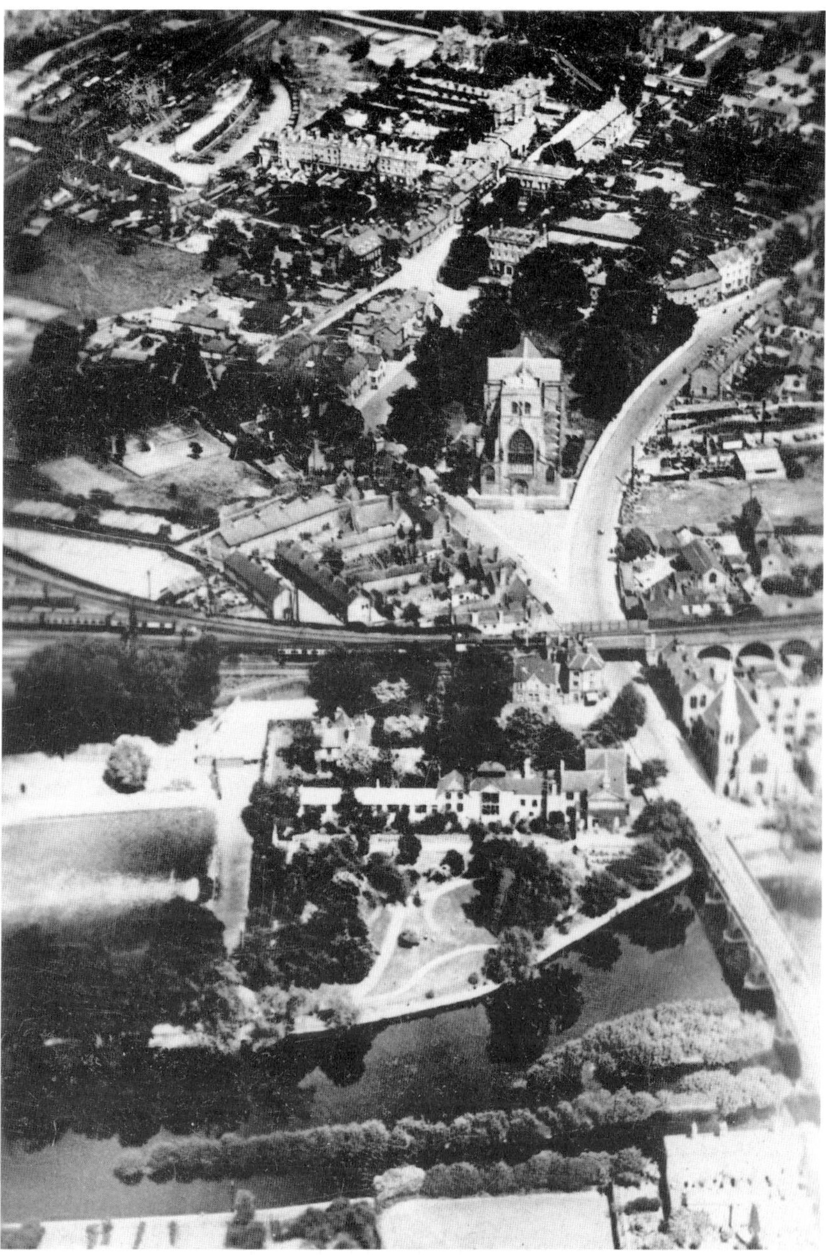

Abbey Foregate, *c.* 1918. This view is looking east over the English Bridge and the railway viaduct towards the Abbey Church. The church is a fragment of a large monastery founded by Roger de Montgomery in 1083. Originally the old road out of town went to the left of the church but in about 1836, to save time, Thomas Telford constructed part of his new London to Holyhead road to the right, sweeping away fragments of the chapter house, cloisters and other historic remains. Abbey Gardens is in the foreground. Above is a side view of John Carline's house, which was converted into a school by William Tutton in about 1890 and into Shrewsbury Technical College in 1899. The building was demolished in 1932 and replaced by the present Wakeman School building.

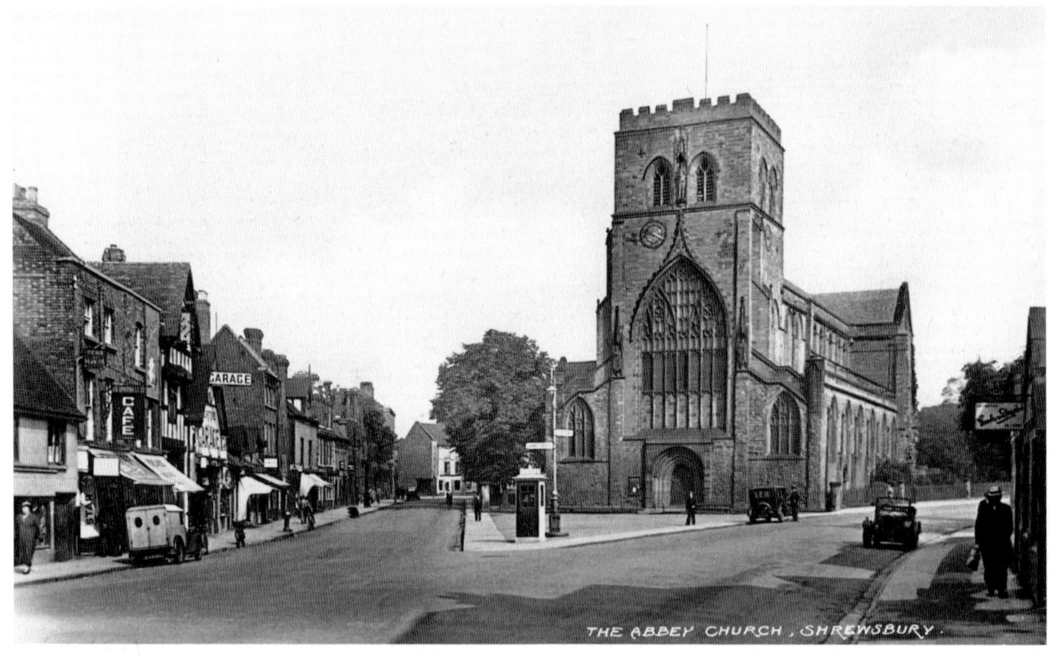

Abbey Foregate, *c.* 1938. The Abbey, which was dedicated to St Peter and St Paul, was founded in 1083. It stands between the old road that ran to the left and rear of the church and Thomas Telford's new one, which was part of his London to Holyhead road, officially opened on the king's birthday in 1836. The van on the left is outside a fruiterer's shop occupied by K.T. Rowland; the café over the top advertising Hovis and teas was run by Leonard Halford. The timber-framed building next door was built as a public convenience out of timbers rescued from old houses being demolished in Barker Street. Cureton's garage to the right was housed in a genuine cruck-framed building dating from the beginning of the fifteenth century.

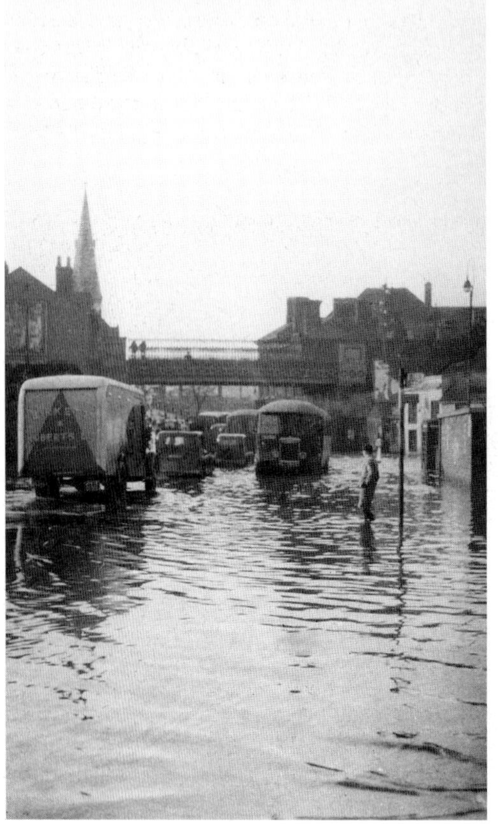

Abbey Foregate, February 1946. Two men on the railway bridge and a boy paddling in the water watch as vehicles struggle through the rising flood. As the waters rose only lorries and buses were able to ferry passengers and they in turn had to give way to hand-propelled assault craft manned by soldiers in areas where the water was deepest. Eventually the force of the water was so great that plate glass windows were smashed and in one shop the till, which was fortunately empty, was swept down the street. The building on the right in the forecourt of the Abbey is a brick public air-raid shelter that was soon to be demolished.

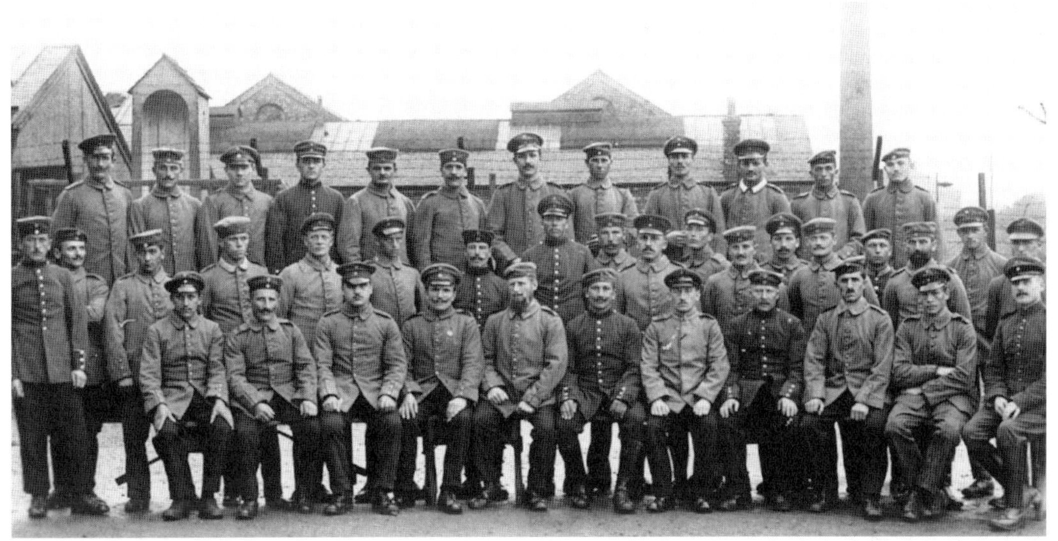

Abbey Foregate, *c.* 1916. Both these cards were sent without a message by Otto Muth, Prisoner of War No. 848, to his sister or daughter Ema Muth who was living in Glatten, Freudenstadt, Württemberg. The soldiers are posing in front of the Midland Carriage & Wagon Works, which was converted and renamed the Abbey Wood Barracks. At Christmas 1914 the War Office banned a proposed concert by the men to raise money to provide comforts for themselves. However, sanction was given for German ladies to provide a Christmas tree for the Barracks. It was said to be 'illuminated and decorated in typical German style' and that the prisoners received seasonal presents. A story circulated the town that the Wednesday before Christmas a German lady and her manservant arrived by car laden with gifts that she distributed to her compatriots. On leaving the camp she carefully handed the guard a penny packet of Woodbines. As the war progressed the prisoners were allowed to organise concerts, which were accompanied by their own orchestra made up of soldiers, sailors and airmen.

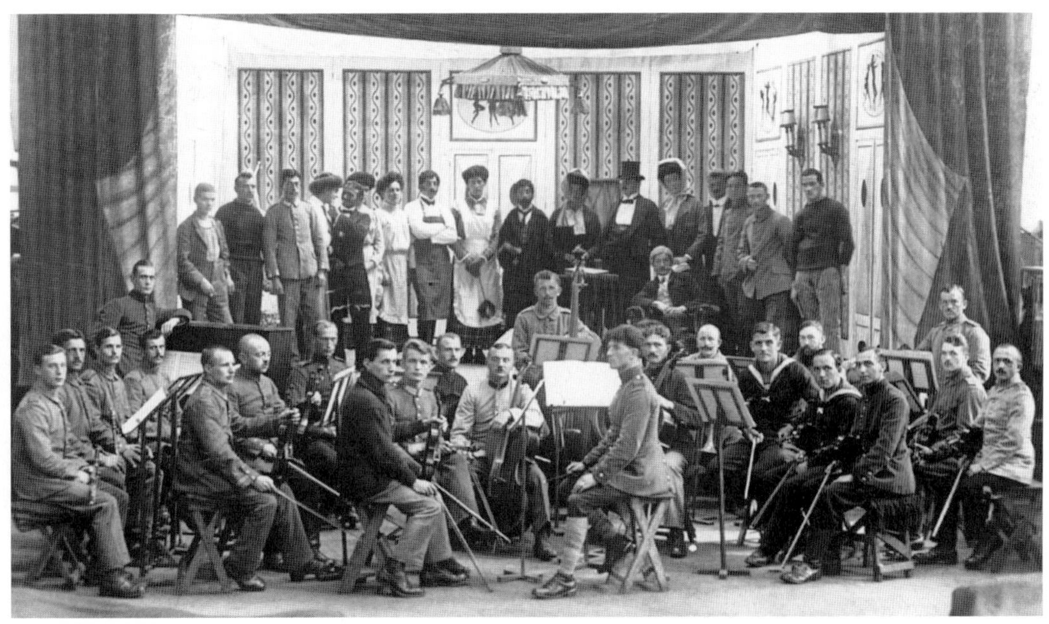

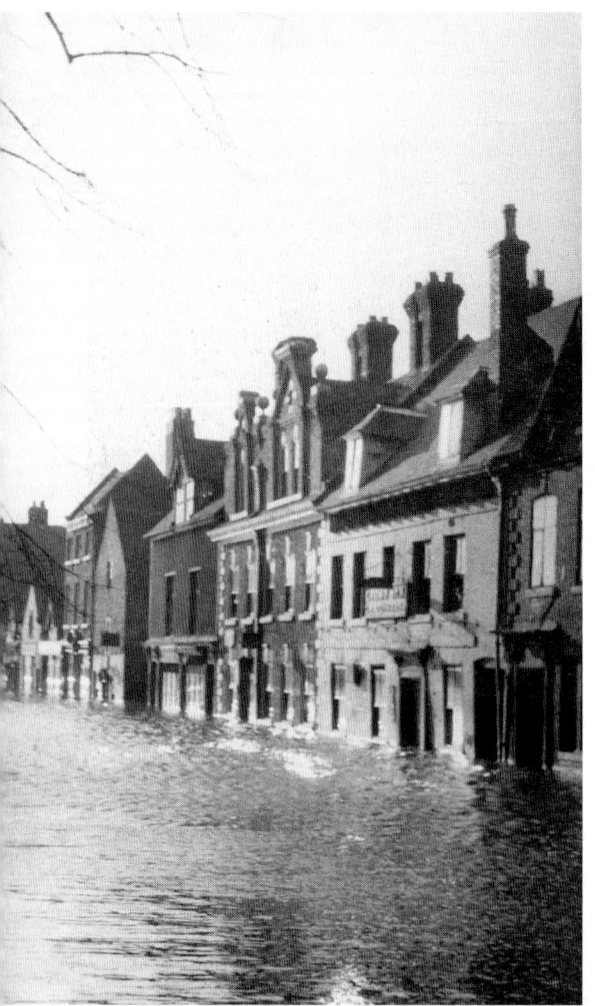

Abbey Foregate, February 1946. Flood waters lap up to the windowsills of the Crown Inn. The inn was first recorded towards the end of the eighteenth century and was known as the Crow until 1861. The building to the left with the Dutch-style second storey is now incorporated into the Crown. Until the 1940s it was known as the Coleham Brush Factory, a firm that was founded in Mardol and located for much of the nineteenth century in Coleham, before moving to these premises after the First World War. The 1946 flood rose to a height of 19ft 6in above normal river height.

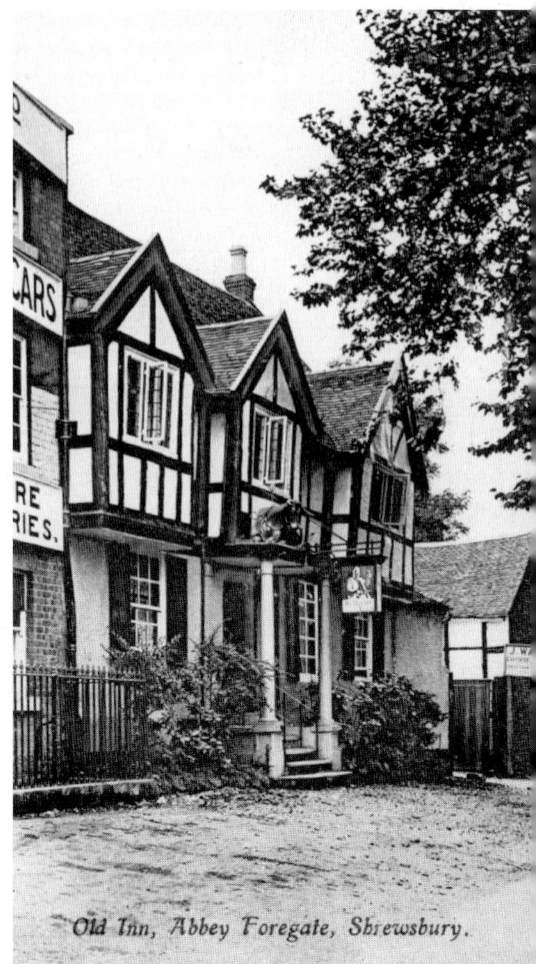

Abbey Foregate, *c.* 1938. The Dun Cow Inn dates from the early seventeenth century and is one of the oldest and most picturesque public houses in Shrewsbury. In September 1900 the inn was put up for auction but when the bidding stopped at £2,500 it was withdrawn. Particulars for the property show it contained an entrance hall, bar, dining room, sitting room, smoking room, kitchen, back kitchen, brew house, lavatory, W.C. and other offices; it also had seven bedrooms and extensive cellarage. It was also reported that there was 'no more pleasingly situated licensed property adapted for hotel purposes in Shrewsbury' and that Abbey Foregate was 'the widest and finest approach to town.' The sign to the right is advertising J. Ward, a carpenter and joiner whose workshop was in the Dun Cow yard.

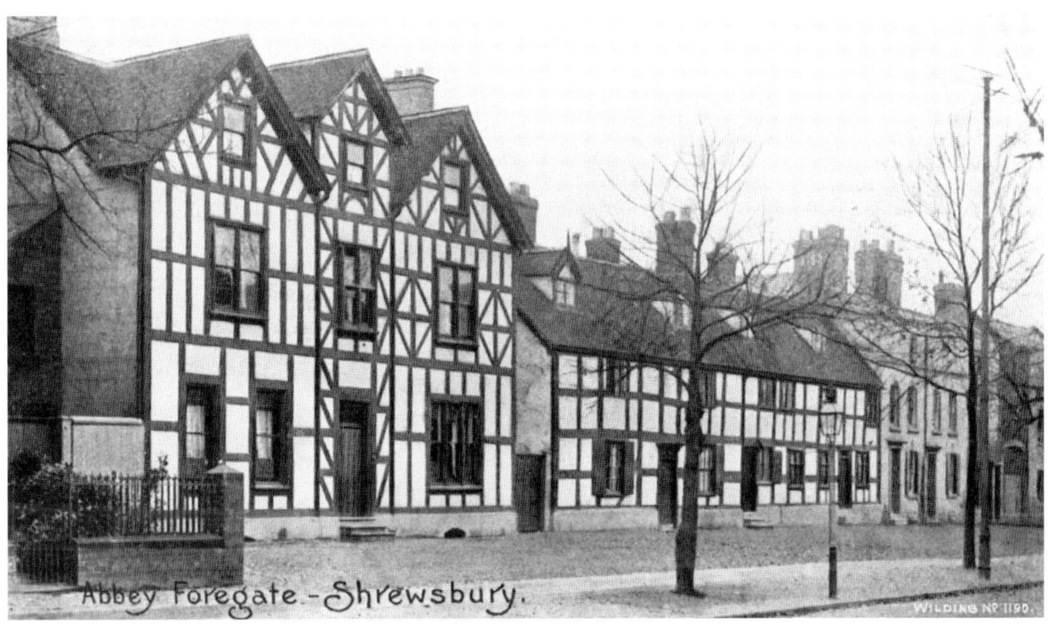

Abbey Foregate, *c.* 1905. The timber-framed building was once the Shrewsbury Collegiate School for Girls that was founded by the Misses White in Lymehurst, a house just to the left. By 1900 it had moved to these premises and was run by Miss Prentice whose aim was to 'give a thorough education to girls; to train them to become conscientious, unselfish, good women, and to develop their powers of character.' It was a day and boarding school and by 1916 there was a kindergarten for little boys. By 1917 it was a hostel for young women working in the Army Pay Corps at Whitehall. It became a private home and later a warehouse for Adams & Co. builder's merchants before being demolished in the 1960s.

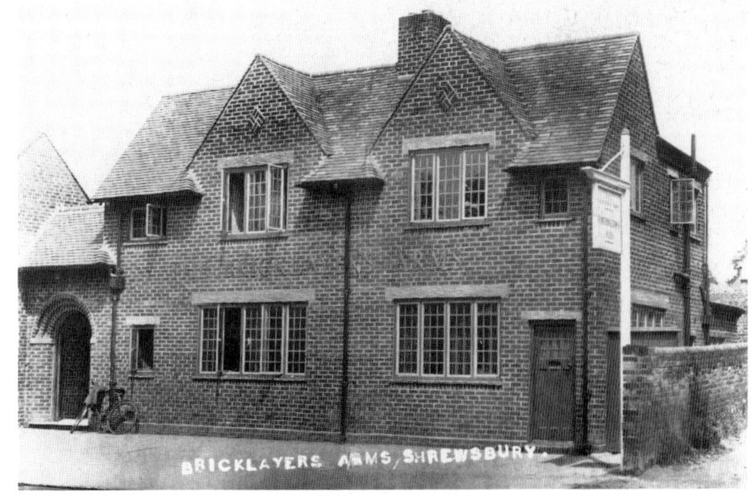

Abbey Foregate, *c.* 1931. The postal date on this card of the Bricklayer's Arms is 30 July 1931. It was sent to Mr R. Littlehales at the Three Tuns in Slough by Alice who writes, 'Dear Dick & Polly, This is our new house.' Alice is probably the wife or daughter of Thomas Price Embrey. He took the licence from Richard Embrey who had been landlord from about 1913. The family continued to run the inn until the 1950s.

The inn was first licensed from about 1780 to 1861 when it closed for a number of years. The name was revived by Thomas Breeze in about 1879. He was landlord until about 1908 when the licence was passed to Charles Chalkley for a short period. The present inn may not be on the same site as the original 1780 building. By the 1930s they were selling Worthington Ales.

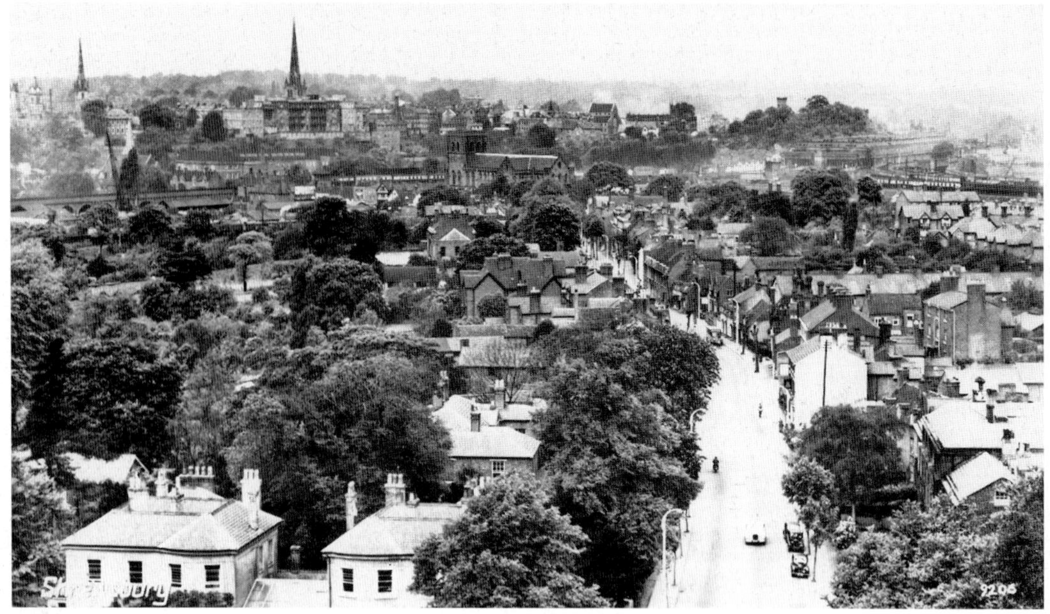

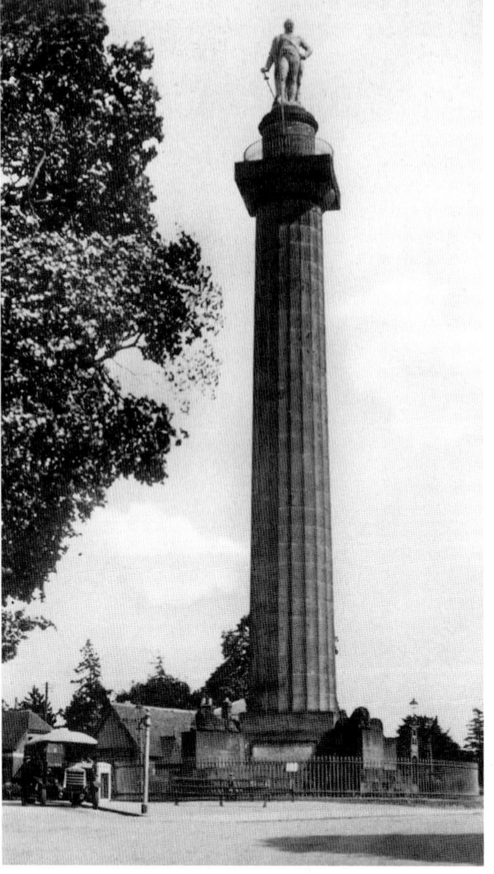

Abbey Foregate, *c.* 1950. This view looking down the Foregate towards the town was taken from the top of the Column. It was described by Samuel Bagshaw in 1851 as 'by far the handsomest approach to the town and containing many genteel residences.' Just above centre are the Abbey Church and a passenger train passing over the viaduct. Close to the horizon are the infirmary and the spires of St Mary's and St Alkmund's. The two houses bottom left were both called The Laurels in 1896 when they were occupied by Laurence Burd and William Bell the postmaster. Just below is Hatton House, a private home until the mid-1930s when it was converted into the Shrewsbury (Shropshire) Refuge Shelter. The old shelter in Crescent Lane was in a house called Chaddeslode, a name they took with them to the new shelter.

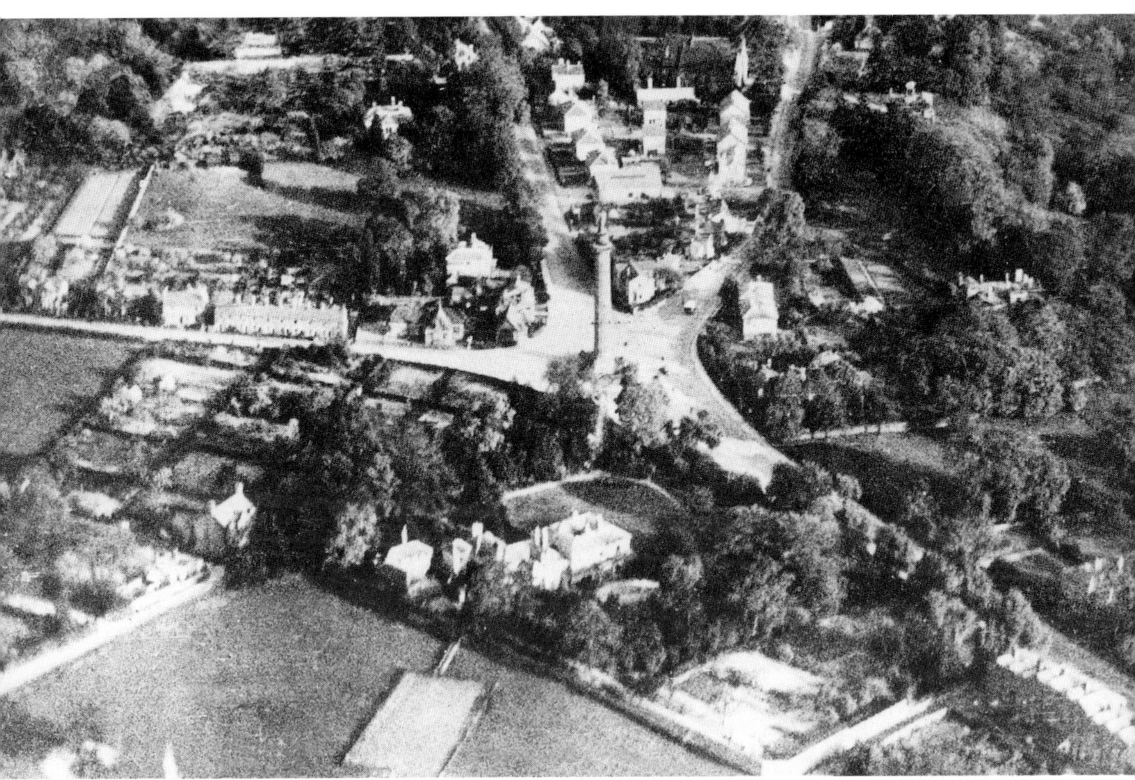

Abbey Foregate, *c.* 1918. The Column stands in the middle of this view at the top end of the Foregate. Lord Rowland Hill was one of Wellington's trusted generals in the Peninsular War and at the Battle of Waterloo. Later many handsome houses were built in the surrounding area such as Nearwell in the foreground on the site of the present Shirehall. It was built by the How family in about 1840 and was their home for over a century. The Column is centred between Abbey Foregate to the right, Wenlock Road, London Road and Preston Street to the left. On the corner of Preston Street is St Giles School and Parish Hall. At the junction of London and Wenlock Road is the Column Hotel while just behind is the old White Horse Hotel. Towards the top right-hand corner is Brooklands, built in the Italianate style in 1831.

Opposite, bottom: Abbey Foregate, *c.* 1925. The Column was built to commemorate the deeds of Shropshire's most heroic soldier, Lord Rowland Hill. The first stone was laid by the Salopian Lodge of Free and Accepted Masons on 27 December 1814 and the last on 18 June 1816, the first anniversary of the Battle of Waterloo. The overall height of the Column, reputed to be the largest Grecian Doric column in the world, is 133ft 6in. The Grinshill stone was carved by John Carline while the builder was John Straphen. The cost including the caretaker's cottage was £5973 13*s* 2*d*. Behind the bus, coming out of Preston Street, are St Giles' School and Parish Hall.

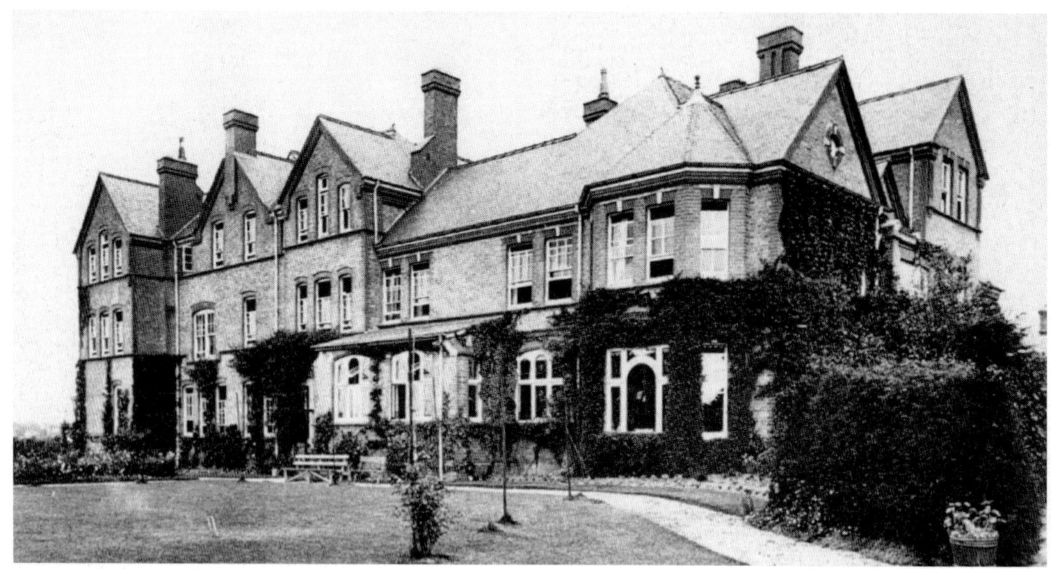

Sutton Road, *c.* 1910. Mill Mead was designed by A.E. Lloyd Oswell in 1899 as a preparatory school for headmaster Wyndham Deedes. He ran the school until 1912 when he was succeeded by joint headmasters F. Folliott Sandford and A.T. Bennion. The aim of the school was to 'teach boys to think and work intelligently, and, while developing their bodies, to influence them to be both gentle and manly.' Fees in 1914 were 28 guineas a term, but if two brothers attended together it was 25 guineas each. The fees included board, tuition, drawing, singing, pens and paper, linen, plate, laundry, games and drill. An extra *7s 6d* a term was charged for medical attention and medicines.

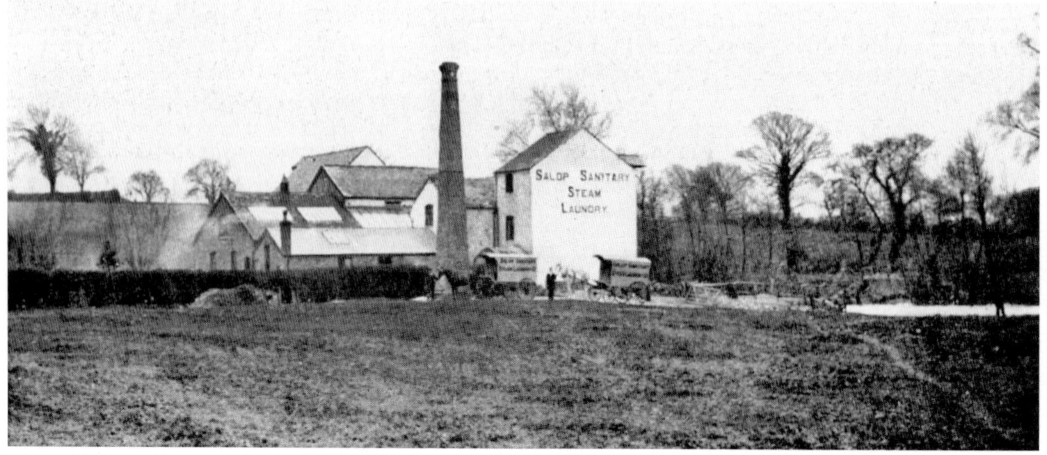

Sutton Road, *c.* 1910. The Salop Steam Laundry was housed in a converted water mill close to the Rea Brook. It was one of three mills under the control of the Abbot of Shrewsbury Abbey that used the waters of the Rea to feed a mill race to power the machinery. This mill was known as Burnt Mill after it was badly damaged in an arson attack in 1801. After repairs it continued to grind corn until 1888 when it was converted into a laundry. In 1914 Miss M.A. McNaught advertised, 'Situated in open country and quite free from smoke and dust. All linen dried in the open air whenever possible. Ladies can view the Laundry on Wednesdays or Thursdays, or other days by appointment. No chemicals whatever used, and all linen kept a beautiful colour.'

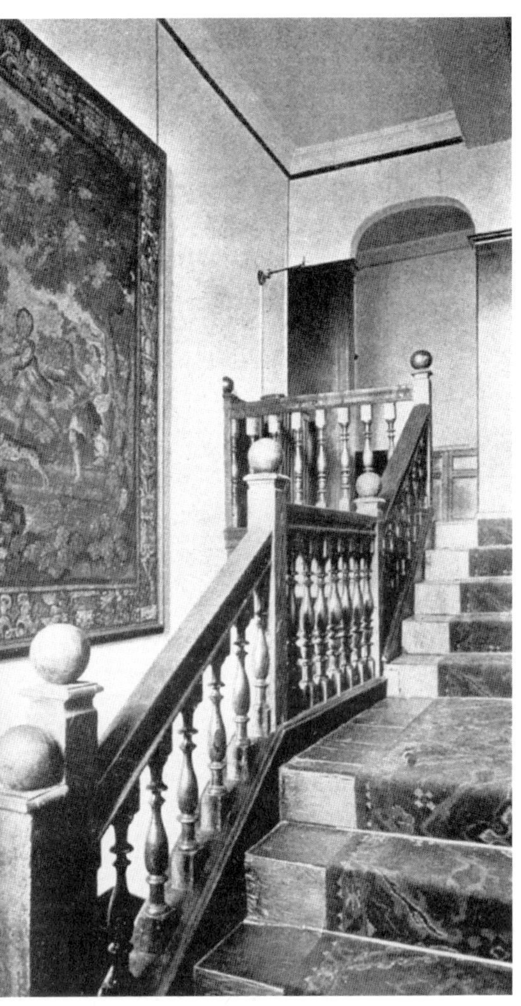

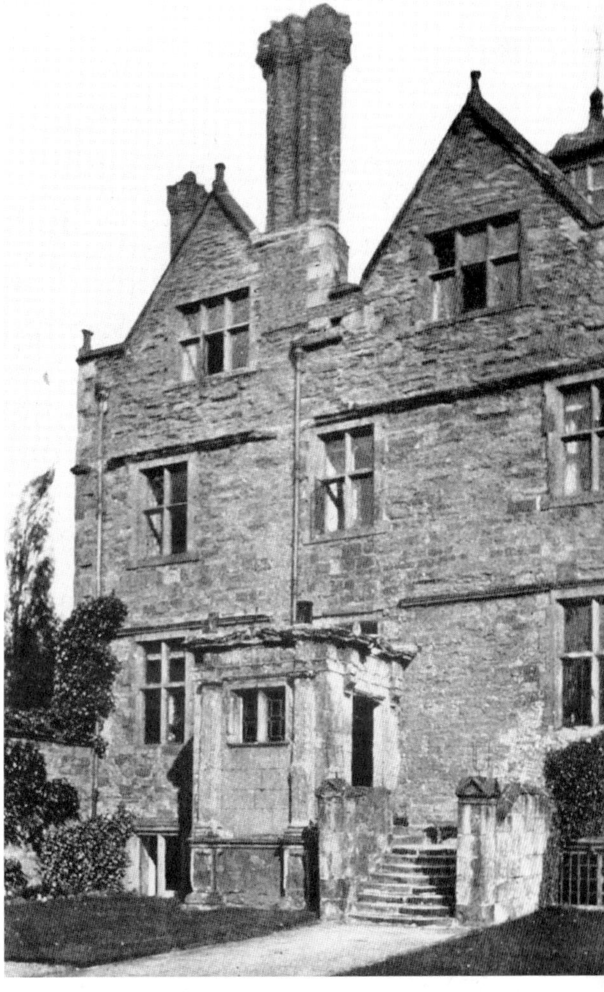

Monkmoor Road, *c.* 1920. Whitehall was erected on the site of the monastic grange between 1578 and 1582 for Richard Prynce, a lawyer. It was built from stone salvaged from the abbey but the interior walls were timber framed and the fireplaces and chimneys built out of brick. Several rooms were oak panelled and the staircase is unusual as the steps are made out of solid wooden blocks instead of boards. The hall was passed on to the Earls of Tankerville who sold it in 1835 to Dr Samuel Butler, the headmaster of Shrewsbury School and Bishop of Lichfield. Several members of the family resided there and at times it was let to a private tenant. During the First and Second World Wars the hall was commandeered and used by the Army Pay Corps. Between the wars the hall was converted into a hotel and restaurant run by a Captain Dugdale and a Mr Ward, and was furnished with antiques, tapestries and works of art. In about 1880, during some restoration work, a secret compartment was found behind one of the chimneys.

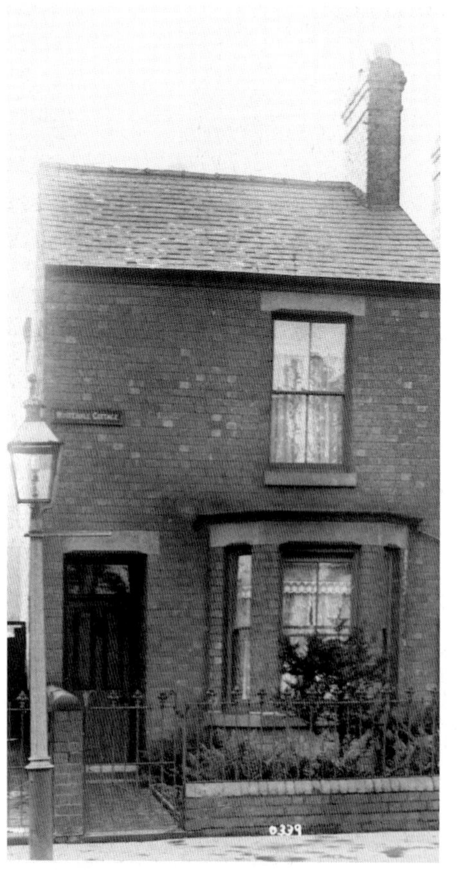

Canon Street, *c.* 1911. Soon after 1886 Samuel Butler, the grandson of Dr Butler, developed the Whitehall Estate on a large field called Walk Croft. The new houses were built along streets named after people close to him – Bishop Street in honour of his grandfather, Canon Street after his father's position in the Church and Alfred Street after his faithful servant Alfred Cathie. This house is number 95 and it has the name Whitehall Cottage above the front door; it was one of three houses called Chirbury Villas. On the reverse of the card, E. Davies writes to Mrs Millar in Lancashire, 'I am sending our cottage for you to have a peep at. I think they might have made it look nicer.' Miss E. Davies was still living there in the 1940s.

Monkmoor Road, *c.* 1930. This view was taken from the top of Cleveland Street looking back towards Abbey Foregate. Crowmere Road is on the left and opposite is Tankerville Street. The building on the corner with the small bell tower is the Abbey Parish Hall, designed by A.E. Lloyd Oswell and erected in the 1880s. It cost in the region of £600, which included fittings. The money was raised locally and the hall was also used by Cherry Orchard Infant School. On the corner of Crowmere Road is the Cherry Orchard post office, which was run by William Lawton Beamand, who was also the local tailor. At this period, the stretch from Abbey Foregate to Crowmere Road was known as Monkmoor Street while from Crowmere Road up to the Aerodrome was called Monkmoor Road.

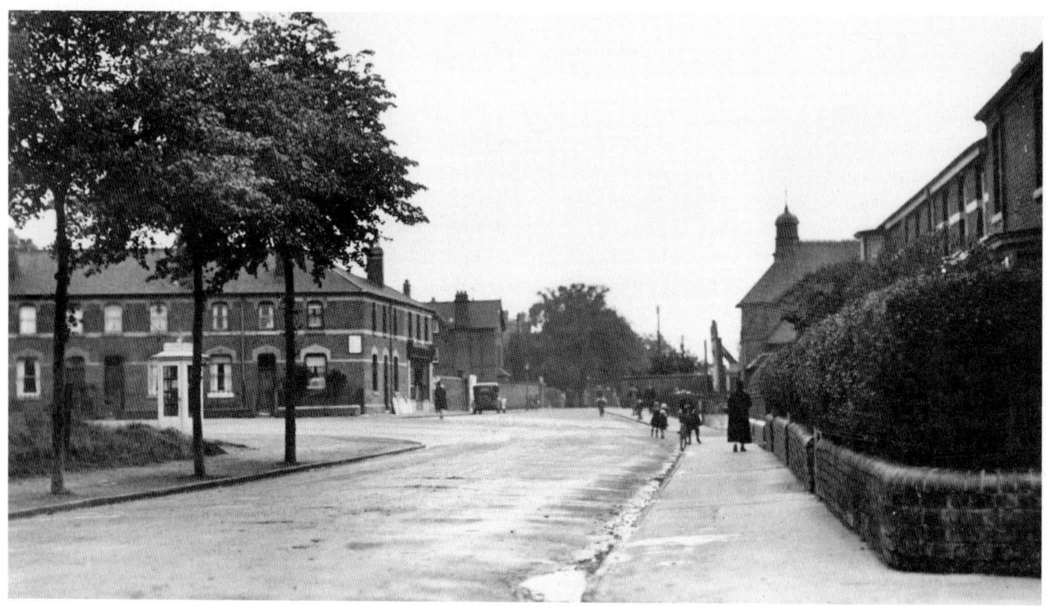

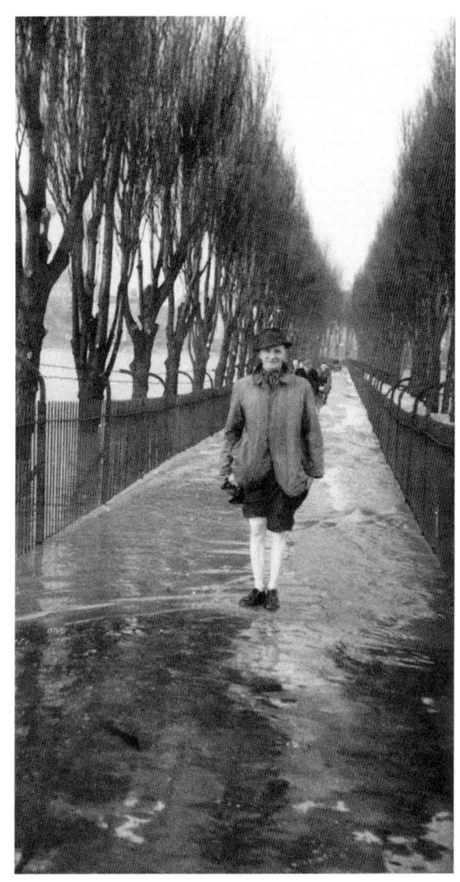

Castle Walk, February 1946. This was the view from Underdale Road to Castlefields during the big flood. The man with the white legs is just about to wade through the murky waters, which in February must have been icy cold. Other members of the public cycle through the flood risking the hazards of mud and potholes. The avenue of poplar trees were planted when the new Castle Walk Bridge was constructed in 1910. Unfortunately they died after the ground around them was raised above the flood level and builder's debris was placed around their trunks. The field on the left called Taylor's Field is now the Wakeman School sports field.

Bradford Street, *c.* 1900. Orchard House was once known as Holywell Cottage and was built in 1819 for John Beck, a local banker. His initials with the date are recorded in a plaque over the porch and he died there in 1821. In 1851 the Shrewsbury Permanent Freehold Land and Building Society acquired the estate and put a road through linking Monkmoor Road to Underdale. It was first called Union Street but was renamed Bradford Street in 1881. Written on the reverse of this card is, 'This is a portion of my family!!' presumably by Henry Pattison who was living there at the time. He was a chemist and seedsman specialising in pansies. The house was later sold to Edwin Murrell, the rose expert.

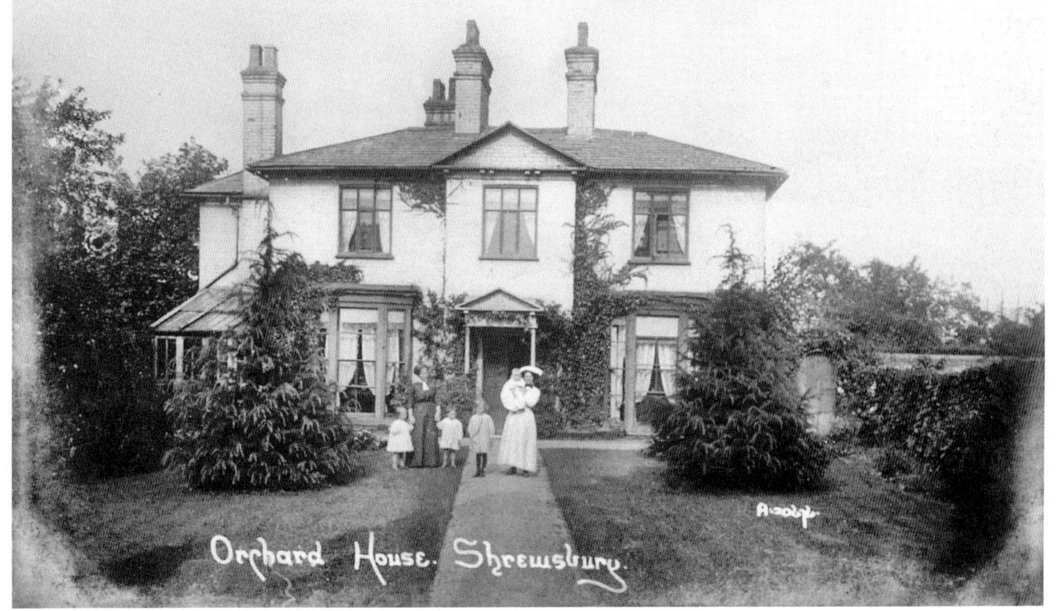

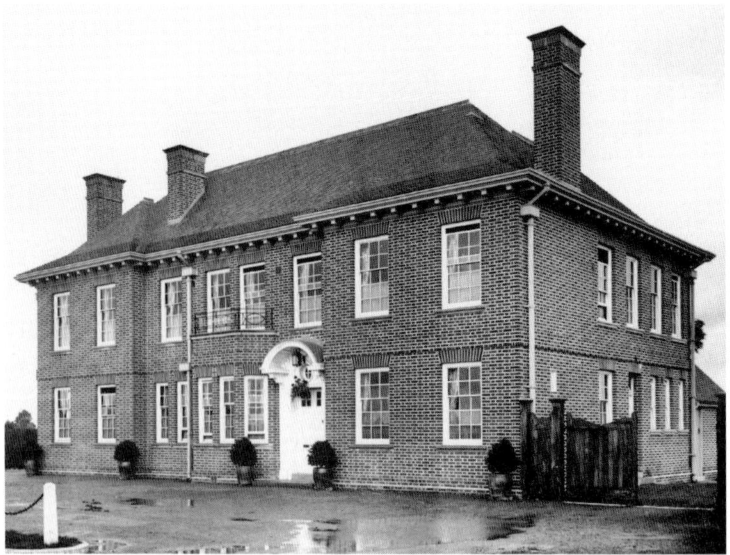

Monkmoor Road, *c.* 1930. This smart new Georgian style building was built by the grandfather of the co-author of this book, A.H. Woodhouse, for William Butler's Brewery. It was opened in March 1930, 'to meet the needs of the growing residential area of which the old race course is the centre.' The hotel was built for comfort and many of the rooms were oak panelled and beautifully furnished by John Blower. There was also a large assembly room overlooking the bowling green, which was to be surrounded by ornamental trees. The licence for the hotel was transferred from the recently closed Bell Inn in Princess Street. The first landlord was Sidney Pace, the son of Thomas Pace a builder and an ex-Mayor of Shrewsbury. He ran the inn from 1930 until 1947.

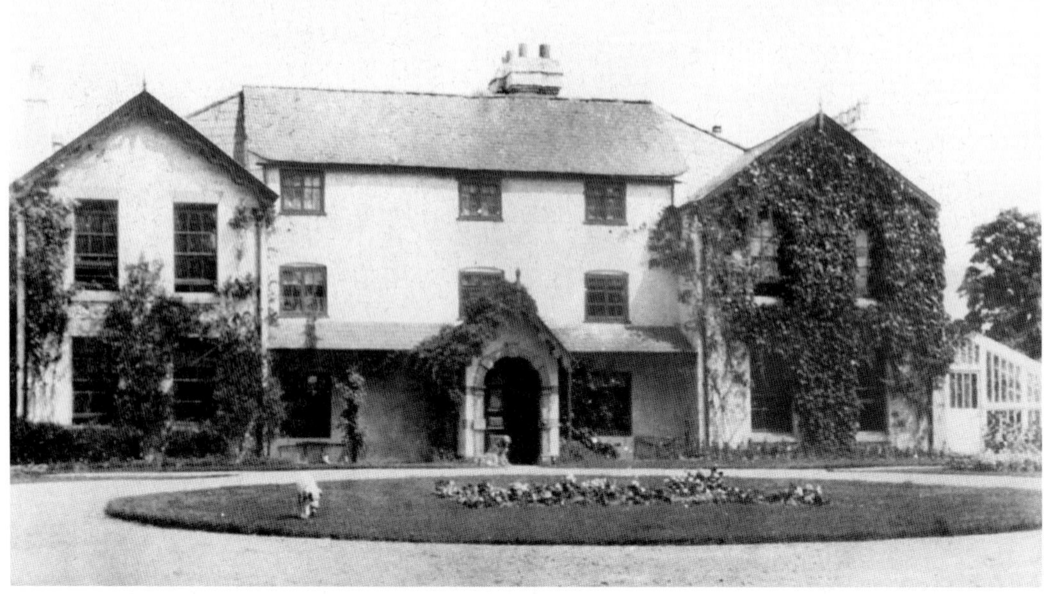

Monkmoor Road, *c.* 1905. Monkmoor Hall was situated at the top end of Monkmoor past the aerodrome and Monkmoor Farm. It was erected in 1840 and was the home for many years of the Butler-Lloyd family. It was a large pleasant house with thirteen bedrooms and spacious grounds. In about 1909 it became the town's isolation hospital with fifteen beds. After the First World War a joint Atcham and Shrewsbury isolation hospital was opened nearby in buildings erected by the RAF as a women's hostel. The hall was again fitted up as an isolation hospital during the Second World War. It closed in December 1944 but the hall remained the property of the council until it was demolished in 1961.

3

TOWN TRADERS

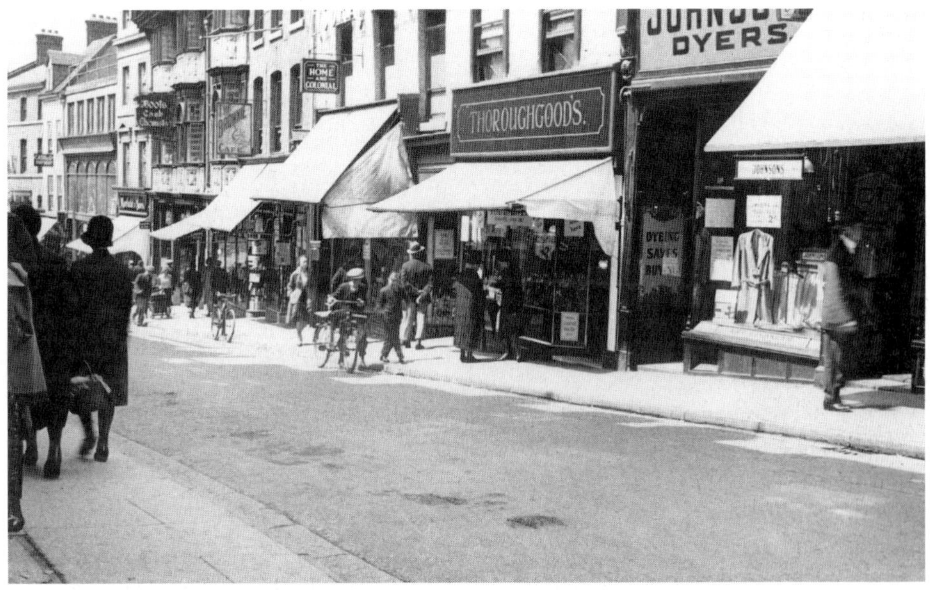

Pride Hill, *c.* 1930. Pride Hill has always been one of the main trading areas of the town. It was named after the Pride family who owned property there in the thirteenth century. Parts of the street have also been known as Butchers' Row and Shoemakers' Row. Johnson the dyers and drycleaners were there for many years. Their motto by the door reads, 'Dying Saves Buying'. Below and side by side are three grocery shops: Thoroughgood's, The Home and Colonial and Hunters the Teamens Ltd. Above Hunters was the popular Brownie Café run by Lois Purslow. Below is Boots the chemist, which also had a café on the upper floor and then Manfield's shoe shop and Shuker's hardware store.

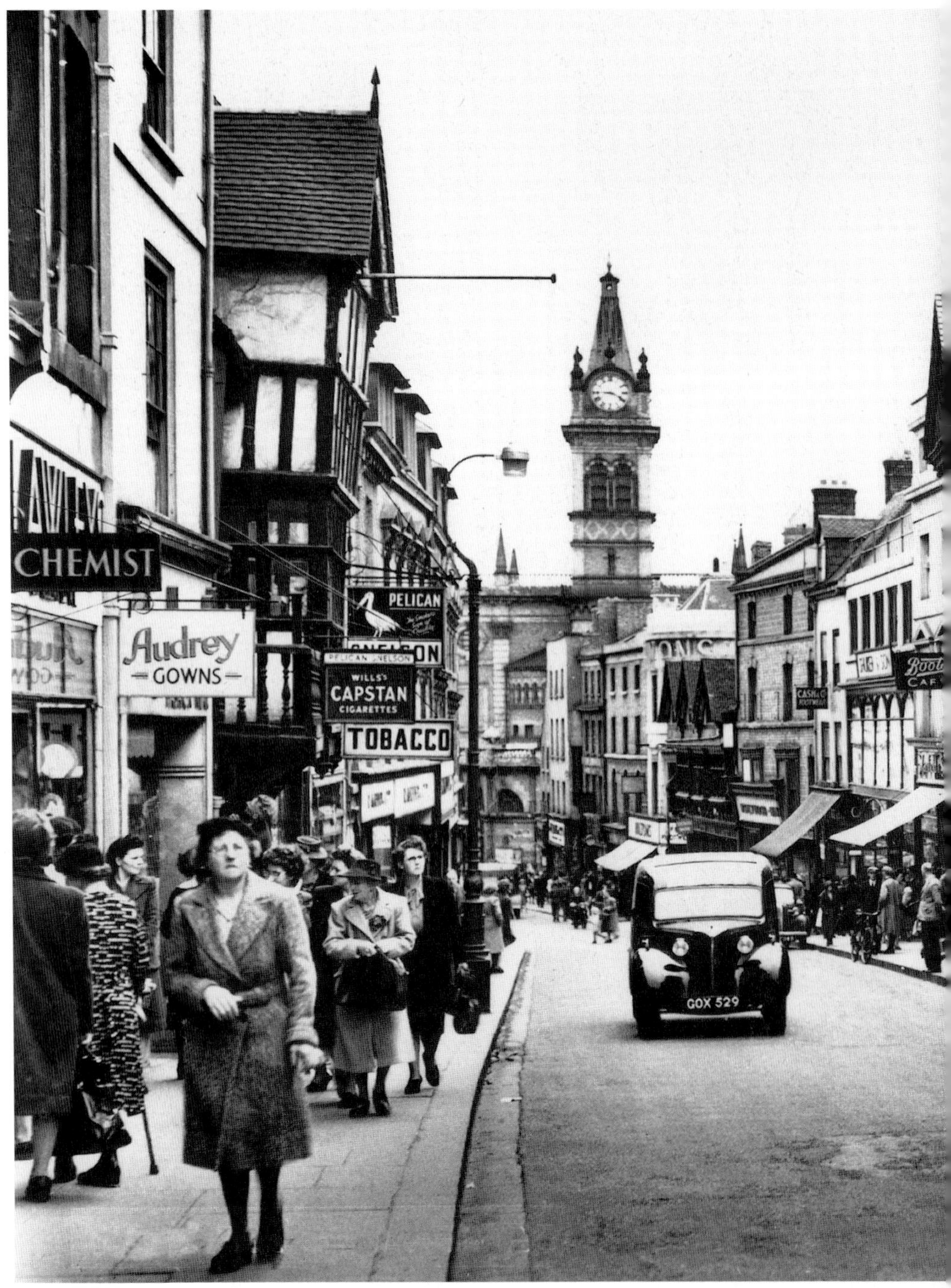

Pride Hill, *c.* 1950. This is a fine view of the street looking down to the Victorian Market Hall. Note the absence of double yellow lines or 'No Waiting' signs and the owner of the bike left unattended on the kerb outside Boots knows it will still be there when he returns. Very little has changed on the right from the last view. On the left is the sign of the pelican, advertising Pelican and Snelson the tobacconists. It is housed in the timber-framed building, built in the

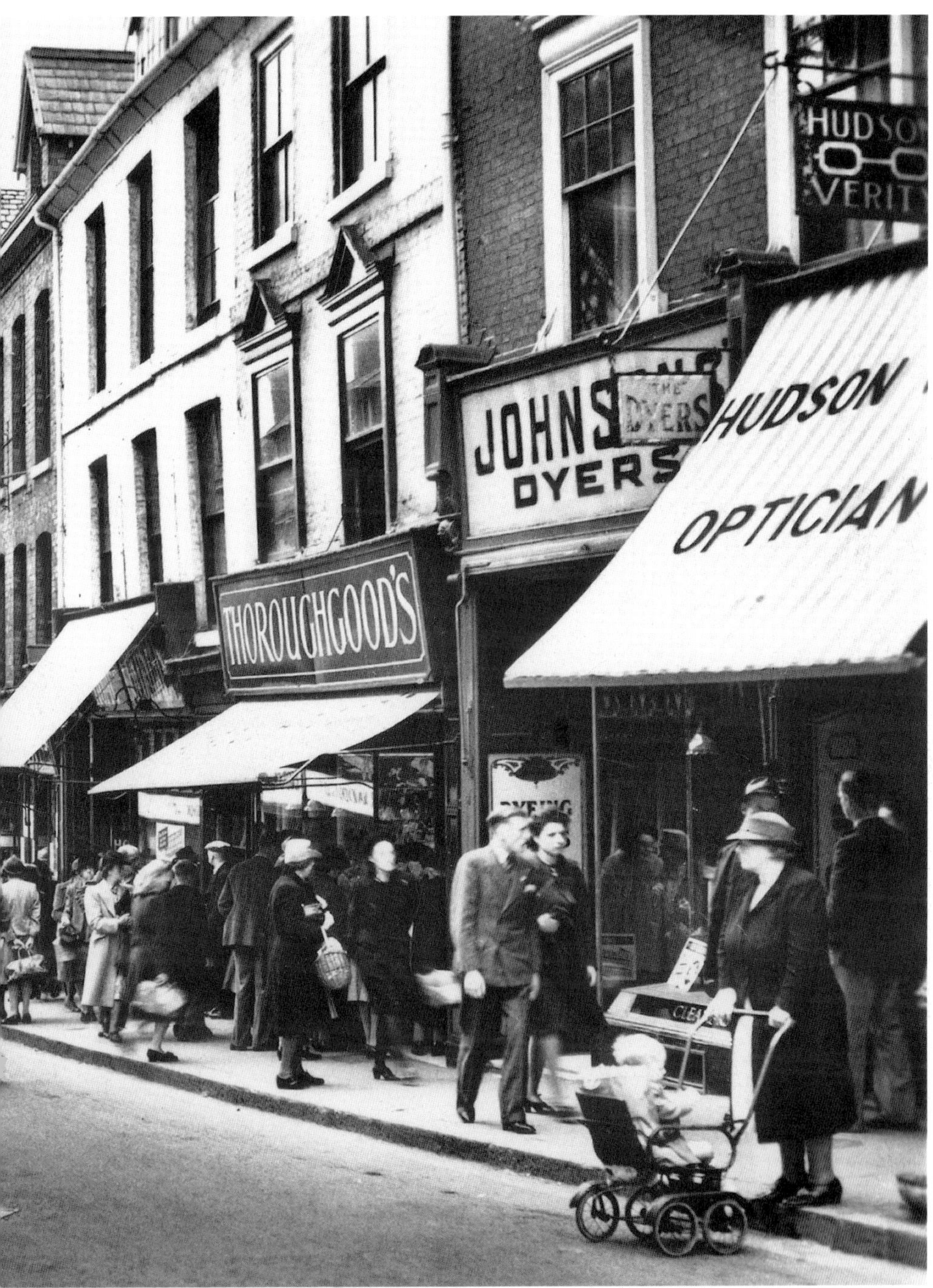

sixteenth century but with an added extension a century later. To the left are two signs, one advertising Audrey Gowns at Paige's ladies' shop, the other the chemist's belonging to C.M. Keenleyside. Between them was Lawleys (of Regent Street) Ltd, the glass and china dealers.

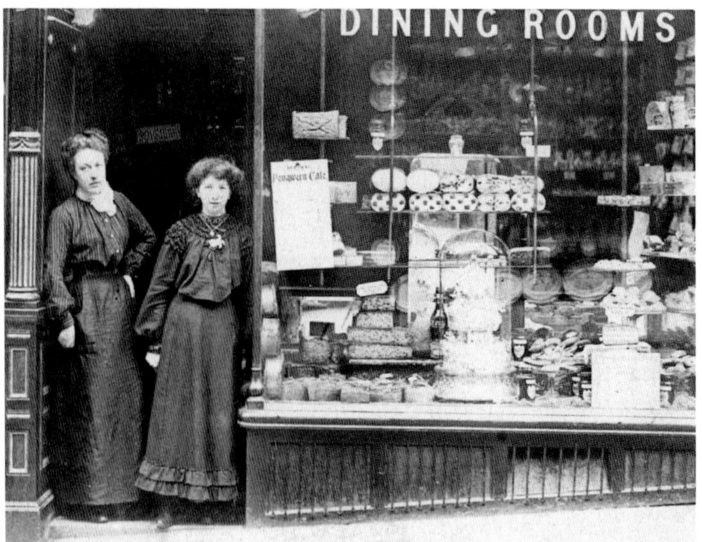

Two shop assistants stand in the doorway of the Pengwern Café and confectionery shop, Pride Hill, *c.* 1903. It was situated at no. 12, which later housed opticians Hudson Verity, seen in the previous view. The shop and café was owned by Thomas Pidduck Deakin who also had another shop at the bottom of Wyle Cop and was listed as a baker and confectioner. He later sold both businesses when he purchased the Crown Hotel in St Mary's Street. He was elected a councillor in 1890 and served twice as Mayor of Shrewsbury, in 1898 and again in 1915.

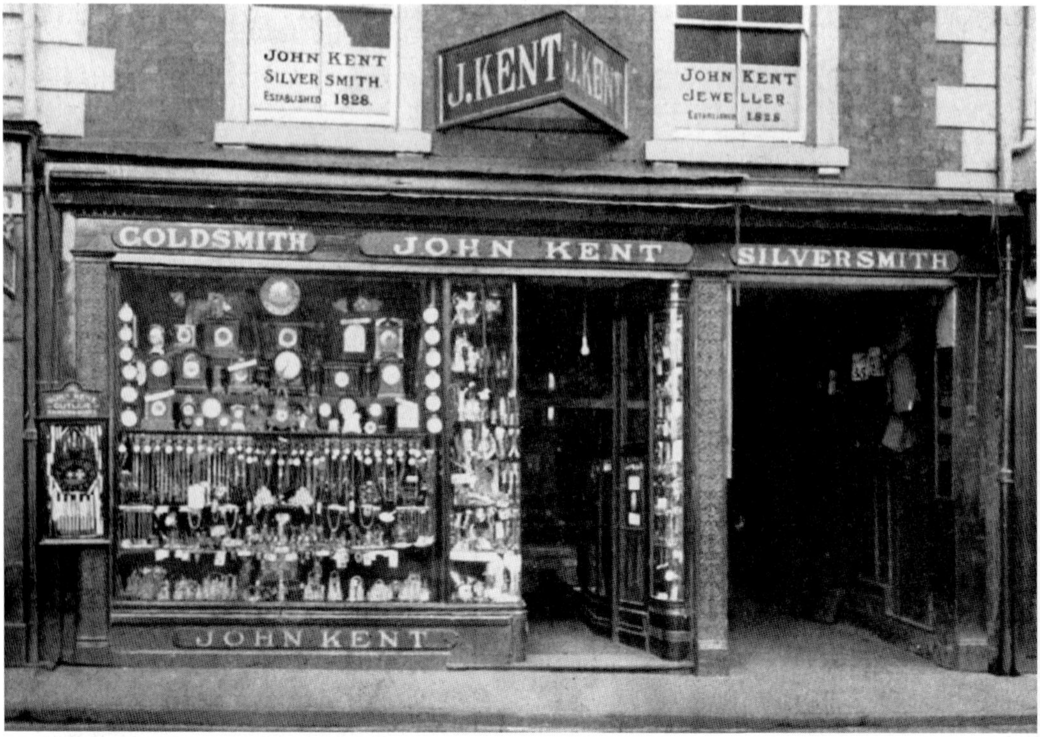

Mardol Head, *c.* 1910. On this trade card for John Kent it was stated that the business was founded in the reign of George III, yet in the windows of the first floor the date of establishment is given as 1826, six years after George III died. He was a jeweller, gold- and silversmith and also a pawnbroker. He advertised that he was the best purchaser for all manner of items including furniture, both modern and antique, pianos, timepieces, books and bicycles. His shop stood next to the Gullet Passage and he was still trading there in 1913 but had gone by 1916.

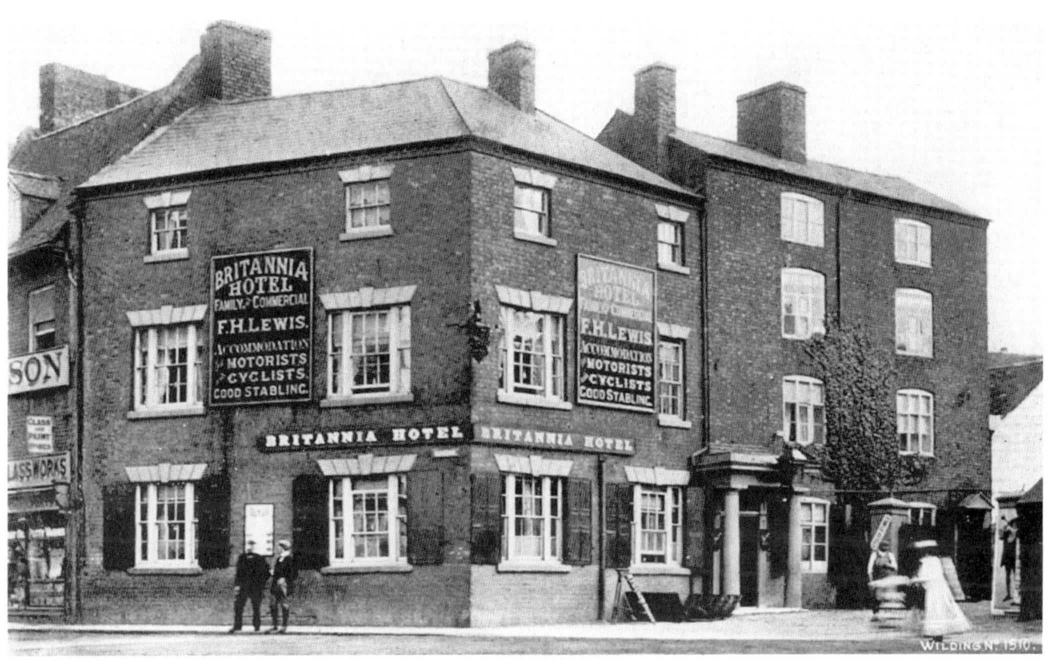

Mardol Quay, *c.* 1910. The Britannia Hotel was first recorded as the Harp or Welsh Harp. In April 1819 landlord Thomas Cartwright went into partnership with William Leighton of the Talbot Hotel and announced that 'Coaches for London, Holyhead, Bath, Bristol, Chester, Liverpool and to all parts of the Kingdom will leave the Britannia Inn every morning.' By the beginning of the twentieth century things were changing with landlord Frank Hemingsley Lewis offering 'accommodation for motorists and cyclists', as well as 'good stabling'. The shop to the left in Mardol belonged to George A. Rowson, an 'Artist In Stained Glass'. Work that he had recently completed were windows for the new Congregational Chapel on Coton Hill and repairs to windows of St George's Church in Mountfields.

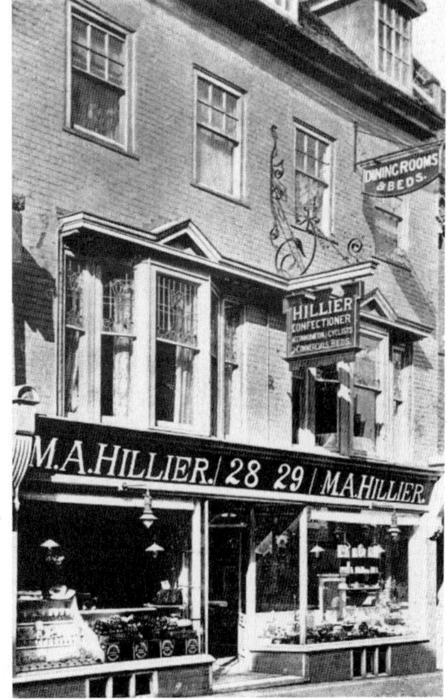

Mardol, *c.* 1912. Mary Ann Hillier and her family ran a café and confectionery shop at no. 29 Mardol for over seventy-five years. They also purchased the grocery shop at no. 28 in about 1907, ran a café and dining rooms and provided overnight accommodation for cyclists and commercial gentlemen. Business was good in April 1914 as Mrs Hillier writes to A.E. Salisbury of Bromsgrove on the reverse of this card. 'Dear Sir, Sorry I cannot oblige you for time stated as I am quite full up.' The dining rooms did a roaring trade on Tuesdays, when farmers in town for the cattle market would sample some of Mrs Hillier's hot dinners, chops and steaks. The café was renamed the Galleon and in about 1960 became Shrewsbury's first Chinese restaurant called Hung Hing.

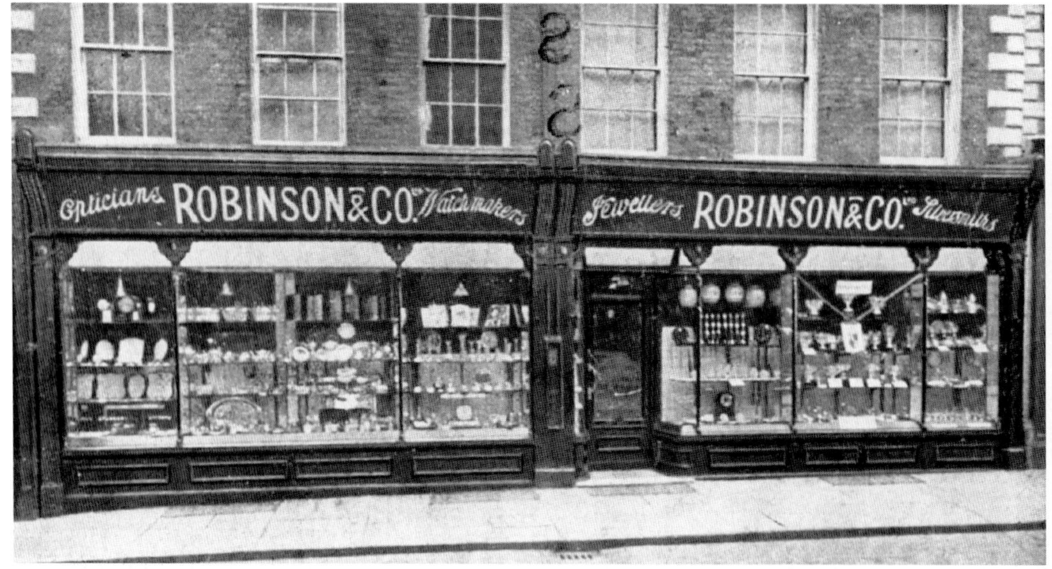

The Square, *c.* 1920. Robinson & Co. were jewellers and silversmiths in The Square for well over a hundred years. In an advert for 1914 they claimed to be 'The oldest established and leading firm of jewellers in Shropshire'. They were diamond merchants, goldsmiths, silversmiths, watchmakers and opticians and one of their specialities was 'Hand beaten silverware in exclusive designs'. On the reverse of this trade card the optician writes to T. Smallman of Onslow on 30 July 1940; 'We have pleasure in informing you that we have a selection of artificial eyes for you to see and shall be glad if you call at your earliest convenience.' The business changed its name in 1997 to Goldsmiths.

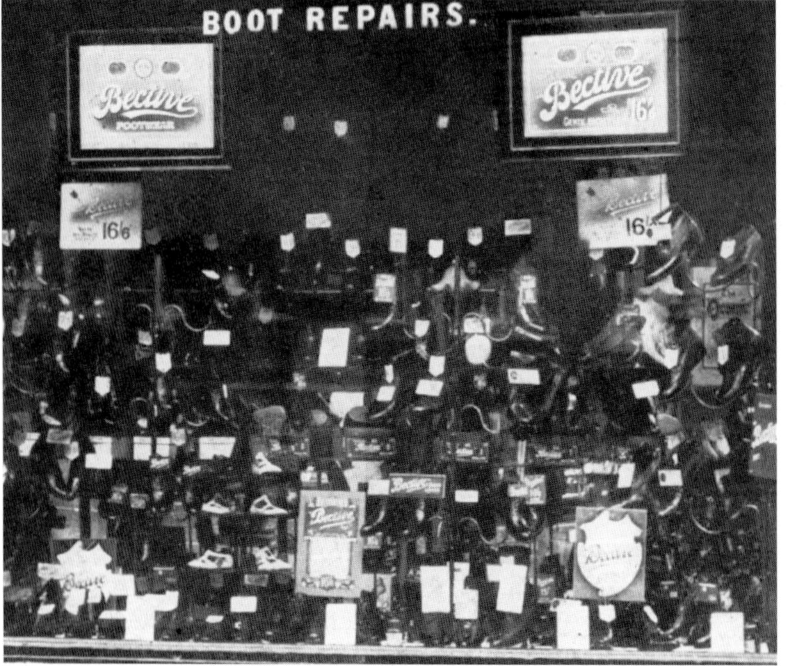

Princess Street, *c.* 1920.This is a trade card for Joseph Della Porta & Son advertising their new range of 'Special Bective' gents shoes priced at 16*s* 6*d*. The printed message on the reverse reads, 'Having received our Season's Stock of Gents' "Special Bective" Boots, we respectfully invite your inspection of the same. These goods occupy a leading position, and are "BRITISH." Made in the latest and most approved Styles, Shapes and most approved materials, in sizes and half-sizes.'

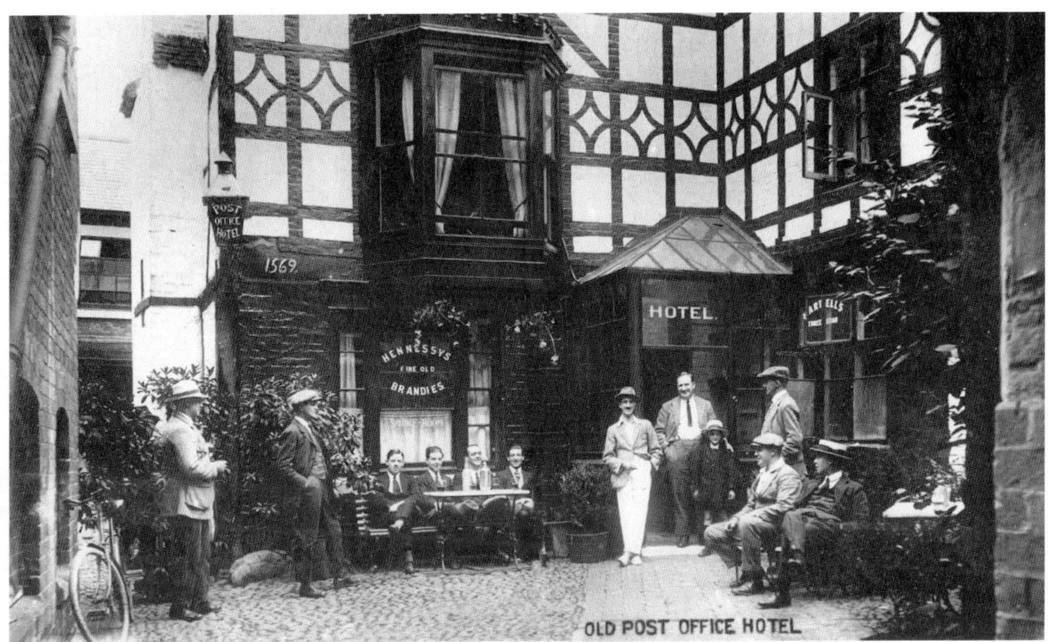

Milk Street, *c.* 1925. This group pose for the photographer and enjoy a drink outside the Old Post Office Hotel. The hotel was first licensed at the beginning of the nineteenth century. It is housed in part of a building known as Proude's Mansion erected for George Proude a wealthy draper in about 1568/9. Note the date on the corner of the building under the lamp. Close inspection of the timbers reveal they were painted on over a skin of brick. The man standing in the door with his arm around the little girl is possibly Charles Davies who was landlord throughout the 1920s and '30s. The cheeky message written on the reverse to Miss Anderson at the Shakespeare Hotel in Nottingham by W.P.R. asks, 'How would you like to spend your Honeymoon here?'

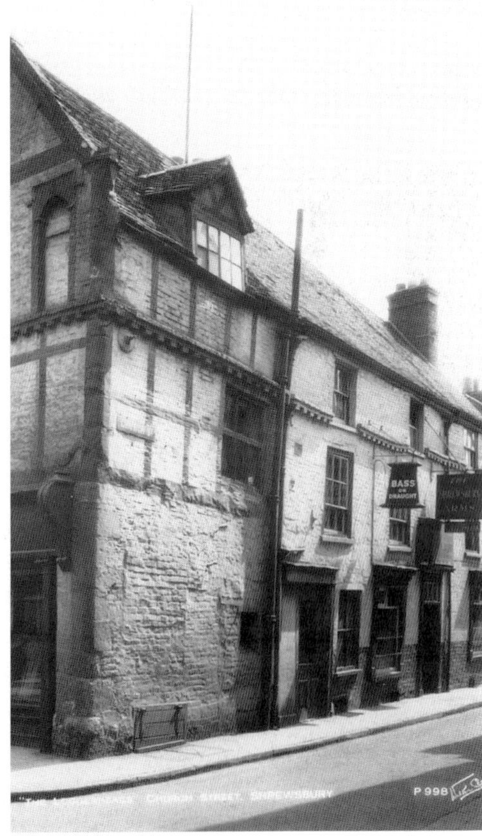

Church Street, *c.* 1930. This building on the corner of St Mary's Street and Church Street has a brick shell over an earlier stone structure. Part of the building is an inn, first licensed in the eighteenth century when it was known as the Greyhound. It was later renamed the Horse and Jockey and then the Lord Hill or the General Lord Hill after Shropshire's most famous soldier. In 1828 it changed its name again to the Shrewsbury Arms, but has been known locally since 1831 by its nickname 'the Loggerheads' (the Loggerheads is the name given to the three leopard or lion heads depicted on the arms of the town).

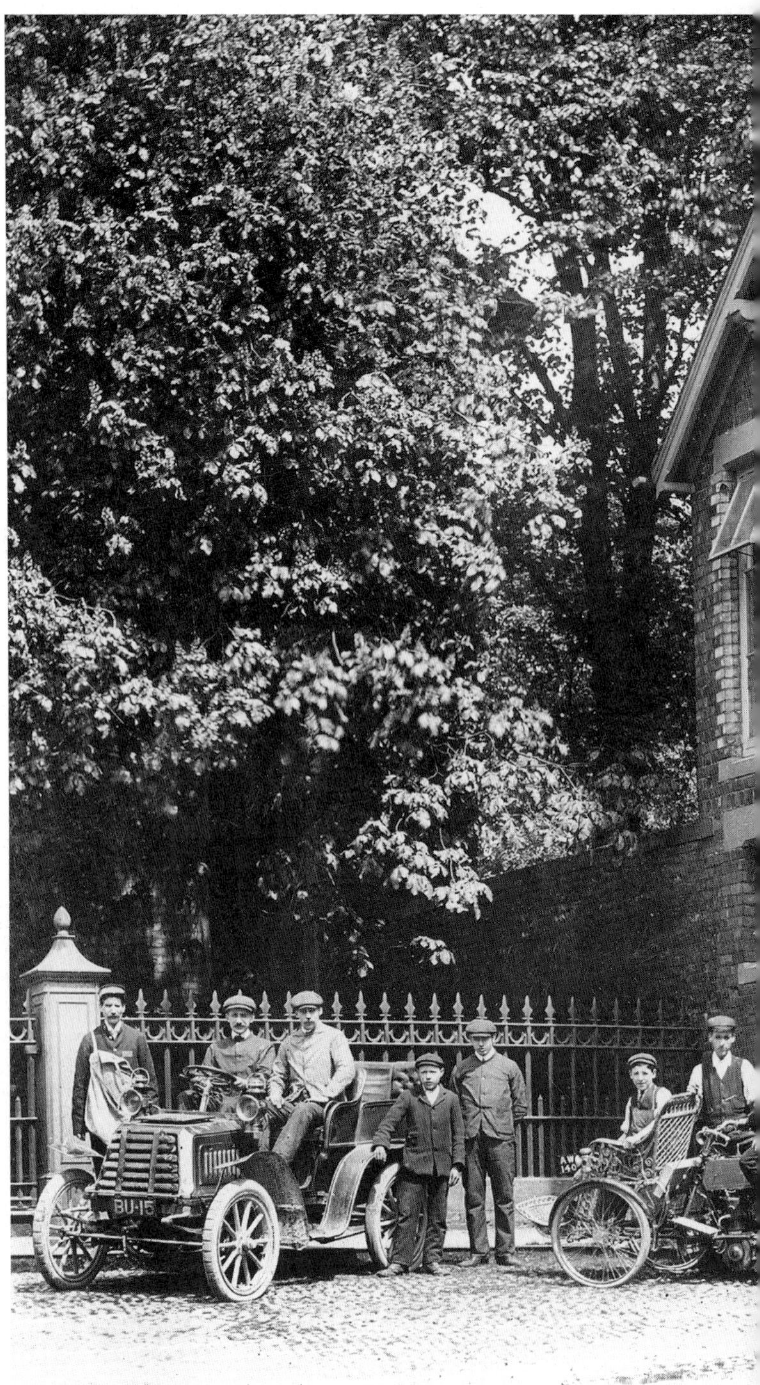

Dogpole, *c.* 1905. Mountford & Co. were established in 1819. In 1896 they advertised that they were 'The Oldest Established Firm of Carriage Builders In The County', and they could not 'Be Beaten For Quality And Price'. It was converted into one of the town's first garages and had connections with the Raven Hotel which was beginning to cater for the new trade brought in by the motor car. Soon after 1900 the firm was taken over by Mark Davies who also had a cycle and motorcycle depot in High Street and Chester Street. He was also responsible for opening a new garage in Benbow House on Coton Hill that was later sold to Furrows. During the 1920s the premises was adapted into offices for the Guildhall that stood to the left in Newport House.

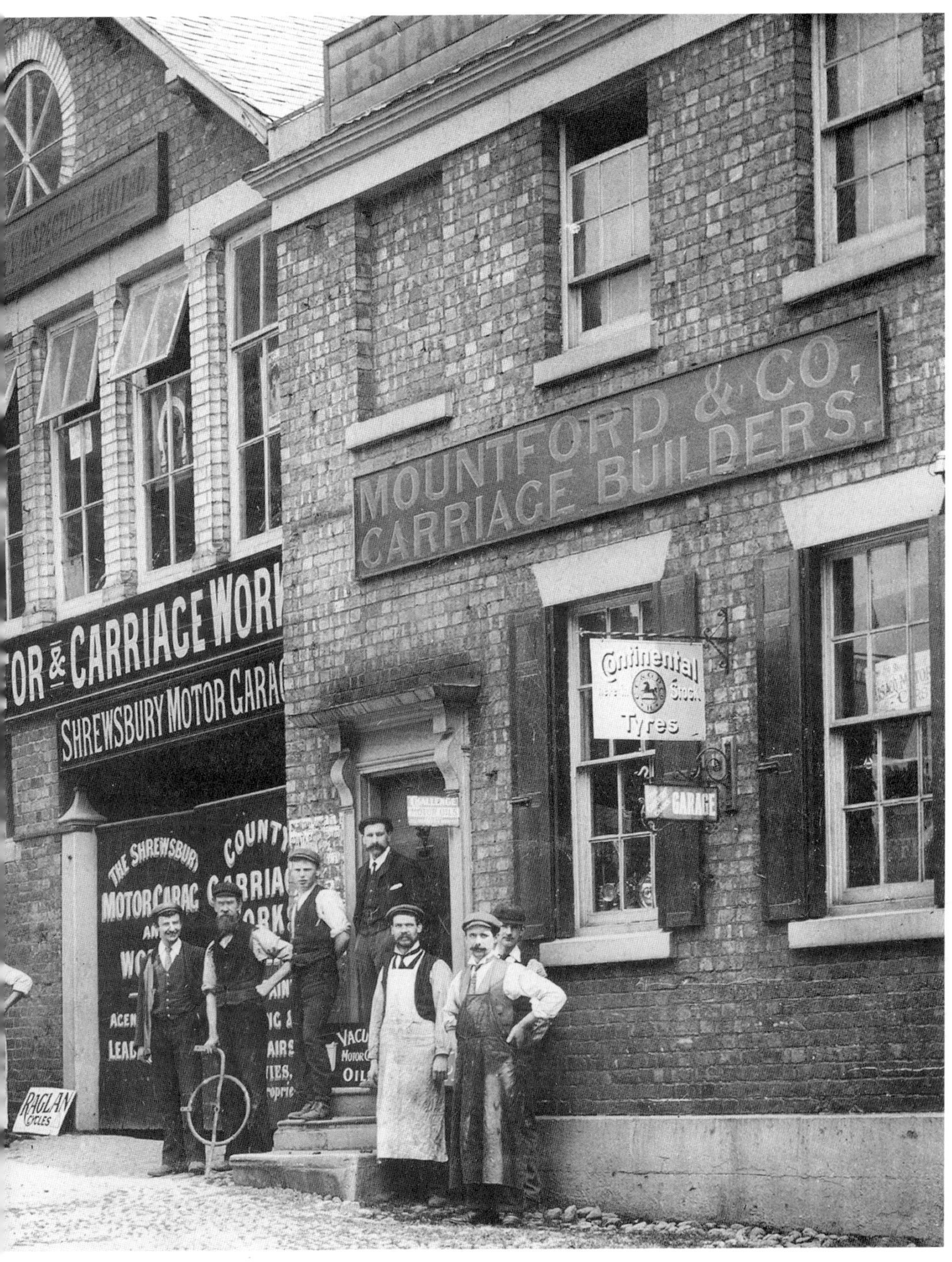
MOUNTFORD & CO,
CARRIAGE BUILDERS.
OR & CARRIAGE WORK
SHREWSBURY MOTOR GARAG
Continental Tyres
GARAGE
THE SHREWSBURY
MOTOR GARAG
COUNTY
CARRIAG
RAGLAN CYCLES

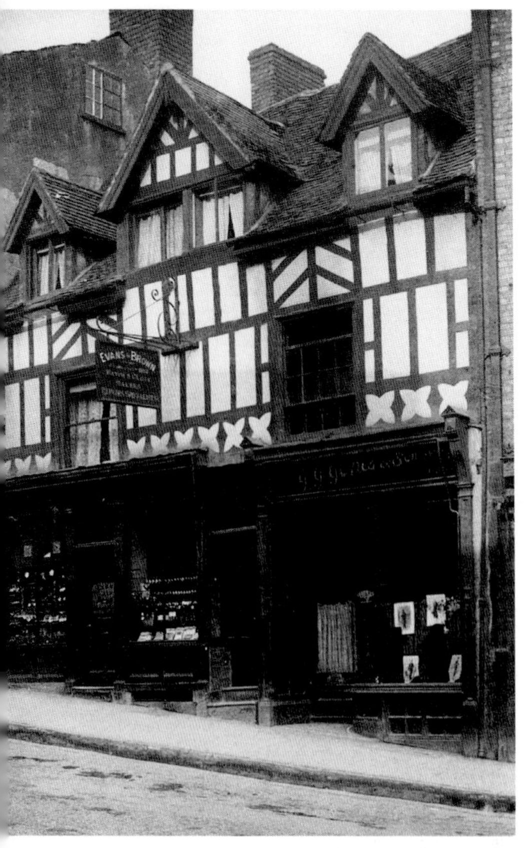

Wyle Cop, *c.* 1925. This building stood on the steep curve near the top of the hill. It was demolished in the mid-1920s when the road was widened at the summit to coincide with the remodelling of the English Bridge. The old timber frame had been covered by plaster but new 'timbers' were painted over the top when they came back into fashion. Evans & Brown were jewellers, watch- and clockmakers and repairers. They were established in 1812 and were trading for nearly 200 years. They advertised in 1916 that they were the oldest and most reliable firm in Shropshire for repairs and that their shop was 'replete with all the modern appliances for the execution of Watch and Clock repairs in a skilful manner.' The business continued well into the twentieth century in the new building. In the 1960s the proprietor was A.E. Campbell. The shop next door changed hands many times. Here it is occupied by J.J. Jones & Son who were ladies' and gentlemen's tailors.

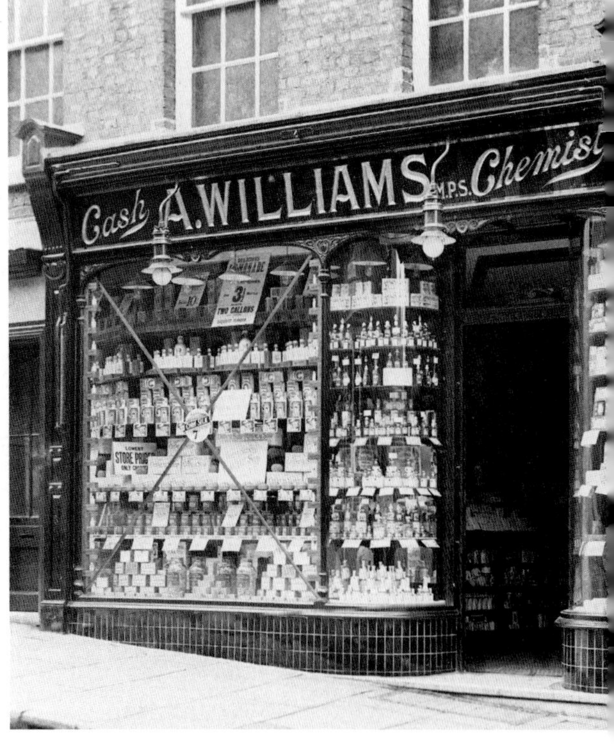

Wyle Cop, *c.* 1913. For most of the second half of the nineteenth century this chemist shop was occupied by the Blunt family. In 1885 Thomas Porter Blunt was advertised as a 'chemist & druggist & public analyst for the counties of Shropshire, Montgomery & Merionethshire'. He also guaranteed that 'Special attention is given to the Dispensing Department, and great care is exercised in ascertaining the strength and purity of the preparations used.' By 1913 the shop was being run by Arthur Williams, although Thomas Blunt continued to work as an analyst from 23A Wyle Cop. In the window he advertises Corn Silk, Violet Soap and a mixture to make two gallons of lemonade with an 'Exquisite Flavour'. He also announced 'Lowest store prices only charged'.

4

COLEHAM TO THE SOUTH

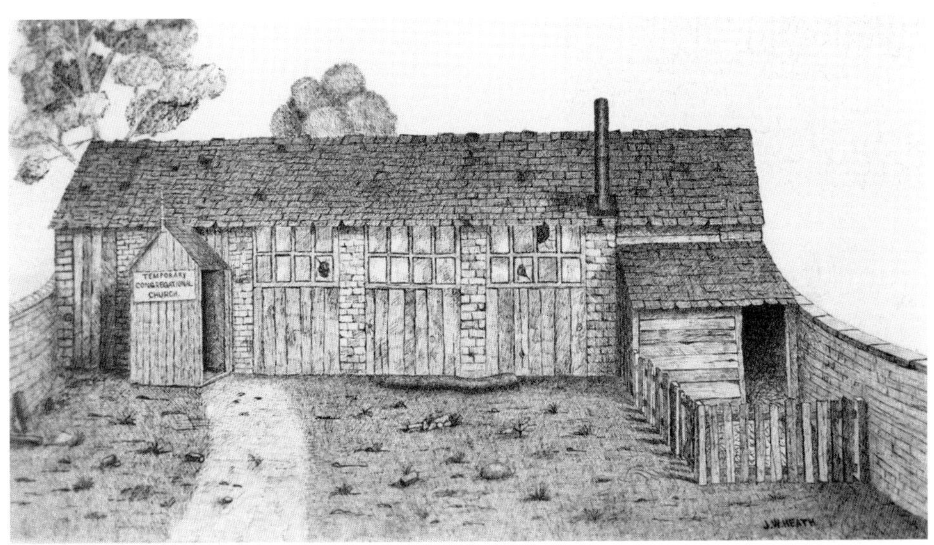

Coleham Head, *c.* 1862. In 1862 the Congregational Church in Shrewsbury decided to celebrate the bicentenary of the removal of over 2,000 clergymen from the established church by erecting a memorial church on the corner of Coleham Head and Abbey Foregate. The site that they purchased for about £750 included the Victoria Inn and adjoining builder's workshop and a timber yard, probably belonging to John Hall. The workshop and stables were turned into a temporary church and Sunday school. The old hay cratch was used as a front piece for the pulpit and 200 chairs accommodated the new congregation for the first service held on 3 October 1862. Note the pigsty on the right.

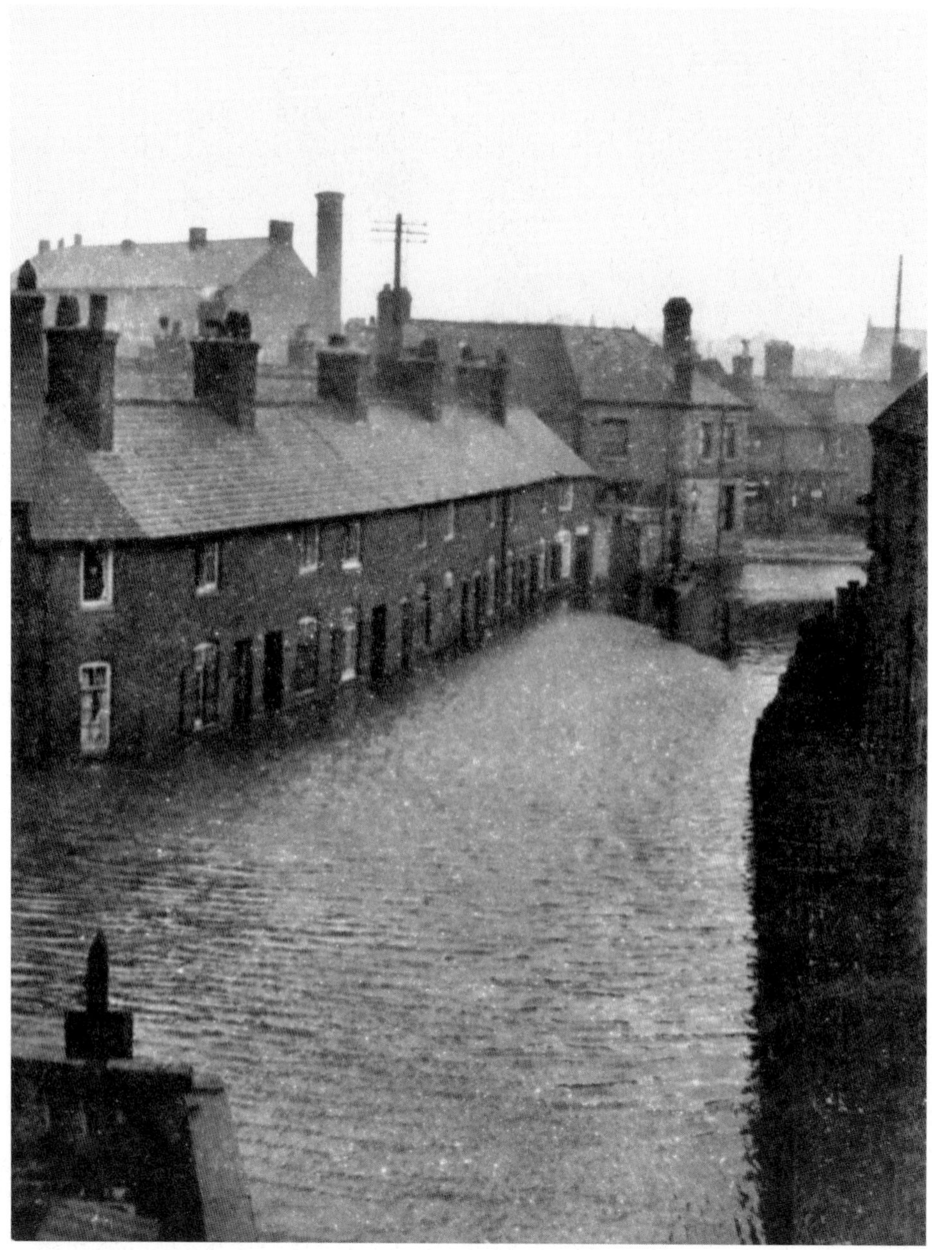

Coleham, February 1946. This view was taken from the railway bridge, looking towards Carline Fields. The chimney to the pumping station in Longden Coleham is visible above the roof line. The *Shrewsbury Circular* that was published in Coleham reported, 'Shrewsbury Floods – The Worst For 150 Years'. Flood water rose to over 5ft in parts of Coleham and flat-bottomed punts were used to ferry people and supplies to affected areas. There were many distressing sights as live animals were swept downstream – a horse was seen striking its head against an arch of the English Bridge and a dog chained to a kennel passed rapidly by, but nothing could be done to rescue them.

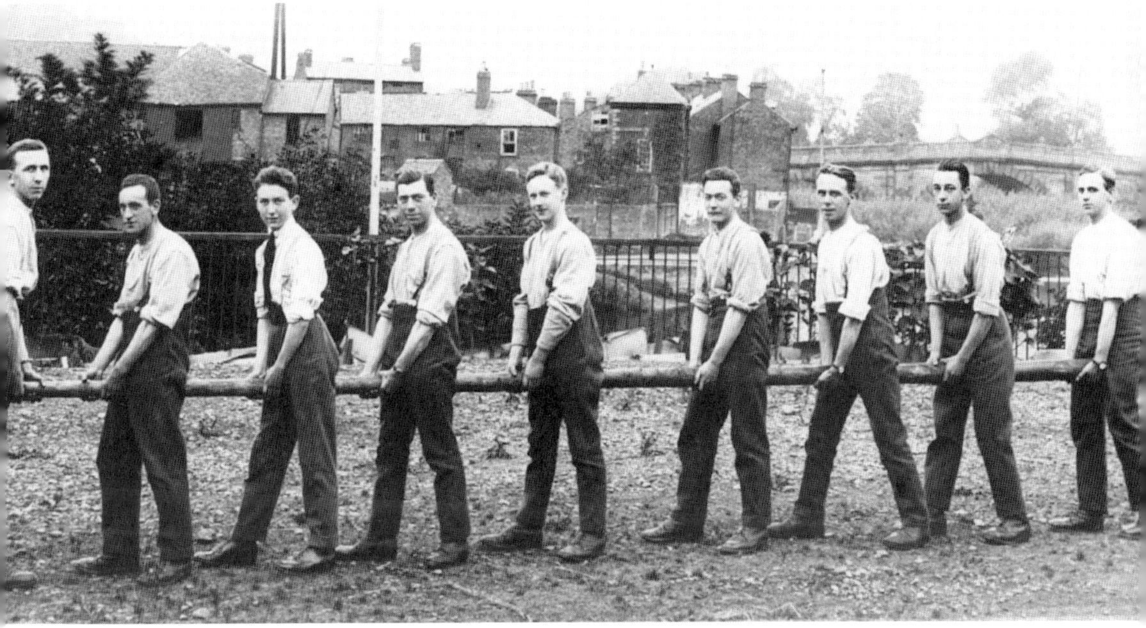

Longden Coleham, August 1918. Both these views were taken on the banks of the River Severn at the rear of the Drill Hall. In the background to the right is the English Bridge with its high central arch that was lowered during rebuilding in the 1920s. In the first view the buildings to the left of the bridge are Marine Terrace, once known as Stant's Row after the builder Joseph Stant. The building directly behind is a square two-storey gazebo that was demolished in the 1950s. It was used as a place to relax and entertain friends in a more informal environment. The two teams were involved in the Military Gymkhana that took place on the playing fields of Shrewsbury School. The event on Kingsland, which attracted a crowd of over 5,000, was to raise funds for men of the King's Shropshire Light Infantry who were prisoners of war. The men of No. 2 Records Office were the winners of the land boat race.

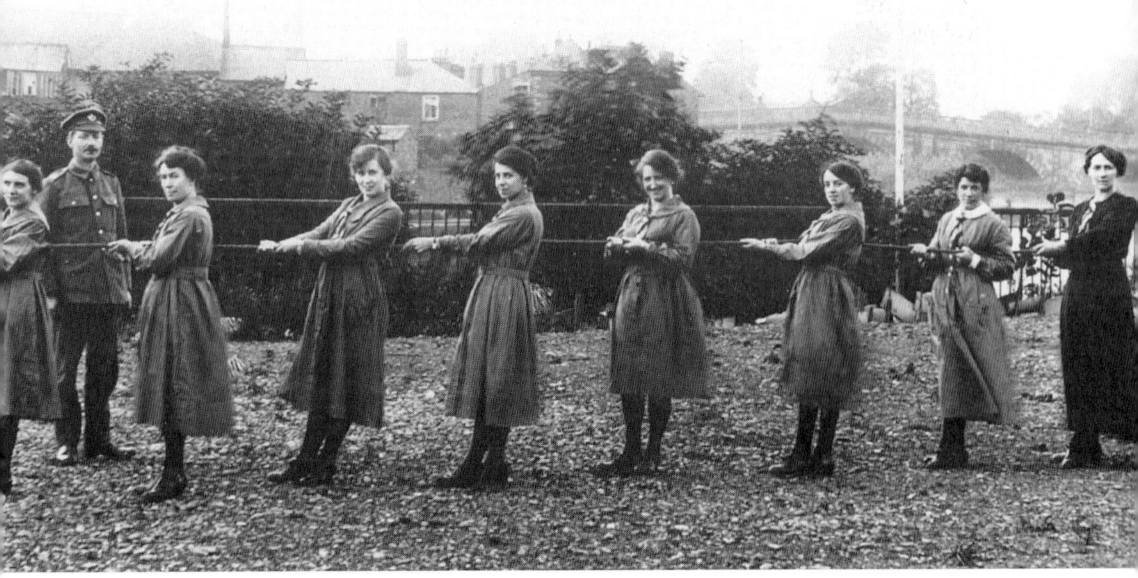

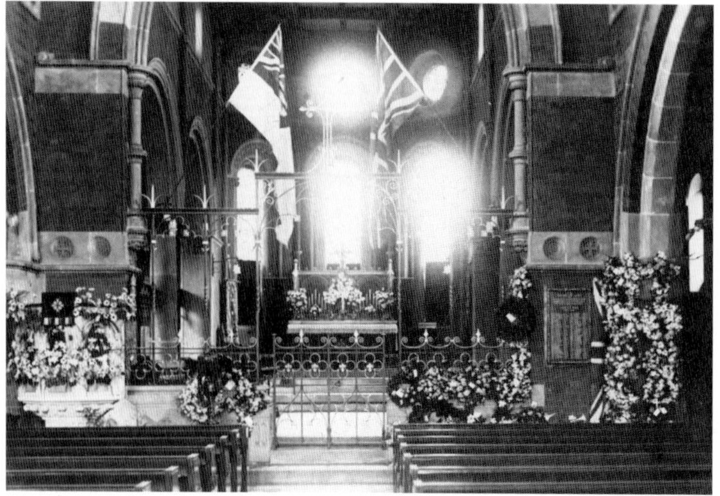

Holy Trinity Church, Belle Vue, *c.* 1925. Sunshine streams through the east window to illuminate a beautifully decorated church during a Flower Festival in the 1920s. Holy Trinity was built in 1837 as a chapel of ease attached to St Julian's Church in whose parish it was situated. It was described as 'Plain Classical' and consisted of a short tower, nave and an elliptical recess for communion. A vestry was added in 1847 and in 1861 a new chancel designed by William Pountney-Smith in the Byzantine style. In 1885 the church was rebuilt with the exception of the chancel, at a cost of £5,012. It was built out of red terracotta brick and was designed by A.E. Lloyd Oswell. Note the memorial on the right listing the names of the men of the parish who sacrificed their lives during the First World War.

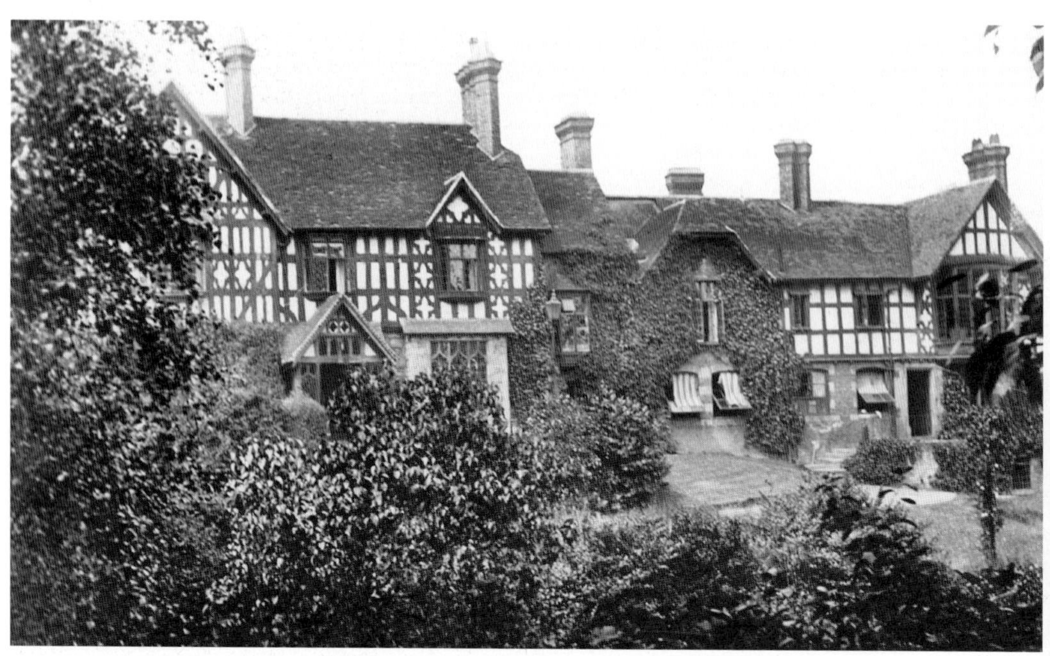

The Limes, Belle Vue, *c.* 1924. The house was designed and built by Samuel Pountney-Smith in about 1880. It incorporated a fragment of an earlier house on that site and also architectural features he had acquired from around the county including from an old mansion demolished next to the Plough in The Square. It became a preparatory boarding school in 1892 and was later adapted into a nursing home until 1955. Afterwards it was used until 1963 as a boarding house for pupils from Shrewsbury Technical College and the Priory School who lived too far outside the town to return home each night. Subsequently it was used by a number of agencies including Trading Standards and the Health Authority.

Montague Place, *c.* 1900. The address on the reverse of this postcard is Miss Smith, Sussex House, Belle Vue, Shrewsbury, with the message, 'Dear aunt standing at the door.' Sussex House is a three-bayed house in the Italianate style built in about 1880 for John Frederick Smith who was originally from Camberwell in London. Throughout the 1880s and early 1890s he held the lease of Shrewsbury Cattle Market in Smithfield Road and was responsible for collecting the tolls due. By 1900 the house was owned by William Smith but by 1905 it was occupied by Mrs Smith, presumably the lady by the door. From 1913 until the mid-1930s the occupant of the house is listed as William Smith.

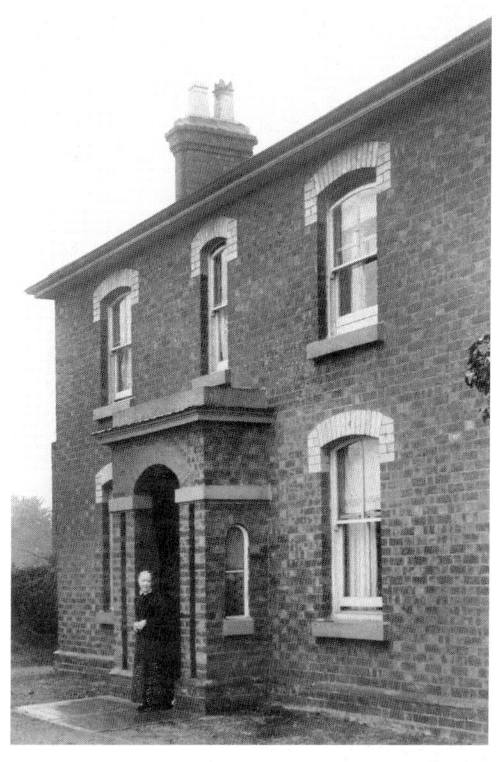

Kingsland, *c.* 1925. This aerial view is looking across Kingsland and over the Severn towards The Quarry and town. Shrewsbury School moved to this site in 1882 taking over a large building erected by Thomas Coram as a foundlings' hospital and later adapted into a workhouse. The school governors paid £8,000 for the building and 16 acres of land. Sir Arthur Blomfield was commissioned to draw up plans to alter the main block and design a new chapel and Master's House. The two trees in the centre of the playing field are known as 'Smokers' Trees', while the three trees to the right are known as 'The Pier' – both are ideal sites for watching cricket matches.

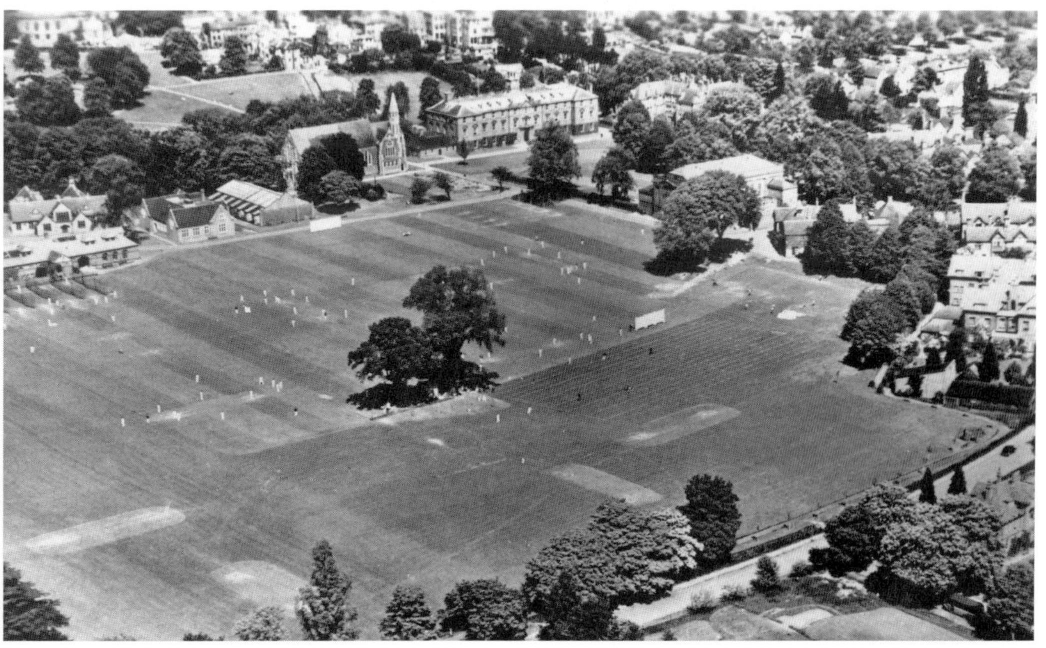

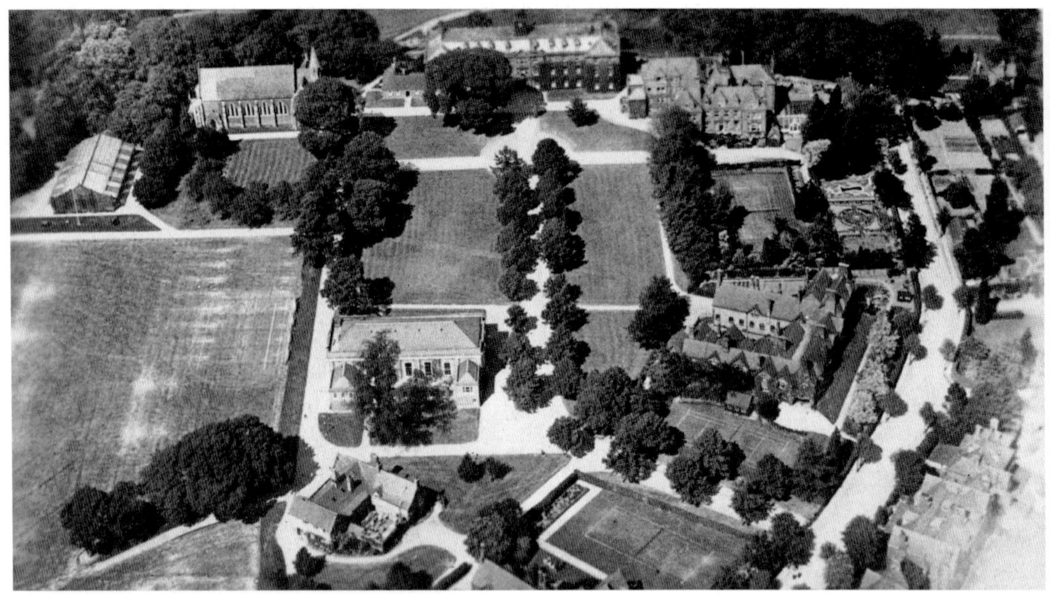

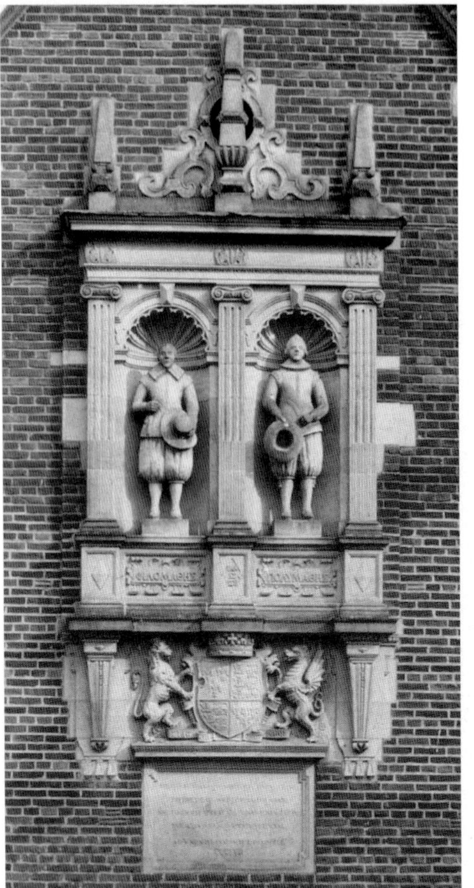

Shrewsbury School, Kingsland, *c.* 1920. Kingsland covers about 27 acres. It was enclosed land belonging to the Crown, from where it takes its name. It was later transferred to the Corporation by royal grant. The main building, top centre, was built in 1760 as a foundlings' hospital. It was later used as woollen manufactory, a Dutch prisoner of war camp and a workhouse, before becoming Shrewsbury School. On the left of the photograph is the chapel designed by Sir Arthur Blomfield and used for the first time on 11 November 1883. He also designed School House to the right. The road on the right is Ashton Road, named after Thomas Ashton a former headmaster.

Kingsland, *c.* 1925. This is part of the Moser building at Shrewsbury School built as a library and reading room between 1914 and 1916. It was designed by W.A. Forsyth and was named after Edward Brandthwaite Moser, a master who donated his collection of watercolours to the school. The foundation stone was laid by George V by means of an electric current, which he turned on from his carriage in The Square while visiting Shrewsbury in July 1914. The library contains some very rare volumes including one book printed by William Caxton. The figures in Jacobean dress represent Philomathes and Polymathes, showing the young scholar as he enters the school and the graduate as he leaves. They are copies of the original figures that stand over the entrance to the old school and still belong to Shrewsbury School.

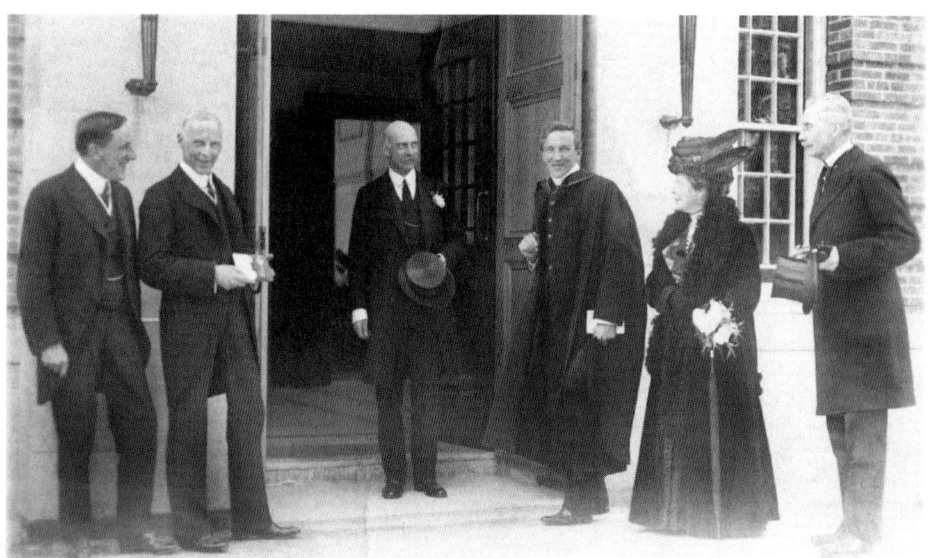

Kingsland, 11 May 1911. Alington Hall was erected opposite the main gates of Shrewsbury School. It was built to hold 900 people and was used for speech days and other large gatherings. It also doubled as a gymnasium and concert hall and had music practice rooms along the side corridors. The foundation stone was laid in 1909 by Lord Barnard, chairman of the governors, and it was officially opened by the Duke of Teck (later known as the Marquis of Cambridge), a brother of Queen Mary. He is seen standing in the doorway. To the right is the Revd Cyril Argentine Alington who gave his name to the new hall and was headmaster from 1908 to 1916. He was a brilliant headmaster breathing new life into the school and raising academic achievement. Note the students relaxing after the opening and the boys sitting on the roof of the hall.

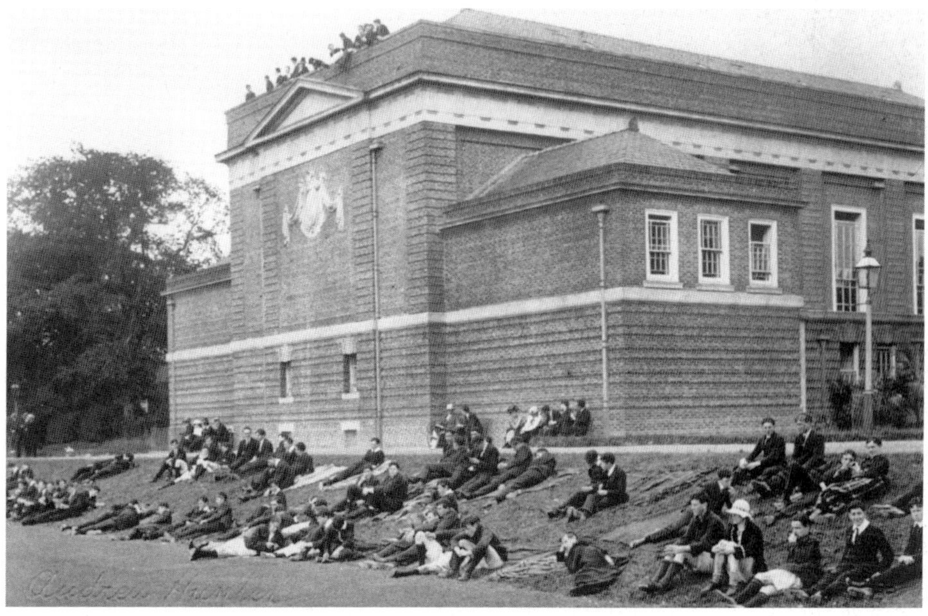

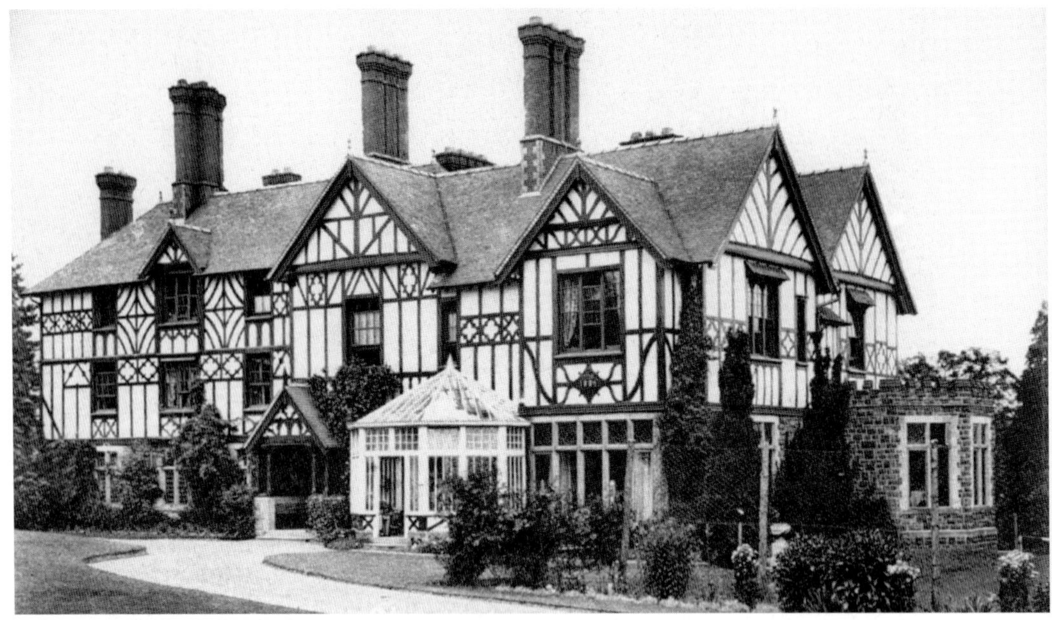

Roman Road, *c.* 1930. Kingsland Grange was built as a private house in 1884 by local builder Henry Treasure for himself and his family. In 1910 W.B.C. Drew, the headmaster of the Limes Preparatory School in Bell Vue, moved his school to this larger site. In 1914 the school was able to accommodate fifty boys between the ages of seven and fourteen. He advertised that, 'It is most conveniently situated, being only a mile and a half from Shrewsbury station, which has a splendid train service from all parts of the country. The grounds consist of 13 acres, which include well laid out football and cricket grounds and a playground for wet weather. There is also a gymnasium, and well ventilated class-rooms have recently been erected. Mrs Drew personally directs all domestic arrangements of the school and is assisted by Miss Drew (a qualified nurse) who devotes special attention to the health of the boarders.'

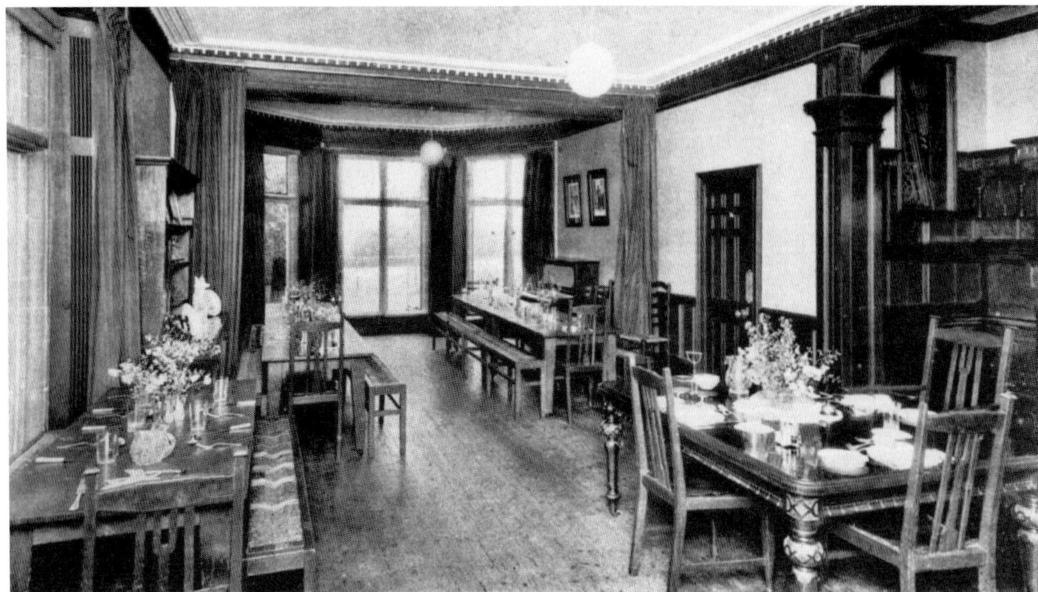

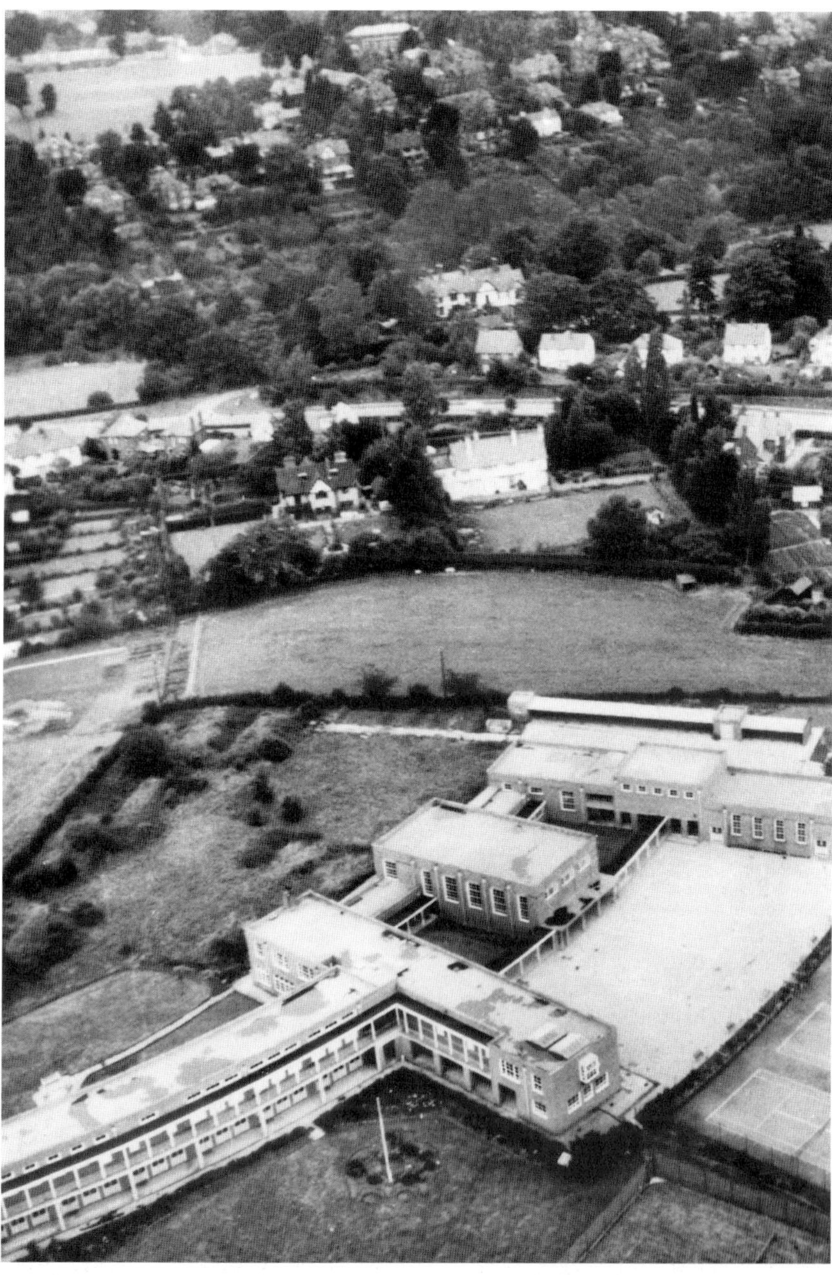

Longden Road, *c.* 1960. The photographer is looking over the Priory Girls' Grammar School, the large building in the foreground, towards Kingsland and the town. The girls' school was founded in 1911 in a building they shared with the boys by The Quarry. Overcrowding at the old school resulted in a new school for the girls being opened in September 1939. The headmistress Miss Hunter wrote, 'we look forward now to entering our "Promised Land" a realm flowing with light, sunshine and fresh air from "a' the airts".' The building was designed by A.G. Chant and built by W. Higley & Son of Shrewsbury and cost £34,977.

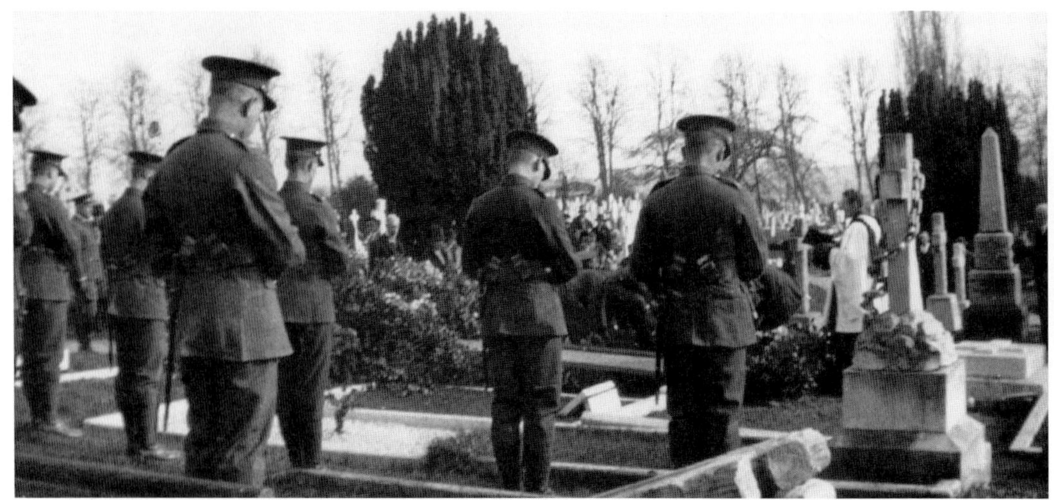

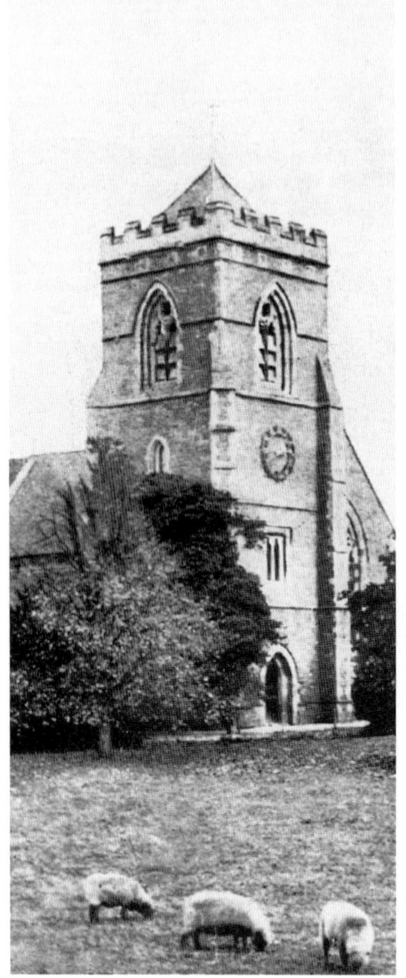

Longden Road, 30 January 1929. Troops stand respectfully to attention at the graveside of Colonel Francis Wingfield Robinson. He was born on 15 January 1846 and died just a few days after his eighty-third birthday at his home on Claremont Bank. He trained at Sandhurst where he passed out ninth in his year. He served in India, Malta, Egypt, Bermuda, Malta, Afghanistan and Hong Kong – the colonel was in Hong Kong during the Bubonic Plague outbreak in 1884. He gathered a party of around 300 volunteers and cleaned almost every building in the native quarter with a solution of chloride of lime and sulphuric acid. For their courage the men were awarded plague medals; in gold for the officers and silver for the men. They were also affectionately nicknamed 'The White Wash Brigade'.

Meole Brace, *c.* 1905. At this period Meole Brace was a village lying 1½ miles outside Shrewsbury. It became part of the borough in May 1934. The church was once in the Diocese of Lichfield but was transferred to Hereford in 1929. This is the third church to be built in the village. The medieval building with its half-timbered upper section was replaced in 1799 by a brick structure, which was then replaced by the present church in 1868. The cruciform church was designed by Edward Haycock junior and was dedicated to the Holy Trinity. The interior contained a semi-octagonal apsidal chancel, a six-bayed nave, aisles, and a south porch. The attractive north-west tower was fitted with a clock and a peal of three bells. The most splendid parts of the church are the beautiful windows designed by Sir Edward Burne-Jones, William Morris and C.E. Kempe. In 1905 the living was in gift of Edward W. Bather and consisted of a vicarage, a net income of £280 a year plus 7½ acres of glebe land. In 1905 the vicar was the Revd William Henry Bather who was the incumbent from 1897 until 1931.

5

THE AGE OF STEAM

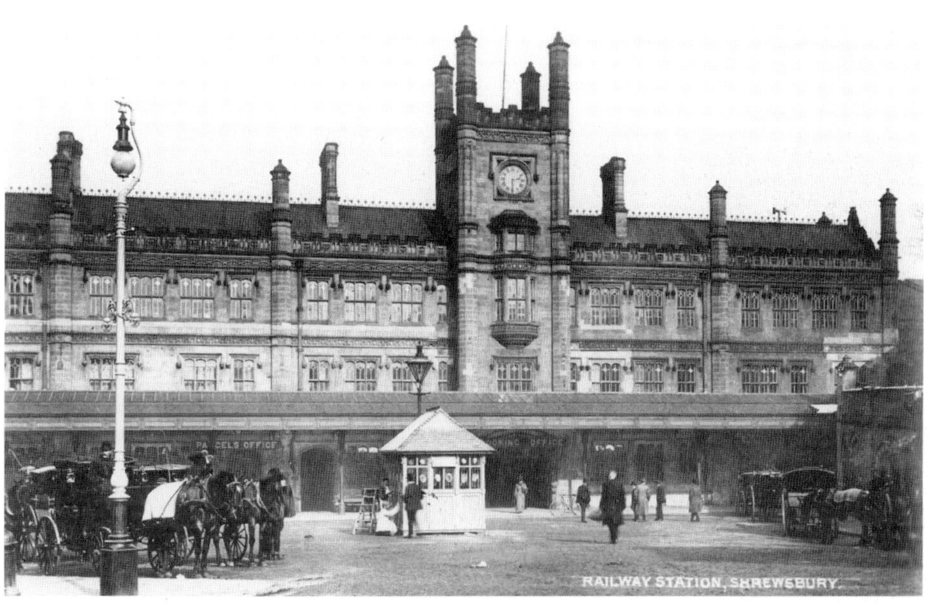

Castle Foregate, *c.* 1910. Shrewsbury station dates from 1848 with the opening of the Shrewsbury to Chester line. It was designed in the Gothic style by Thomas Penson of Oswestry and built out of Grinshill stone. Originally it was a two-storey building with a central tower with two bays of three and four windows on either side. The main ground-floor entrance was just below the oriel window of the tower. In the 1850s an extension in the same style was built to the left that joined Castle Foregate. A further extension was built between 1899 and 1902. The whole of the forecourt was excavated to a depth of 20ft in places to open up the cellars. The new ground floor was then faced with Grinshill stone in the same style as the upper storeys and provided a new entrance along with booking, parcel and other offices. Note the men painting the new cabbies' shelter in the centre.

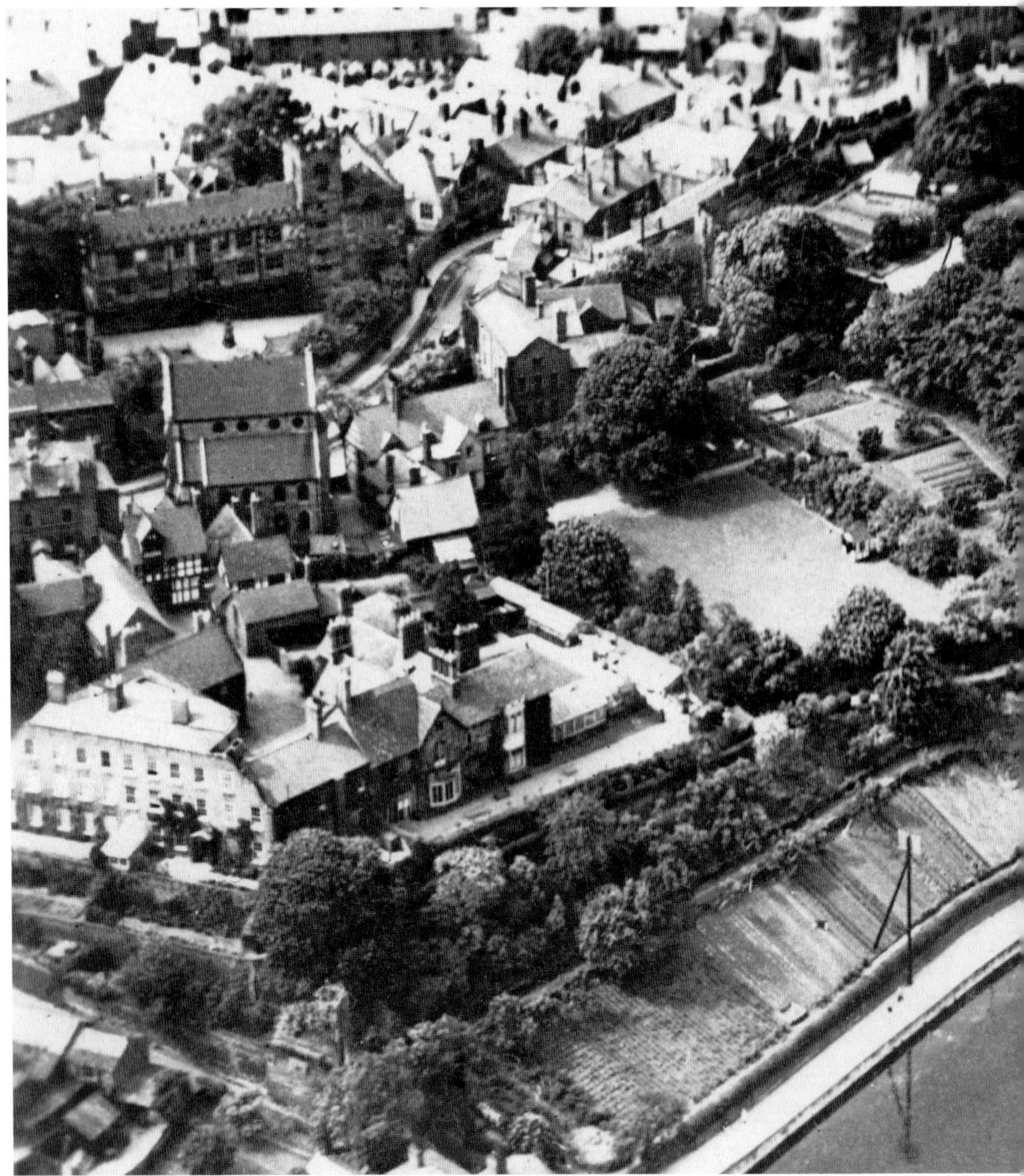

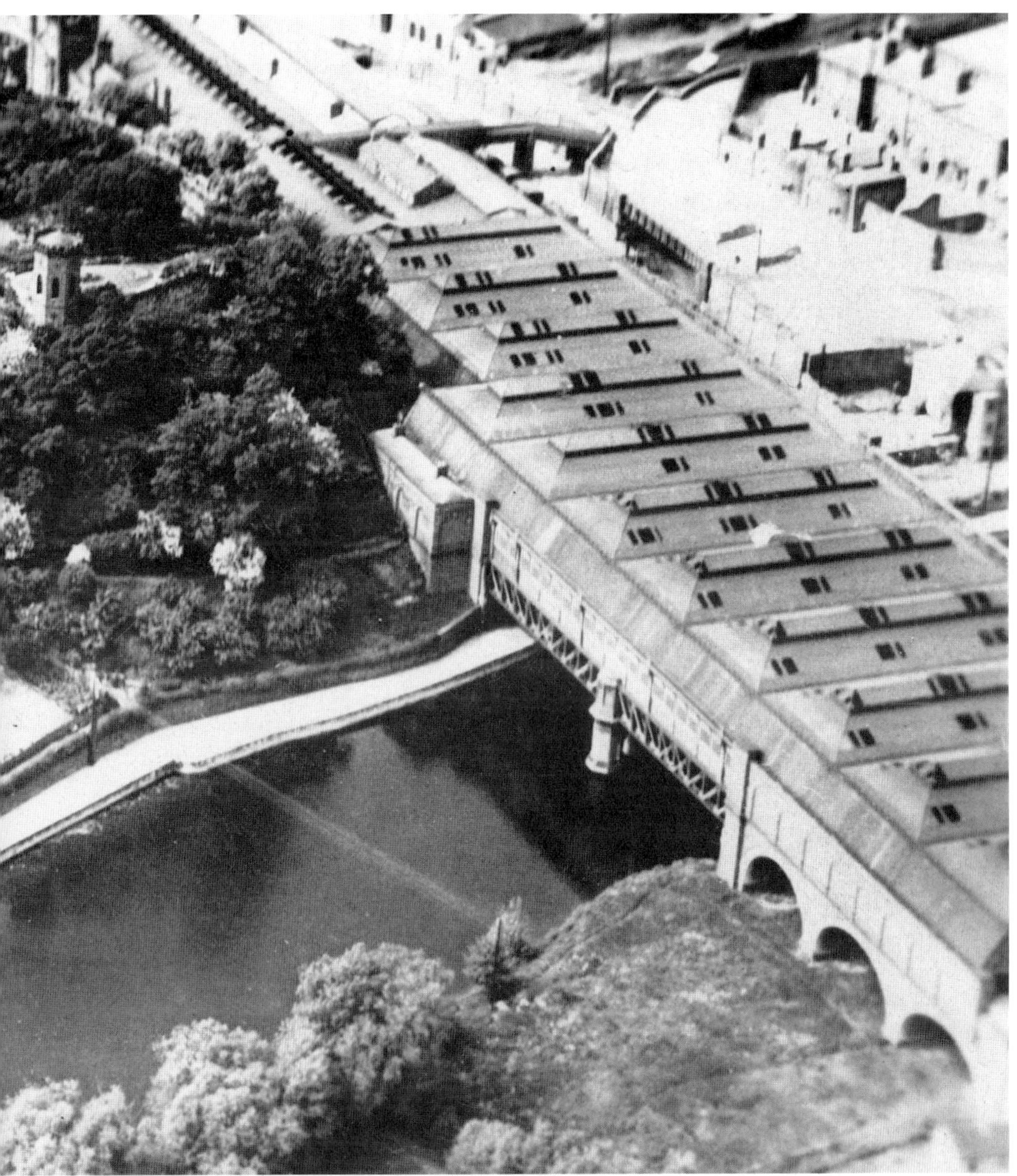

Shrewsbury, *c.* 1918. This view shows the full extent of the roof that once covered Shrewsbury station and was removed between 1961 and 1962. The bridge spanning the roof at the top of the view is the Dana, linking the town centre to Castlefields and the prison in the top right corner. To the left of the station is the castle with Laura's Tower standing above the trees. On the far left centre is a complex known as the Council House where the Council of the Marches met when in Shrewsbury. It was once known as Lord's Place and parts date back to 1502. Above is the roof line of St Nicholas' Church and in the top left corner is the library that is housed in the original Shrewsbury School founded in 1552.

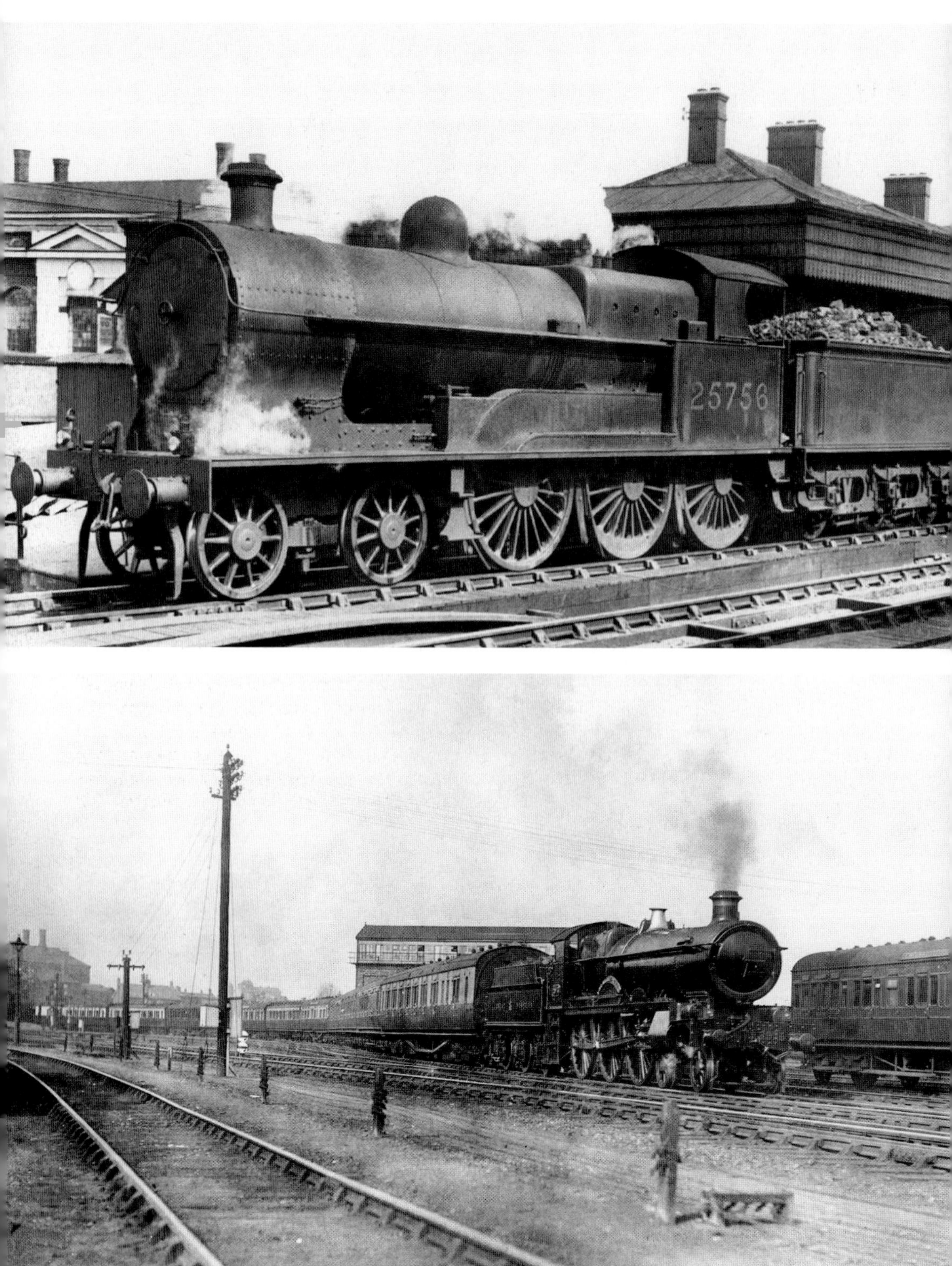
25756

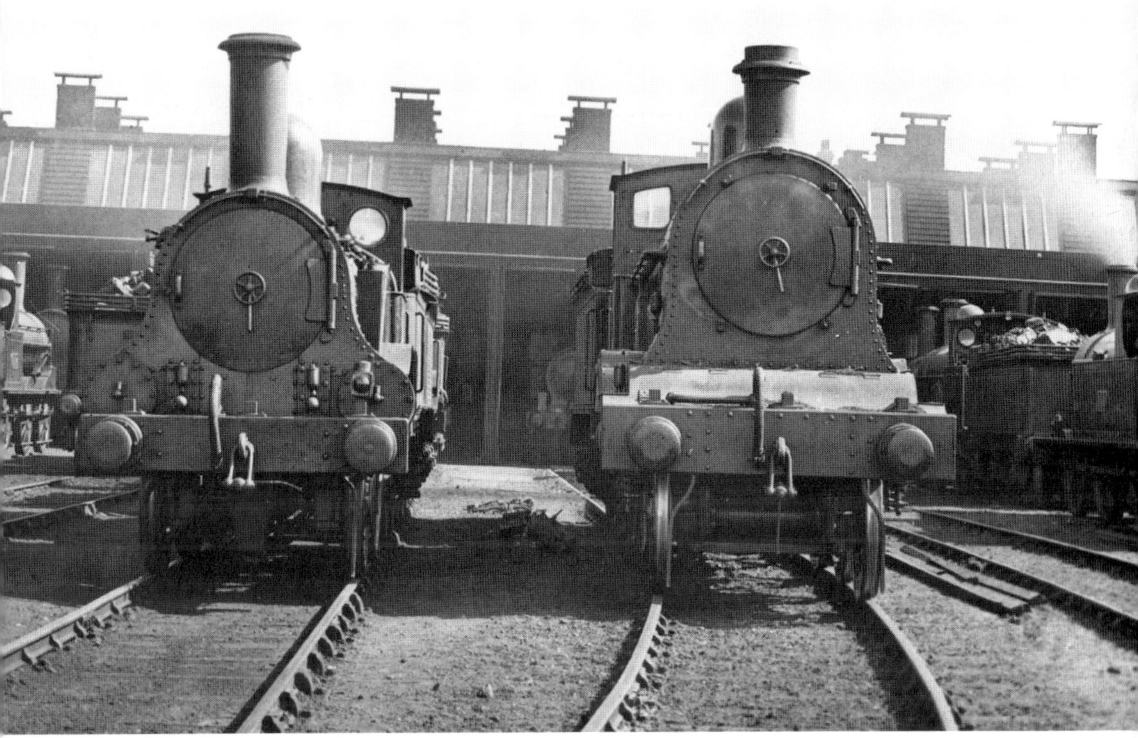

Shrewsbury engine sheds, *c.* 1930. This view captures the great days of steam at the engine sheds just off Scott Street and Sutton Lane. Many people living in the area were employed by one of the railway companies and the area was known as the 'Back of the Sheds'. Day and night it was a hive of activity, full of noise and smells so familiar to the people who once lived there. This is the London & North Western Railway shed that was taken over from the Shrewsbury & Hereford Railway. By 1866 the company had fifty-one engines stationed there. The engine on the left is a 'Lady of the Lake' class 2–2–2 while the one on the right is a 'DX' goods, rebuilt by Francis William Webb.

Opposite, top: Shrewsbury station, *c.* 1930. An LNWR 'Prince of Wales' class engine built in about 1915 stands alongside platform 4 at the head of a passenger train heading towards Crewe. At the rear left is the Butter Market built at the terminus of the Shrewsbury Canal in 1835. The London & North Western Railway purchased it in the 1850s turning it into a warehouse and part of the canal basin into a railway goods yard. Above the Butter Market are the chimneys of Shrewsbury prison that was built by Thomas Telford in 1787.

Opposite, bottom: Shrewsbury station, *c.* 1930. This view shows a North Wales to South Wales express passing the Severn Bridge signal-box as it leaves the station. Pulling the large passenger train is a Great Western Railway 'Saint' engine. It is no. 2975 *Sir Ernest Palmer*, built in May 1905 and withdrawn from service in November 1944. The original Severn Bridge signal-box straddled the lines of the viaduct over the Severn until the rebuilding of 1899 to 1902, when it was moved to the junction of the Wellington line and the line leading to Hereford and Wales. With 180 levers it was one of the biggest in the country.

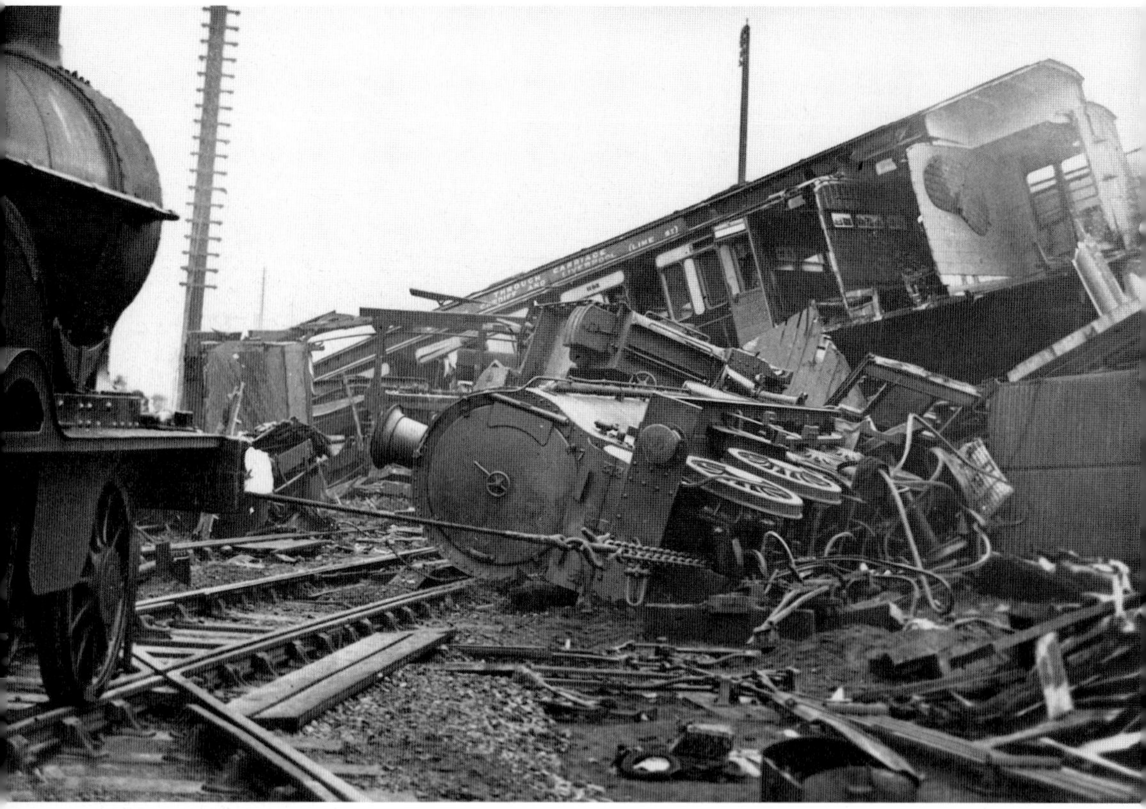
THROUGH CARRIAGE
LIVERPOOL

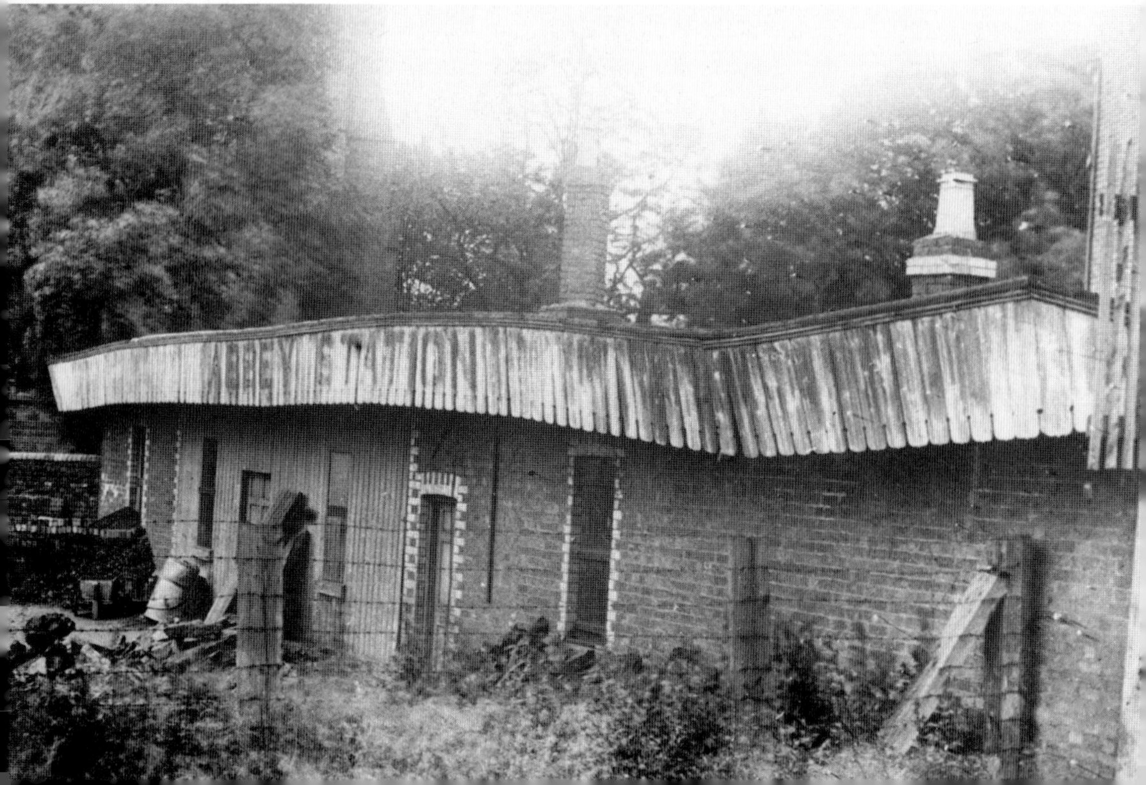
ABBEY STATION

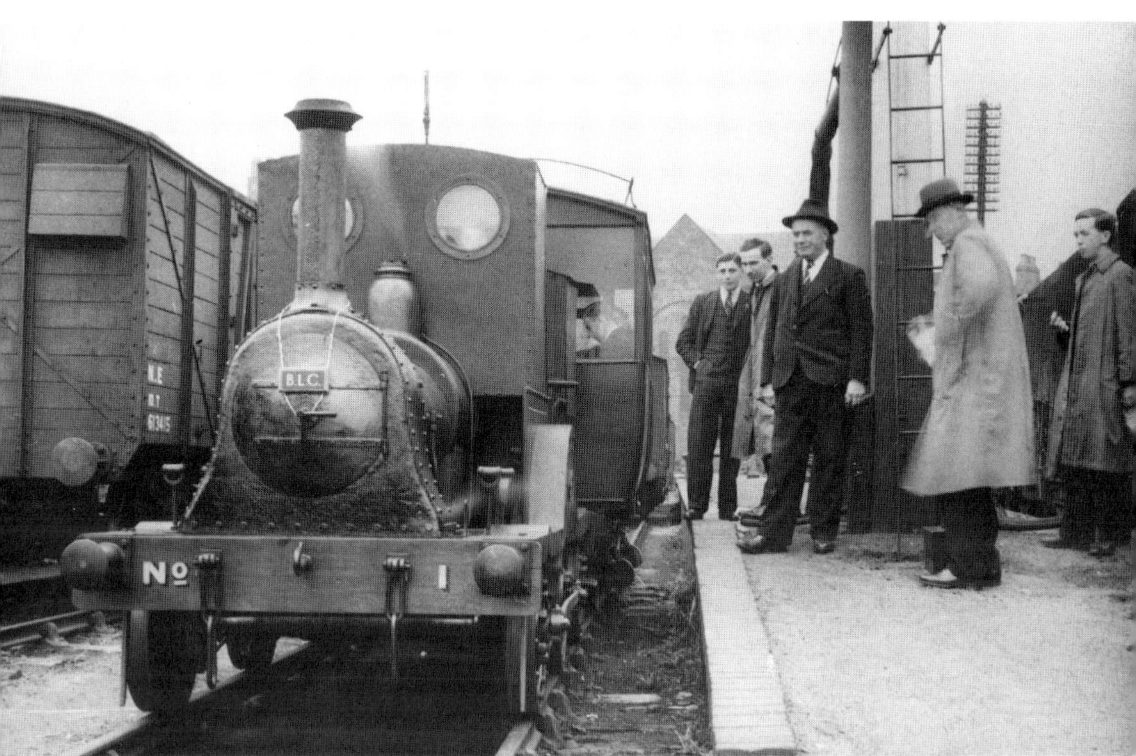

Abbey Foregate, *c.* 1939. The line was closed for thirty-one years until it was reopened in 1911 as the Shropshire & Montgomery Railway by Colonel H.F. Stevens. The line was closed to passengers in 1933 and was taken over by the War Office. The final excursion train ran on 20 March 1960 but a short section of track from the main line to an oil depot in Abbey Foregate was used until the 1980s. The engine is the *Gazelle* that was nicknamed 'The Coffee Pot' and was reputed to be one of the smallest standard gauge engines in the world. It was built in 1893 by Alfred Dodman & Co. at their Highgate Works in King's Lynn, Norfolk. It is about to leave the Abbey station pulling an inspection carriage. For a number of years it was the first engine out to make sure the track was ready for the other trains.

Opposite, top: Castle Foregate, 15 October 1907. This is the aftermath of Shrewsbury's worst ever rail disaster. The express left Crewe eight minutes late at 1.28 a.m. and was due in Shrewsbury at 2.05 a.m. On a very stormy night the train, carrying mail and over 100 passengers, approached the station at about 60mph. It passed a danger signal near Crewe Bank and went around a sharp bend with a 10mph limit. There the engine left the rails, ploughing a deep furrow over 100 yards long and derailing all the carriages. Twenty people were killed with around forty injured. The engine being towed away is a Stevenson 'Experiment' class, no. 2052. Although badly damaged it was repaired and continued in service. The cause of the accident was never fully explained.

Opposite, bottom: Abbey Foregate, *c.* 1903. This is a view of the railway station during the years it was closed. The line was opened in 1866 and was supposed to link the Welsh coast to the Potteries. This never happened and only a short section between Shrewsbury and Llanymynech was built. The line flourished at first carrying around 70,000 passengers and over 90,000 tons of goods a year. But by the 1870s the company was struggling to make a profit and in 1880 the line was closed and it was recorded that, 'The trains ceased running and the trucks and carriages remained in various sidings along the line, and a decadence of ruin commenced. Soon the silent track presented a melancholy spectacle, the station buildings falling into disrepair, and it seemed as if the line was doomed to sink into obscurity.'

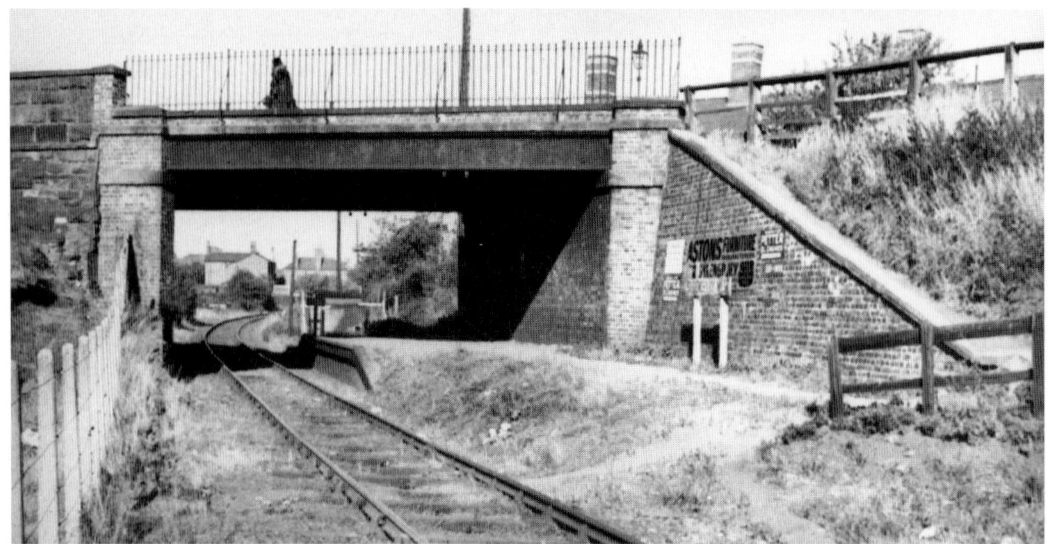

Belle Vue, *c.* 1937. The photographer is looking back towards the Abbey station along the old Shropshire & Montgomery line. This station was Shrewsbury West and it stood underneath the bridge that took the main road over the railway to Meole Brace at this point. The main line railway into Wales is to the left. The station, known locally as 'Belle Vue Platform', never attracted a great deal of trade and was closed in about 1933. Note the adverts for Petter Oil Engines and Aston's furniture store who were then situated at 29 and 30 Pride Hill.

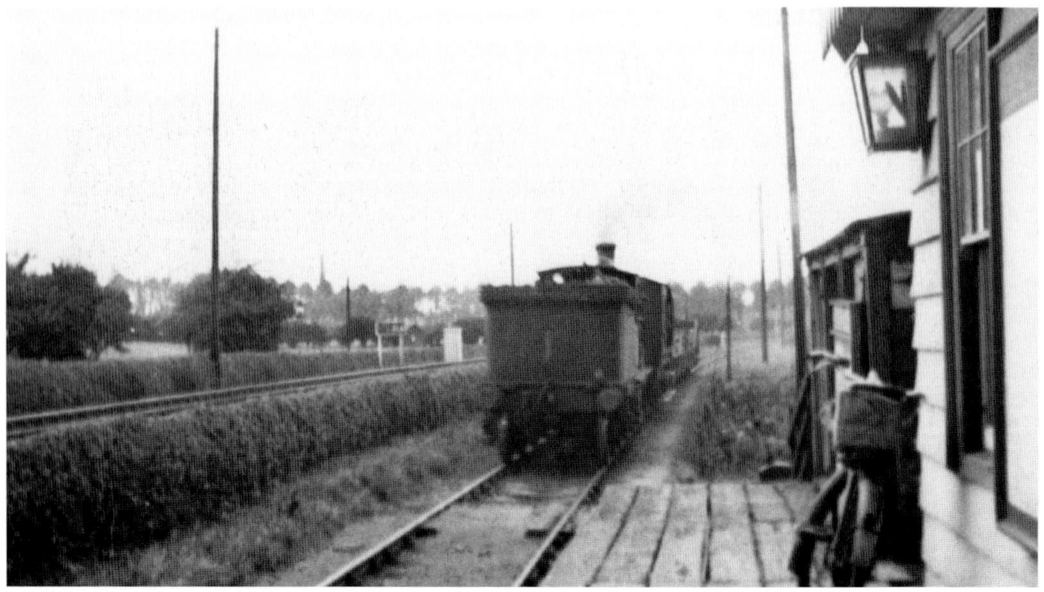

Meole Brace, *c.* 1937. This station was opened by the Shropshire & Montgomery Railway in 1911. It stood under the railway bridge that carries the road over Stanley Lane from Longden Road to Meole Village. For many years the people from the village found this to be a cheap and regularly timetabled way to get to Shrewsbury. The train is travelling out of town towards the photographer; the main line can be seen on the left over the hedge. Behind the cameraman was a single siding used mainly to unload domestic coal.

6

CHURCHES & CHAPELS

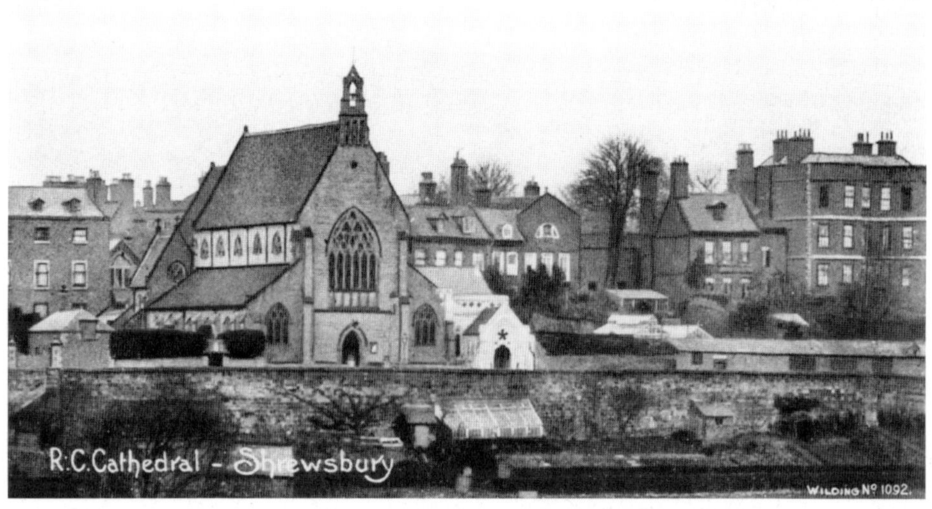

Town Walls, *c.* 1910. The Catholic Cathedral is dedicated to Our Lady Help of Christians and St Peter of Alcantara. It was designed by Edward Welby Pugin and financed by Bertram, 17th Earl of Shrewsbury. The foundation stone was laid by Bishop James Brown on 12 December 1853, the day after the earl's twenty-first birthday. The plans included the building of a large tower and spire but due to the poor quality of ground on which the foundations were to be placed, the idea was modified. The cathedral was opened on 29 October 1856 with a Mass conducted by Bishop Brown and a sermon preached by Cardinal Wiseman. Note the new stone of the Centre Porch on the right, which was added by Bishop Samuel Allen in 1907.

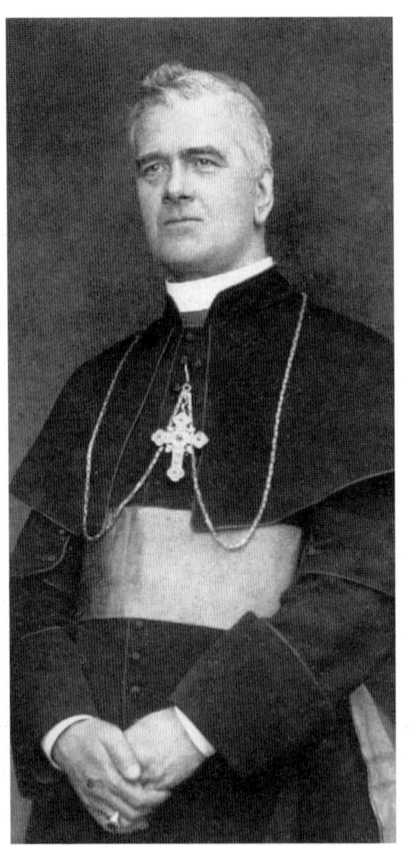

Town Walls, *c.* 1905. The Right Revd Dr Samuel Webster Allen was born in Stockport on 23 March 1844. He was the fourth Catholic Bishop of Shrewsbury, serving from 1897 until 1908. He was ordained in 1870 and spent the whole of his priesthood in Shrewsbury and was consecrated bishop on 16 June 1897 by Cardinal Vaughan. The Shrewsbury diocese thrived under his leadership with many young men seeking to enter the priesthood and several new churches and missions were established. The bishop died at a relatively young age and was interred in Shrewsbury cemetery on 16 May 1908. This card sent by Patrick to Miss Bromley of Picklescott just a month after the bishop's death informs her that the bishop 'was buried in that lovely cross & chain.'

Abbey Foregate, *c.* 1910. This is Telford's new road put through the south side of the Abbey and shortcutting the old road that ran to the east and north of the church. In doing so he destroyed what remained of the chapter house, cloisters and dormitory of the old monastery dissolved by Henry VIII on 24 January 1540. The whole of the east end was rebuilt and the roof restored to its original height between 1886 and 1888. The architect was J.L. Pearson who had intended to restore the central tower and transepts but had to modify his plans through lack of funds. After Telford's new road was built, speculators wanted to build to the rear of the church. Fortunately the land was purchased and consecrated as Shrewsbury's first general cemetery, the first burial taking place there on 18 October 1841.

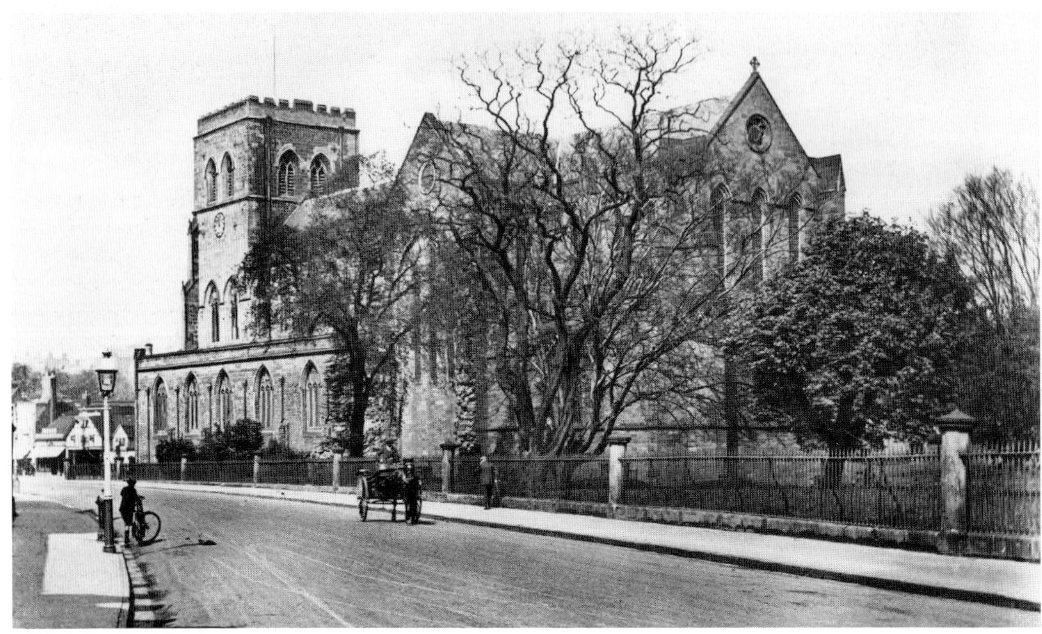

Right: Abbey Foregate, *c.* 1910. The lower section of the picturesque north porch is Norman while the upper storeys are perpendicular in style. Above the door there are two canopied niches; the left-hand one is empty while in the right is a statue of St Margaret. The wooden doors bear the date 1640 and the legend 'Reverence My Sanctuary'. The top room of the porch was once used for sleeping guests and was known as a 'Parvise', a corruption of the Latin word for paradise. One of the rooms was used as a study by Richard Prynce the builder of Whitehall and in the 1980s it acted as the Abbey shop and tearoom. Today it is used as office space. In 1900 the *Chronicle* reported that the north porch was unsafe.

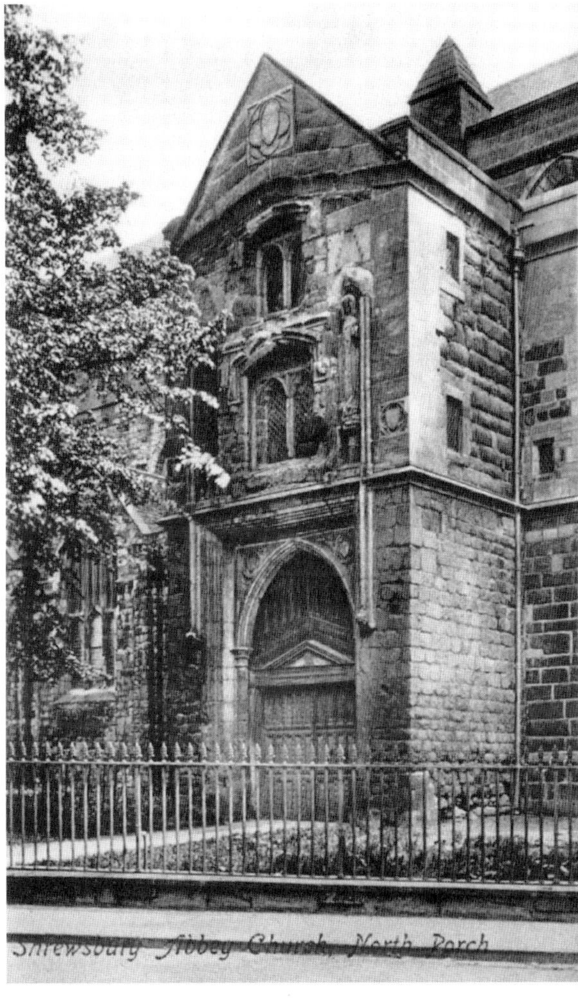

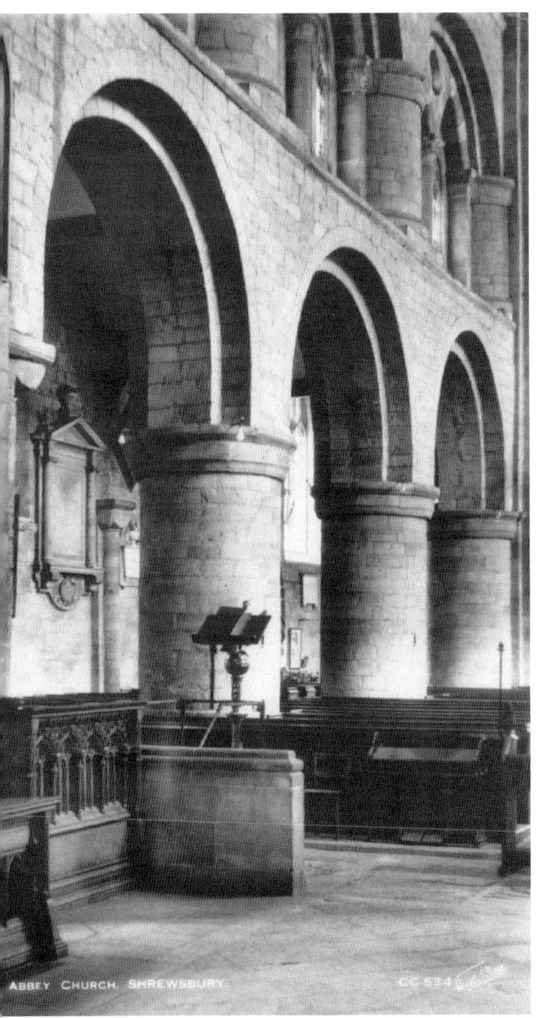

Left: Abbey Foregate, *c.* 1920. This view of the nave and south aisle of the Abbey is taken from the newly built east end. The massive round pillars supporting the semi-circular arches are early Norman. The triforium above is also Norman but has been modified over the years and now contains work from 1862/3. Through the first arch, on wall of the south aisle, which is also Norman, you can see one of the vaulting shafts that show the aisle once had a vaulted roof. The painting on the left of the Angels at the Sepulchre is early nineteenth-century and the work of John Bridges. It was once used as the reredos before the new east end was built. The brass eagle lectern was presented to the church on Christmas Day 1865 by John Loxdale.

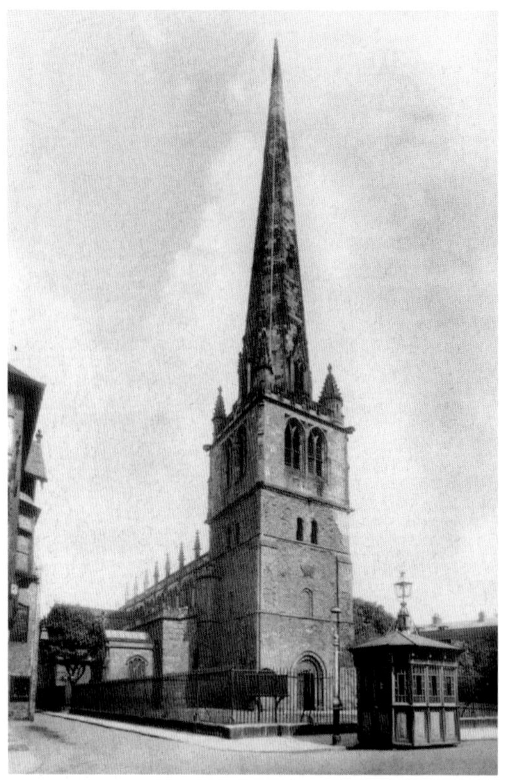

St Mary's Street, *c.* 1930. The church dedicated to St Mary was founded by King Edgar in the second half of the tenth century. The foundations of the Saxon church still lie beneath the present structure that was started in about 1150. The church has been added to and altered many times over the centuries to produce the beautiful building we have today. At 222ft, the spire is the highest point in Shrewsbury and reputed to be the third tallest spire in the country, after Salisbury and Norwich. The outstanding feature of the church is the stained glass, from the Jesse window in the east, made up of fourteenth-century English glass, to the fine windows bought in the nineteenth century from Belgium, France and Germany. The structure by the kerb is a cabbies' shelter used to keep warm and dry while waiting for a fare. Apart from the door end a bench ran around the interior and there was a stove in the middle. Note the chimney vent under the gas lamp on the roof. There were several of these shelters dotted around the town.

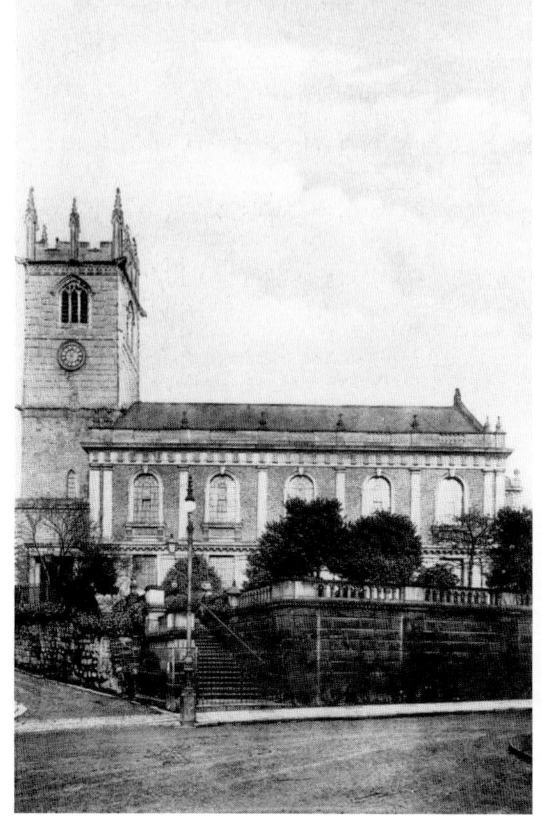

High Street, *c.* 1905. St Julian's is another church founded by the Saxons. Originally it was the church dedicated to St Juliana, a young woman from Nicomedia, a place in modern Turkey, who was martyred in the fourth century. A later church was built but by 1748 it was in a dilapidated state and was pulled down, with the exception of the tower. The new building was designed by Thomas Farnolls Pritchard who lived in the parish and is buried in the church. The outside of the building was very plain but this side was beautified by the addition of pilasters, cornice, balustrade and urns in 1846. The bottom section of the tower in red sandstone was built in the late twelfth century while the upper section, which is slightly narrower and built out of white Grinshill stone, was built in the fifteenth century.

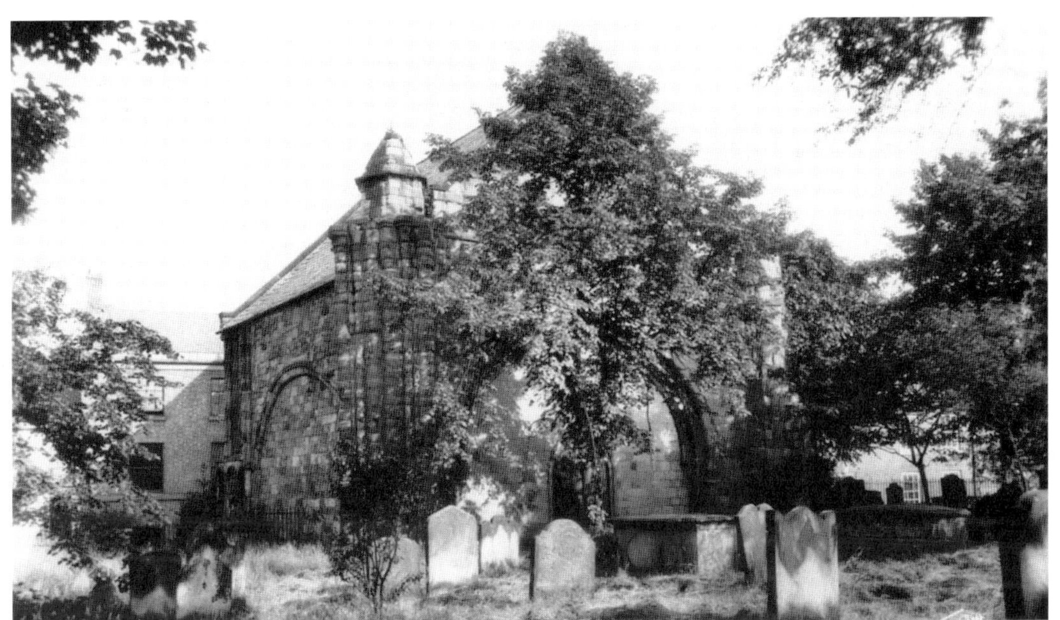

Princess Street, *c.* 1920. The Lady Chapel is all that remains of old St Chad's Church. It was founded in the late eighth century and was named after a former Bishop of Lichfield who was canonised in 779. It was a collegiate church with a chapter of ten canons and a dean until it was dissolved in 1547. On 9 July 1788, as the clock struck four in the morning, the great tower collapsed taking with it most of the building. The *Chronicle* reported, 'The whole of the tower, except the wall to the south side, together with the floors, roof over the principal part of the body of the church, and part of the side walls are entirely in ruins.' After the Reformation the Lady Chapel was often called the Bishop's Chancel. The arch on the left led from the chapel into the chancel while the arch on the right led into the south transept.

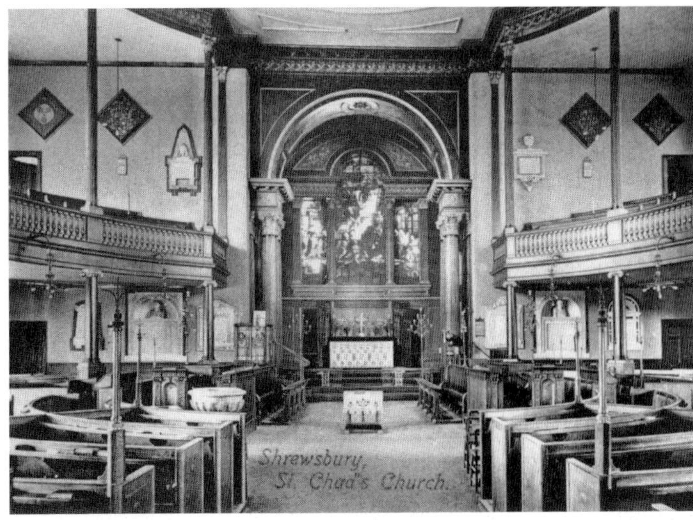

St Chad's Terrace, *c.* 1925. After much debate a new St Chad's Church was erected overlooking The Quarry. It was designed by George Steuart, cost just under £20,000, and is a rare example of a round church. The first stone was laid on St Chad's Day, 2 March 1790, and the church was consecrated on 19 August 1792. The chancel is shallow and flanked by a pair of Corinthian columns on each side of the arch. The east window is the work of David Evans, a Shrewsbury man with a workshop on Wyle Cop. The central light depicts Rubens' 'Descent From The Cross', while the side windows show the 'Visitation' and the 'Presentation'. The font, just left of centre, is an oval bowl carved out of Silurian marble. It was bought in 1843 from a church in Malpas for just £10.

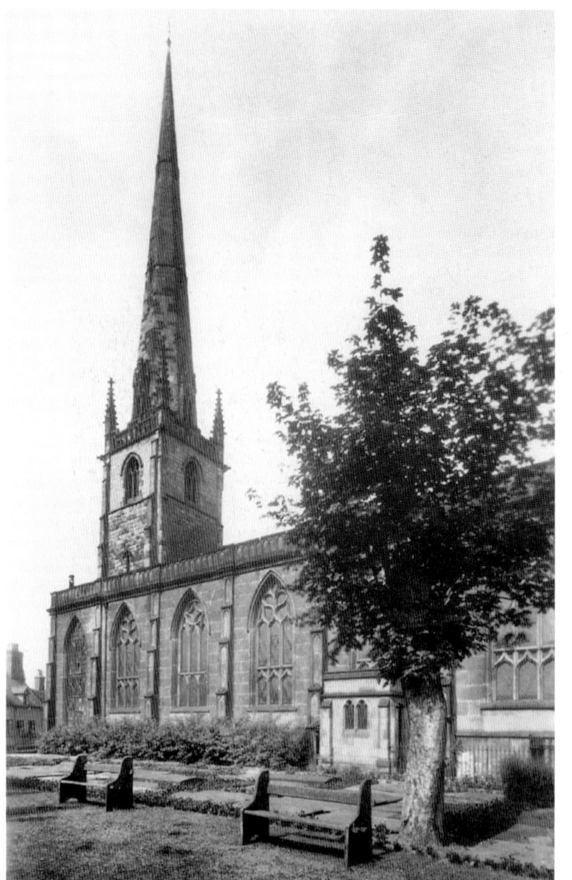

St Alkmund's Square, *c.* 1925. It is thought that St Alkmund's Church was founded by Ethelfleda the daughter of Alfred the Great. Over the foundations of the Saxon church, a fine medieval church was built; but after the fall of old St Chad's the main body of the church was demolished leaving just the tower and spire that date from the late fourteenth century. Demolition began in 1794 and parishioners worshipped in St Julian's Church until Sunday 8 November when the new church was opened for service. It was rebuilt by Tilley and Carline who used cast iron tracery in the windows that was made by the Coalbrookdale Company. The interior is fairly plain but the east window is remarkable. It is a copy of the Madonna from Guido Reni's 'Assumption of the Virgin' in Munich Cathedral. It is painted onto glass and is the work of Francis Eginton of Birmingham. The font and the pinnacles around the tower are memorials to the Revd J. Wightman and his son C.E.L. Wightman who were vicars of St Alkmund's for seventy-five years in the nineteenth century. In 1904 the tower arch was uncovered as a memorial to Julia Wightman, the great temperance campaigner and wife of C.E.L. Wightman.

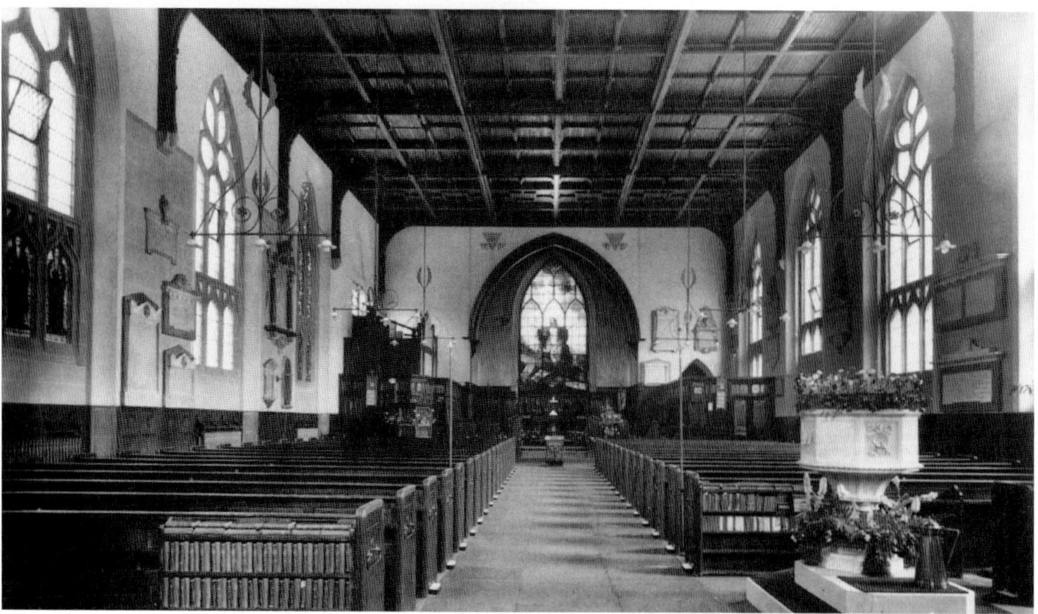

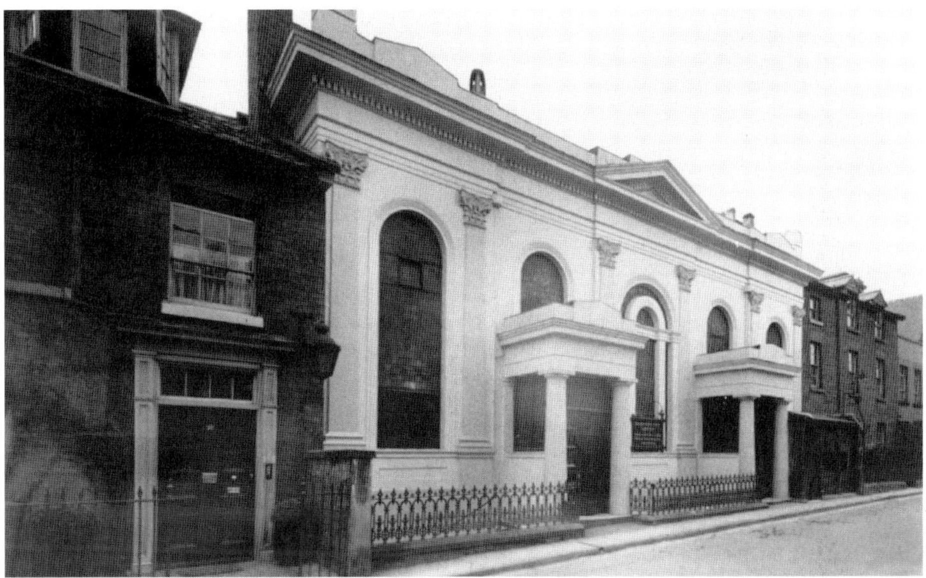

Town Walls, *c.* 1925. The Methodist New Connexion was founded in the Ebenezer Chapel in Leeds in 1797. It arrived in Shrewsbury in 1832 and services were first held in a house on Union Wharf and then in Cole Hall in Hill's Lane before moving to this chapel, which was opened in 1834. It is built out of brick, which has been plastered at the front and decorated with Corinthian pilasters. The two porches are supported by fluted Doric columns. It was able to accommodate 500 people and was opened for worship on 20 June by the Revd John Bakewell. The collection at that service amounted to £122 10*s* 3*d*, which went towards the building fund, leaving a debt of £1,600. Towards the end of the 1930s it became a meeting house for the Christian Scientist Church before being redeveloped for secular use in 1983 by Shrewsbury Girls' High School. A message on the back of the second card reads, 'been closed owing to burst pipes. So shall be in there Sunday for the first time.'

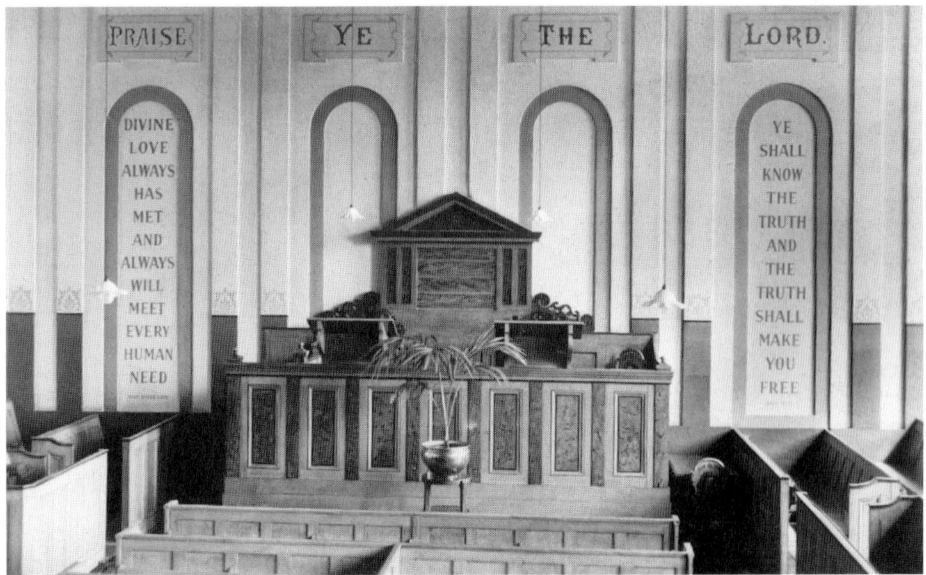

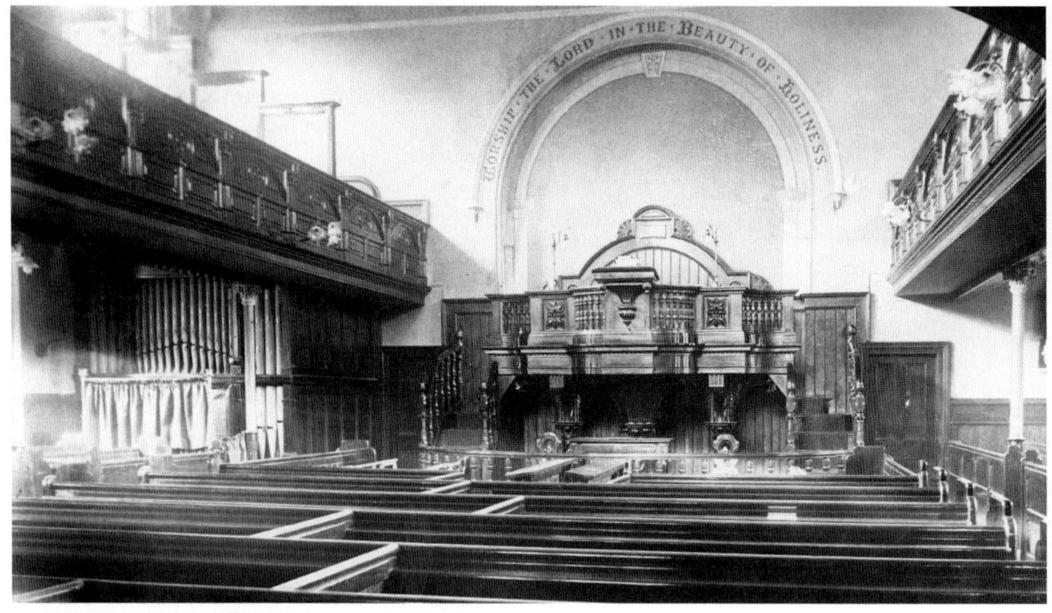

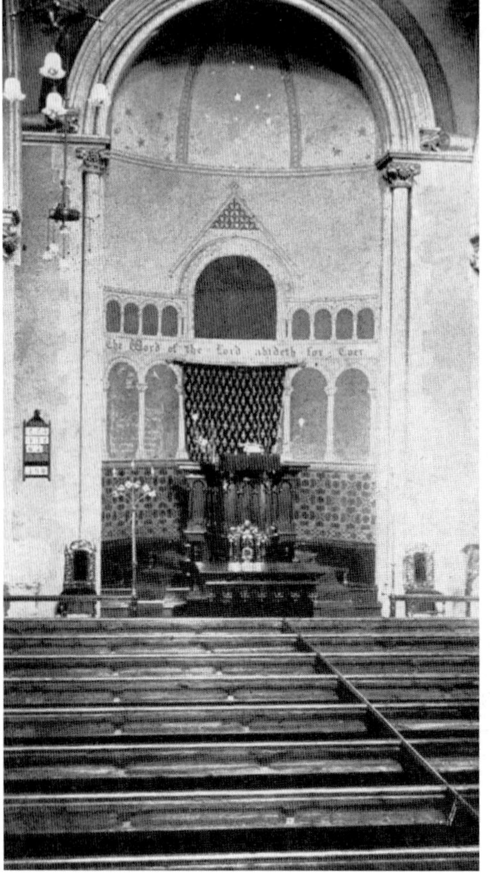

St John's Hill, *c.* 1925. John Wesley came to Shrewsbury on 16 March 1861 and preached in a small cottage in Fish Street. As Methodism grew in the town, Shearman's Hall in Milk Street was converted into a chapel. In 1781 a purpose-built chapel was opened in Hill's Lane by John Wesley. It was built at the expense of a local tanner from Roushill known as 'Good' John Appleton. As the congregation grew at the start of the nineteenth century a new chapel was erected on St John's Hill in 1805 at a cost of over £2,000. It was rebuilt in 1879 with a school room and office space. The legend over the arch reads 'Worship The Lord In The Beauty Of Holiness'.

Castle Street, *c.* 1920. St Nicholas' Presbyterian Church stands on the site of a medieval chapel that was connected to the castle. The congregation of this church was formed in 1865 and held their services in the Music Hall until this church was opened in 1870. The church was designed in the Romanesque style by Robert Bennett of Weymouth. It was built out of stone with a tiled roof. The frontage had a wide-arched entrance with pilaster buttresses and a circular tower at the western corner. It had galleries and could seat 500 people. The chapel closed when the Presbyterians united with the Congregationalists to form the United Reformed Church, holding their services in Abbey Foregate. The church was redeveloped into offices for the borough council and is now the Well Woman Centre.

7

FRANKWELL TO THE WEST

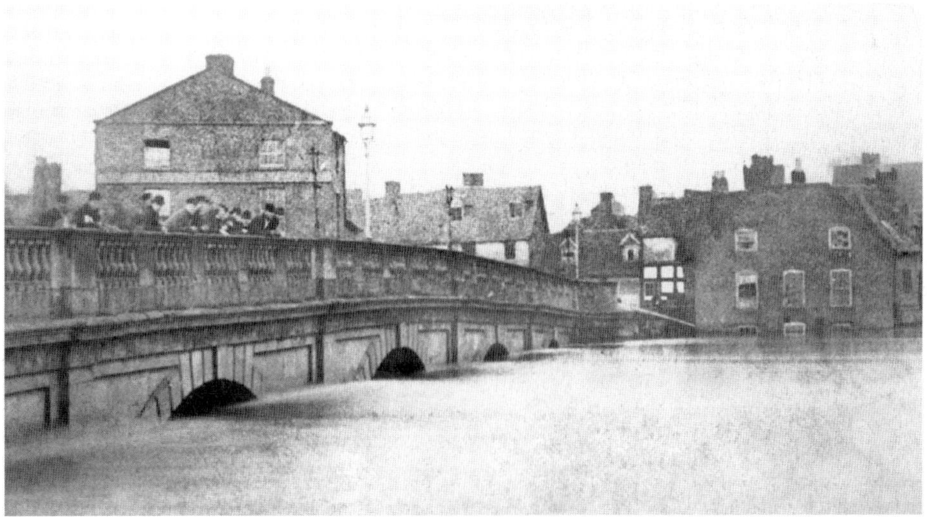

Frankwell, December 1869. When writing 'Recollections of the Great Flood of 1869' for the *Shrewsbury Chronicle*, H.E. Forrest recalled that, 'The Severn sounded like thunder and the Welsh Bridge shook as the river passed underneath.' The large house on the left of the bridge is where Hall's auction house now stands. The warehouse to the rear was built in 1888 a date when perhaps the house was rebuilt or modified. On the right is a very substantial house with its own little footbridge from the first storey that would have been so useful when the ground floor was flooded. It was demolished to make way for Frankwell Forge that was there by 1885. The house may have been occupied by a Mr Hudson a boat-builder who had a timber yard and boat loft next door. The timber-framed building is now a restaurant called Franks of Shrewsbury.

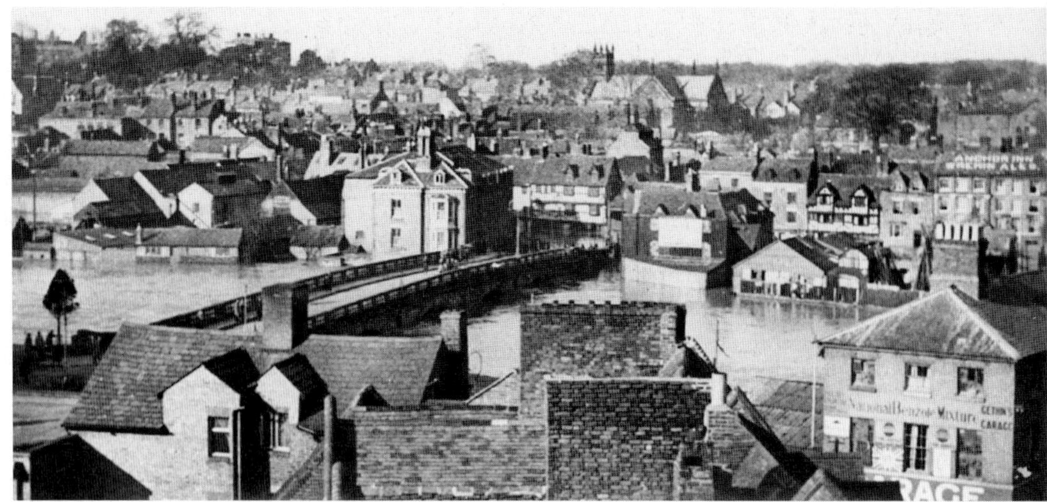

Frankwell, February 1946. The floods reached a peak of over 19ft above normal. Note the buildings on either side of the bridge on the Frankwell side. The house was occupied by Mrs George who let out rooms while the large sign over the corrugated iron building advertises H. & E. Davies' Frankwell Forge. The buildings nearest the camera are in Mardol and Mardol Quay. The garage on the right belonged to Frank Gethin whose petrol tanks were often polluted by floodwater. The writing on the roof across the river advertised the Anchor Inn and Wrekin Ales while on the skyline centre is St George's Church.

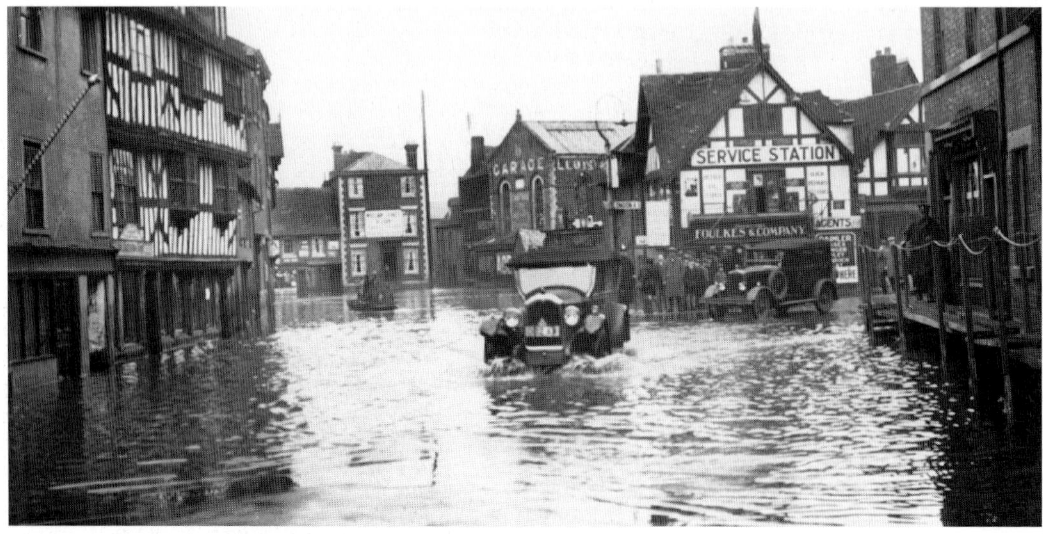

Frankwell, *c.* 1928. There were six floods in the 1920s (1923, two in 1925 and 1928 and another in 1929); all reaching a peak of between 15ft 9in and 16ft 9in. The service station belonged to Foulkes & Co. who later went into partnership with a Mr Gornall. They sold petrol, oil and tyres, guaranteed quick repairs and were agents for Riley, Singer and Daimler. They were also electrical engineers but in about 1940 they sold that part of the business to Medlicott Brothers. Another garage was established by Lewis & Froggatt in the large building with the rounded windows. They were ironmongers with two other premises in Frankwell, including an indoor cycling school. They shared part of the building with Lloyd & Son printers. The large house in the centre was occupied by William Jones, a chimney sweep. Just to the left is an alley leading through to St George's Buildings.

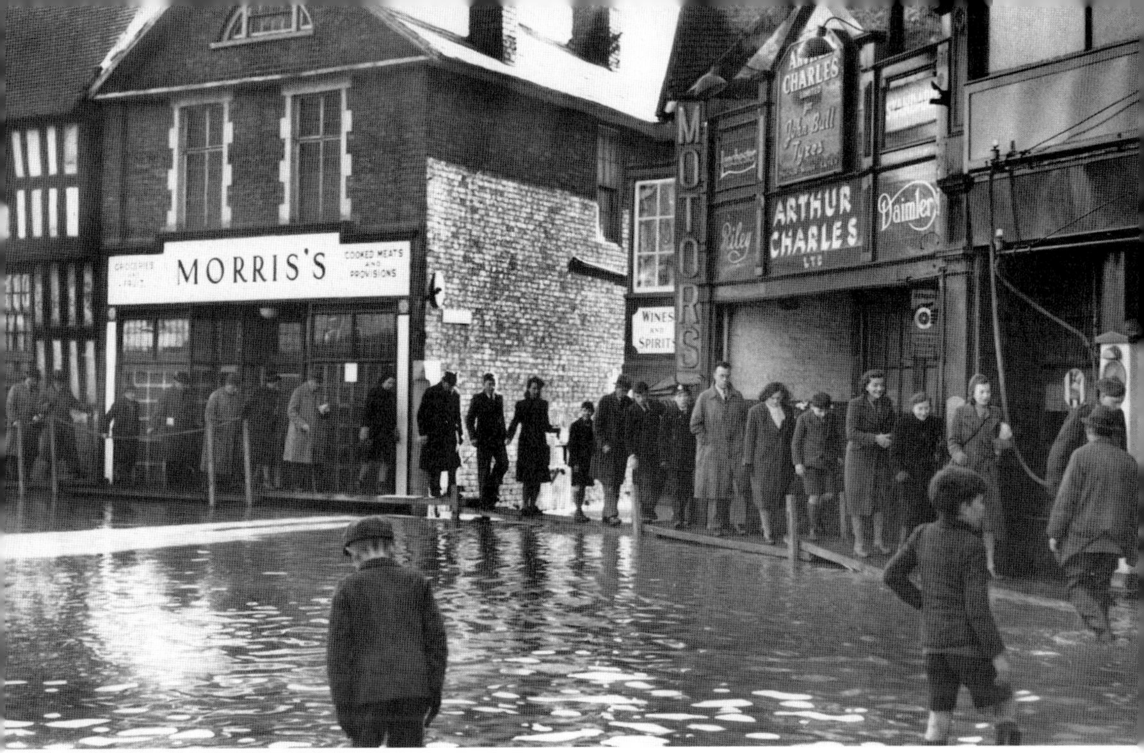

Frankwell, February 1941. Duckboards are needed to convey pedestrians from the Welsh Bridge into Frankwell. Morris's shop sold groceries, fruit, cooked meats and provisions. It was where James Kent Morris, who was born in Ruyton-XI-Towns, established his first business in 1869. To the left are the timbers of the Fellmonger's Hall. On the other side of Water Lane is a sign for wines and spirits on the wall of the Old Crow Inn that was first licensed in the eighteenth century. It closed in September 1971 and has been converted into flats. The garage next door was opened by Lewis & Froggatt who sold it to Wales and Edwards in 1929. By the 1930s the name of the business had changed to Arthur Charles, which was connected to Wales and Edwards at the bottom of Wyle Cop.

Frankwell, *c.* 1910. This suburb has a wealth of timber-framed buildings. The house with the tall gable, far left, is the Plough Inn, which dates from the early fifteenth century. The two buildings on the corner were built as single units about a hundred years later but have since been divided into pairs. At this period the house with the projecting windows was occupied by J. Evans, a carpenter, and a Mrs Bowdler. Next door was occupied by John Probert who was a boot-maker and his wife who let part of the house as apartments. To the right is another of Lewis & Froggatt's shops; note on the window, 'Ironmonger & Cycle Agent'. The building was once occupied by the Prince of Wales Inn before becoming the Club House, a working men's club providing a wide range of activities.

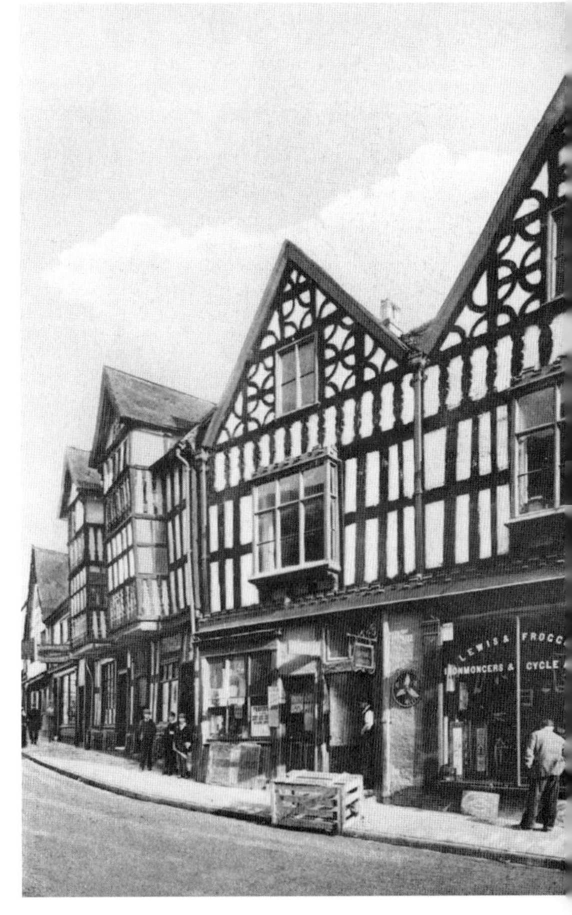

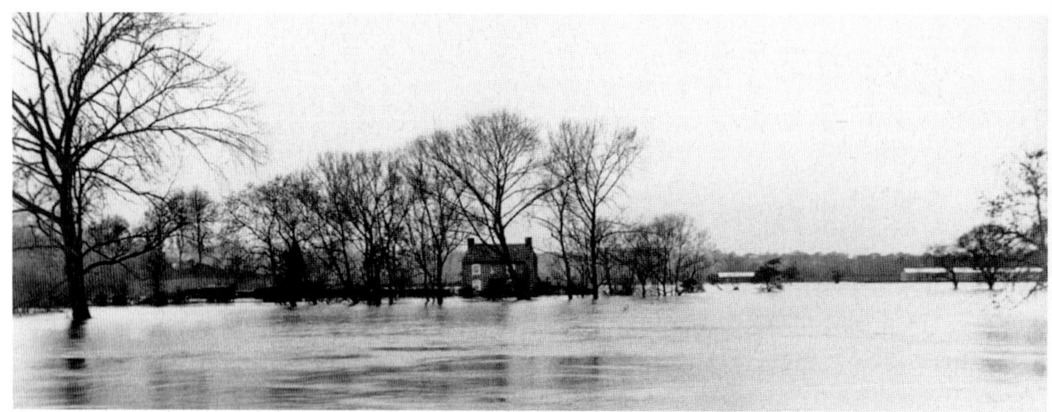

Frankwell, *c.* 1925. Beneath the flood is the Barge Gutter that runs just to the right of the house. It created an island on the right opposite Coton Hill called the Isle of Poplar, known locally as the Popsey Island. The gutter was built to take barges past a fish weir that was built across the main stream. The house was once an inn called the Barge but was delicensed in about 1860 and later divided into two cottages. The left-hand one was occupied by Neddy Powell who was reputed to have one of the best coracles on the river. During one flood he carried himself, his son, a hundredweight of coal and a gallon of water to his marooned house. Neddy was one of the last bird catchers and an amateur taxidermist. When bird catching was made illegal he turned to making garden ornaments out of concrete.

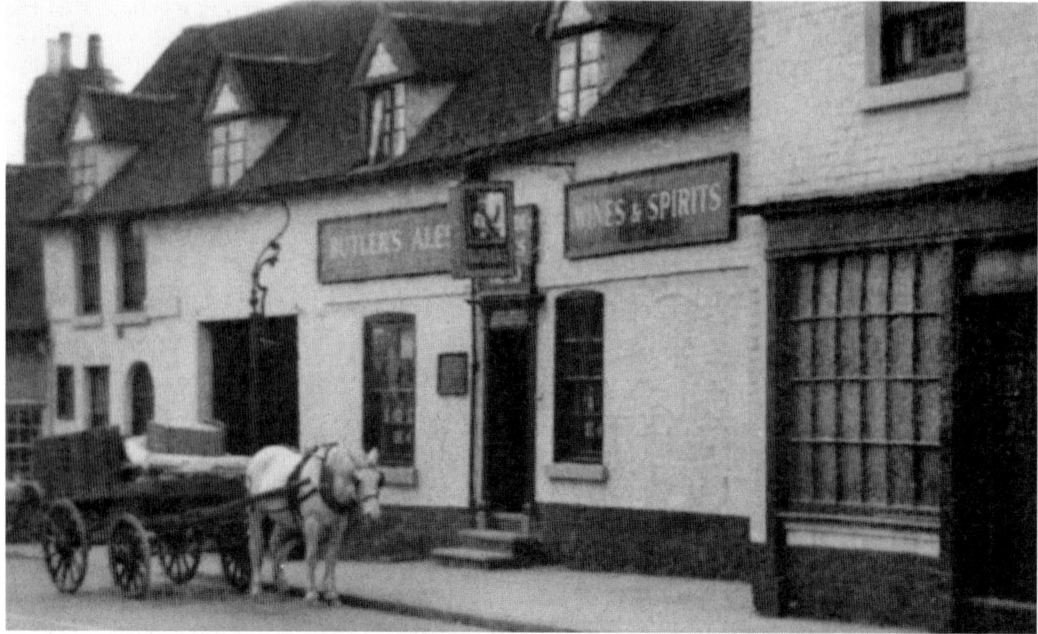

Frankwell, *c.* 1905. The Old Buck's Head was first licensed in the early part of the nineteenth century. It is timber framed but was refaced in the eighteenth century. In 1851 the landlord was James Birch who was also a blacksmith with a smithy at the rear of the building. In 1900 the owner was Sarah A. Richards who lived at Gordon Villa in Copthorne. The landlord was William Felton who was also a cab proprietor and ran a posting stable. In 1906 the cottage to the left of the arch was occupied by John Wilding, a carpenter, while the shop to the right was occupied by M.J. Evans, a grocer. Both properties were incorporated into the inn in the 1970s.

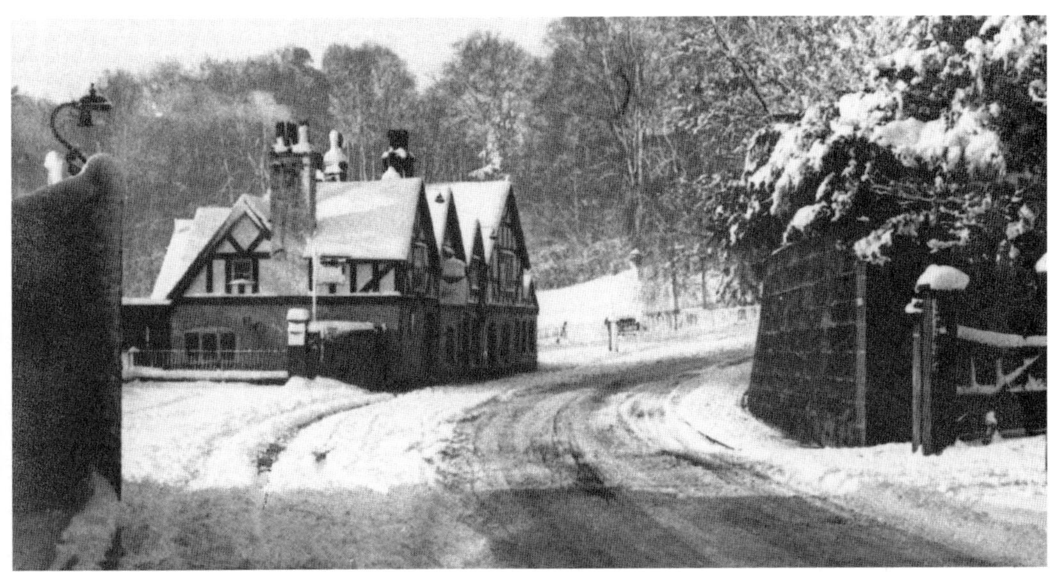

New Street, *c.* 1950. The wintry scene was taken at the point where the street meets Porthill. The gateway on the right is the entrance of Park Avenue that was laid out in about 1913. The sandstone wall to Maes Fron was built on land that was once part of Oscar Pritchard's nursery that can be seen above the inn on the second view. The nursery occupied much of the north side of New Street and was run by the Pritchard family from the 1870s until the 1940s. In the early twentieth century a great deal of the nursery near Porthill was sold for the building of Maes Fron, Sandhurst and Lilleshall House. The Boat House Hotel was first recorded in 1806 but records indicate it was trading from a much earlier date. The building was restored in the nineteenth century. The road-facing side is modern but there are original timbers at the rear and inside the building. Before the opening of the Porthill Bridge in 1923 a manually operated ferry took pedestrians across the river from the inn. In the 1920s and '30s the Abley Brothers kept a fleet of rowing boats for hire and ran a pleasure boat named the *Lady Sue* after their mother. It was 50ft long and able to carry 83 passengers.

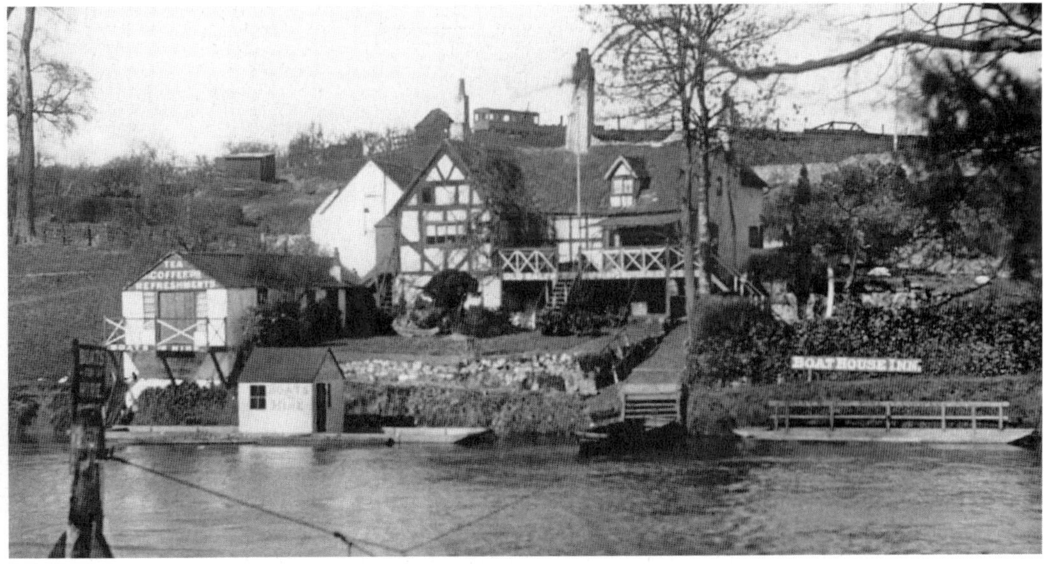

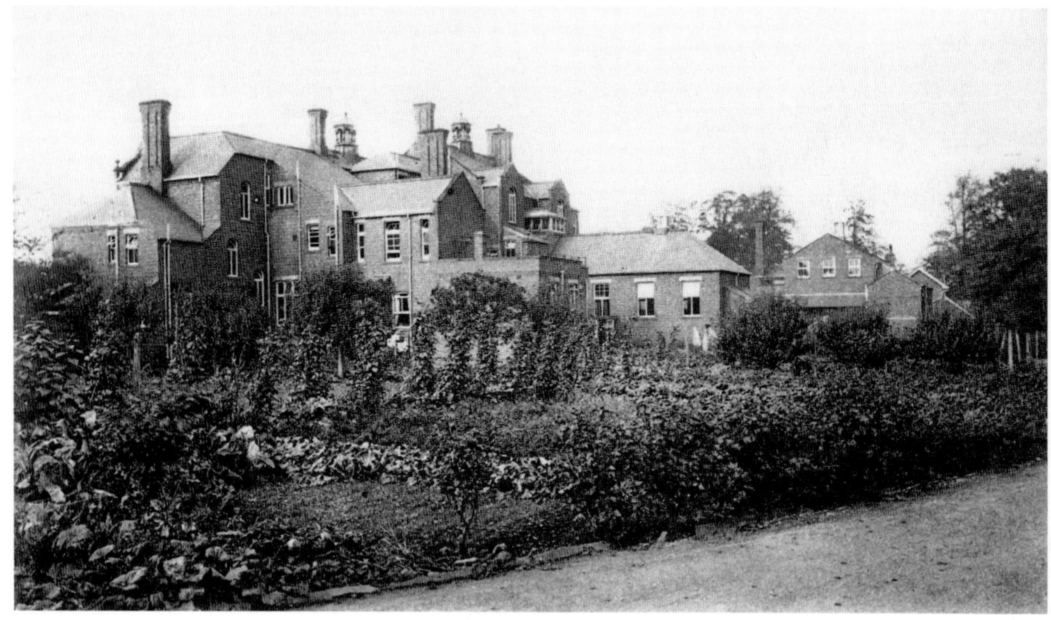

Radbrook, *c.* 1910. The Shropshire Technical School, School of Cookery and the Domestic Arts for Girls, was opened in 1901. It was situated just over a mile from the town in 10 acres of ground set out as gardens, playing fields and tennis courts. There was accommodation for twenty-six boarders, sixteen of them County Council scholars. There was also a cottage hostel where sixteen dairy pupils and a dairy teacher lived. The school year was divided into three thirteen-week terms and the students were prepared for the Housewife's and Housekeeper's Certificate that was granted by the National Union for the Education of Women in Domestic Science. The college later became a teacher training college for Domestic Science and Rural Studies.

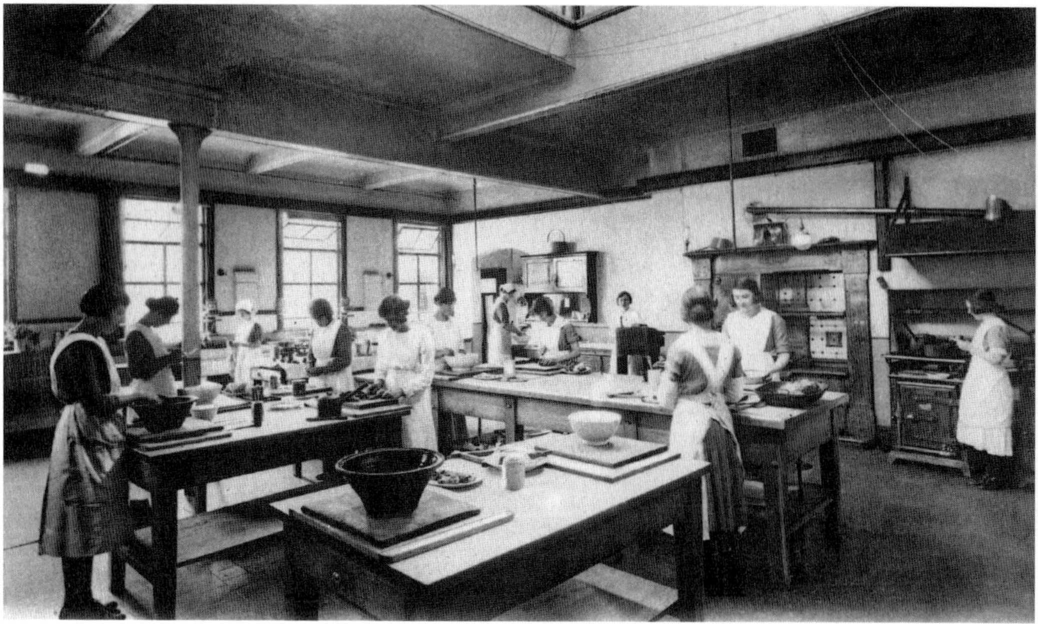

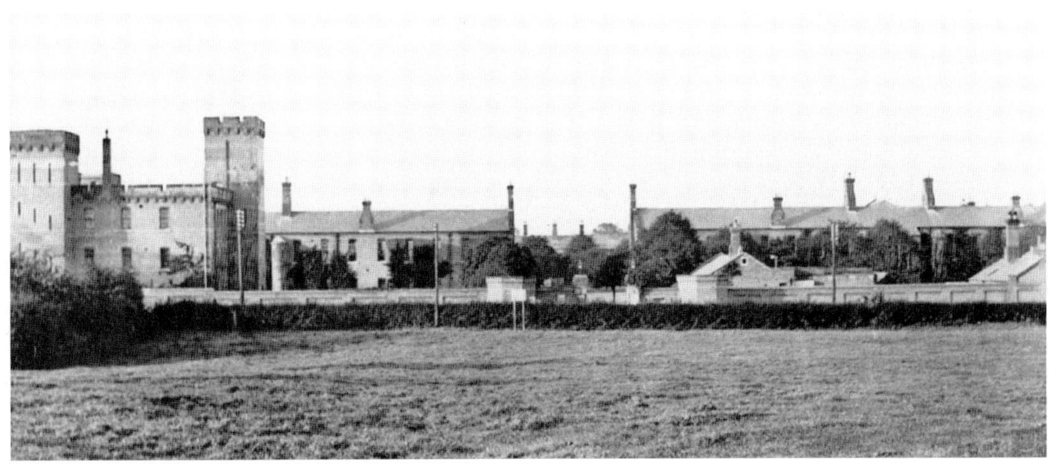

Copthorne, *c.* 1912. The Barracks were built on a 9-acre site and cost in the region of £65,000. Four million bricks were used in its construction and it was first occupied on 30 December 1881 when the Depot Companies of 43rd Monmouth Light Infantry and the 53rd Shropshire Regiment marched in from Shrewsbury station. The open field, where Copthorne Drive now stands, was for fourteen years the home of Shrewsbury Town Football Club from 1895 until April 1910. At the final game played at Copthorne, Bert Dobson scored the last goal in a 2–0 victory over Walsall. The message on the reverse from Arthur Lea to his mother informs her he had arrived safely back at the Barracks and that he was orderly of the day and that his barracks room is on the right.

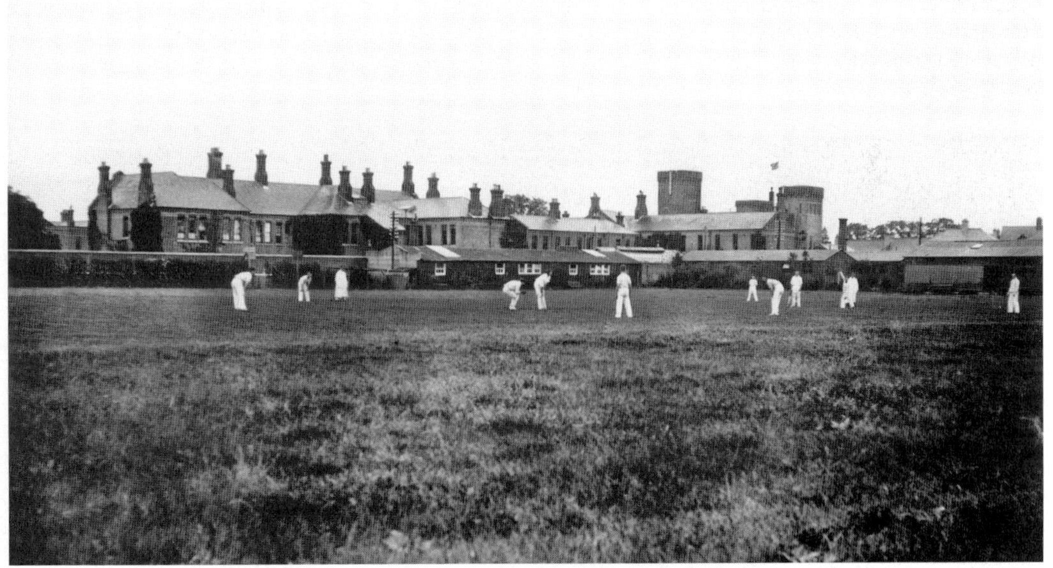

Copthorne, *c.* 1935. This is a view across the cricket field towards the main block on Copthorne Road. During the summer of 1937 the cricket team stationed at the Barracks had a good season. The Regimental journal records they had nearly two months cricket uninterrupted by rain and of the sixteen games played they won eleven, lost four and drew one. Their match against Shrewsbury YMCA was very one-sided, scoring 106 to their opponents' 37. On 21 July a match was played between the sergeants and the corporals who were assisted by Private Higgs. He proved to be the top scorer but the sergeants still won by 12 runs.

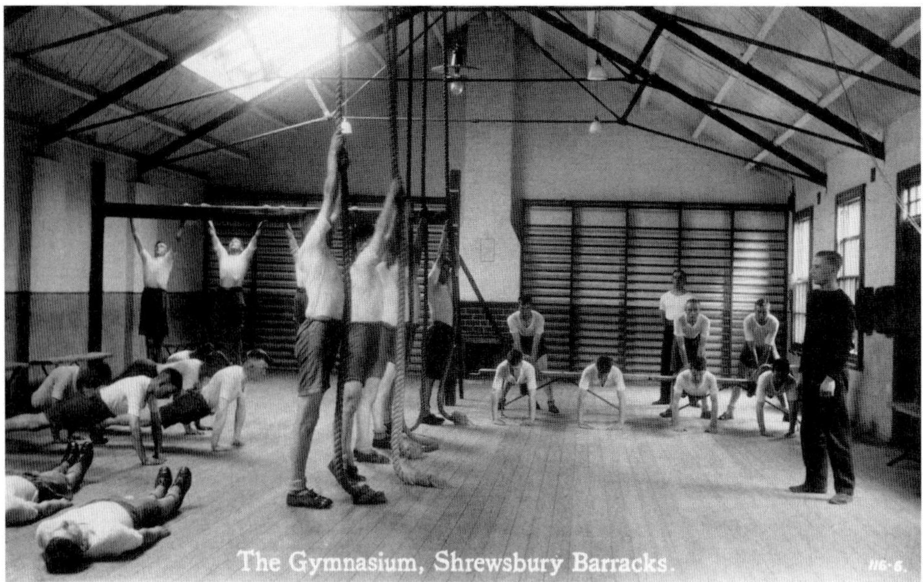

Copthorne, *c.* 1935. Here we see soldiers at the Barracks being put through their paces in the gymnasium. As well as compulsory physical training a Physical Culture Club was organised 'to provide indoor games and physical training, including work on the horse, ground and parallel bars, for those who have any spare time in the afternoon or evening.' Every month a cup was presented to the man who had made the most progress by gaining the highest number of points from a series of tests set in 1937 by Corporals Gough, Blackman and Chambers.

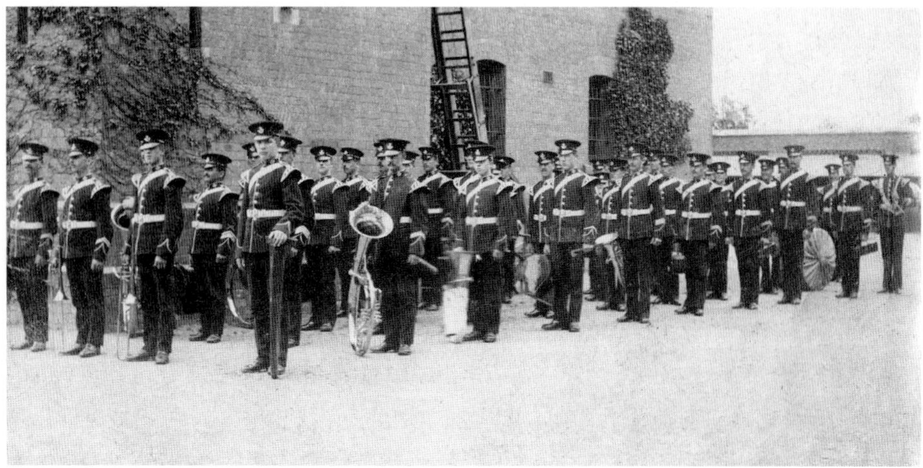

Copthorne, July 1914. This photograph was taken by Alfred Wright whose studio was in Bridge Street. It was taken at the Barracks and shows the band of the 1st Battalion KSLI who were performing at the Royal Show being held on the Racecourse in Monkmoor. They played a wide selection of music on four of the five days of the show and were conducted by Bandmaster A.J. Wilson. There were three sessions each day from 11.30 a.m. to 1 p.m., 2.30 p.m. to 4 p.m. and 5 p.m. to 6.30 p.m.

8

THE LOOP OF THE SEVERN

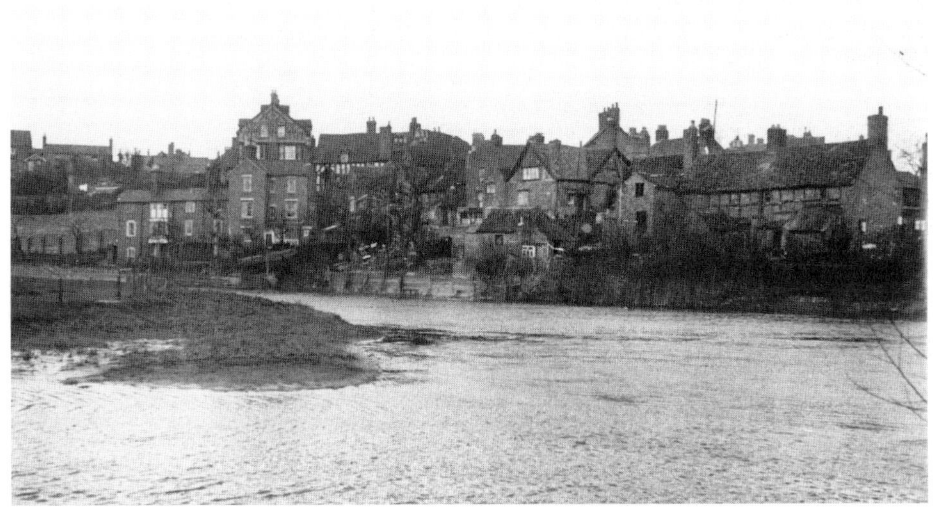

Coton Hill, *c.* 1930. This view shows the rear of the houses and cottages on Coton Hill and the Pig Trough. The timber-framed cottages on the right stood almost opposite the London Apprentice Inn until they were demolished. One of the buildings was once the home of William and Impy Bryan, two of the best coracle makers in the town – this despite William only having one arm. The tall building just left of centre stands between the Pig Trough and Berwick Road but is approached through a driveway off Coton Hill between the Pig Trough and the Royal Oak. Its split into two houses, Thorneycroft House after Lt-Col. Thorneycroft who was living there in the 1890s, and Mytton House named after the family who owned the land there in the fifteenth century.

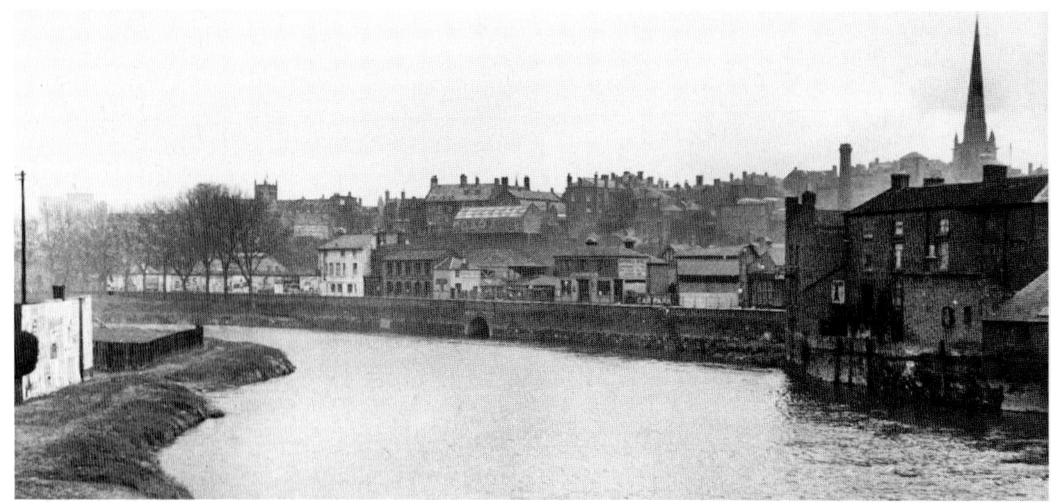

Smithfield Road and Mardol Quay, *c.* 1930. This view taken from the Welsh Bridge shows a length of Smithfield Road before it was widened over the river. Note the large hole that drained the abattoir. The cattle market wall with the advertising hoarding is behind the trees. The white building just left of centre is the Victoria Hotel, first recorded in 1856. Other businesses to the right included Potter Bros, tarpaulin makers, George Edwards, building contractor, the Smithfield Hotel and the Britannic Bottling Co. The buildings on the right are built on Mardol Quay and were demolished in the 1950s. The fence of sleepers was known locally as 'the Muck Yard', an area where the people of the 'Little Boro' deposited their rubbish. It was later used as a recreation area with swings for the children.

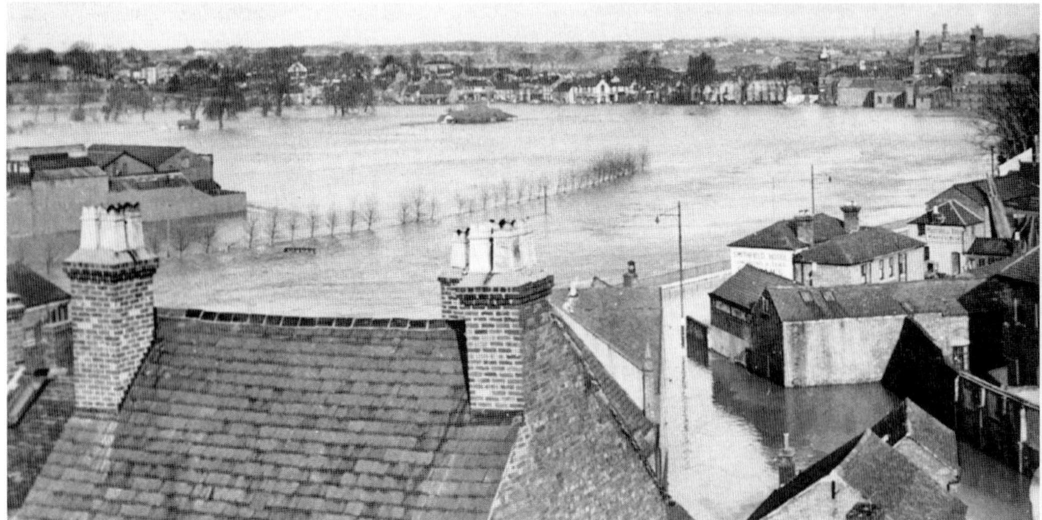

The Severn to Frankwell and Coton Hill, February 1946, looking over the river from Smithfield Road. The building with the writing on the white wall in Smithfield Road is the Smithfield Hotel. It was once known as the Globe Inn but changed its name in about 1916. As well as alcoholic drinks it also supplied luncheons and teas. It was owned by Southam's Brewery and later changed its name to the Proud Salopian, having a portrait of Thomas Southam in his mayoral robes on the inn sign. His brewery is the large building on the bank of the river on the right with all the windows. The building above the chimney pots is the Atlas Foundry in Frankwell and in the centre of the flood is the roof line of the cricket pavilion.

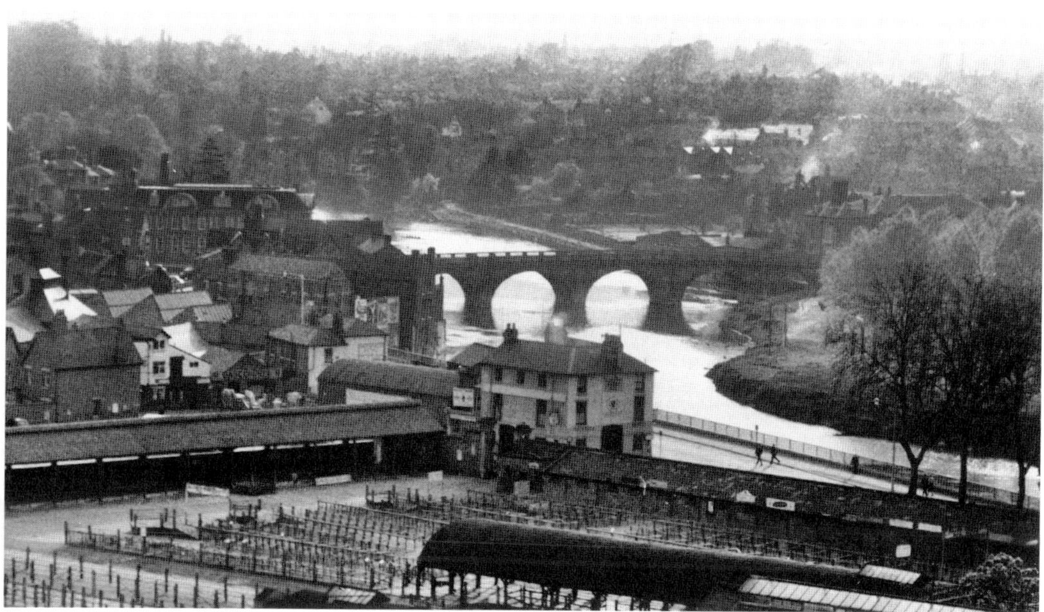

Smithfield Road to the Welsh Bridge, *c.* 1950. This view taken from the rear of Pride Hill looks over the cattle market that was opened on 19 November 1850. The covered area to the left housed the pig pens. By the 1920s Shrewsbury was one of the largest markets for pigs in the country. Pedigree sales were held on a Tuesday but grew so rapidly they moved to a Friday to give extra accommodation. Held in the spring and autumn when over 400 pigs were auctioned, the favourite breeds were Large White, Wessex and Saddleback. The large white building in the centre is the Victoria Hotel that was licensed from 1856 until the mid-1960s – the lifespan of the market. The five-arched Welsh Bridge was opened in September 1795. It replaced a medieval bridge that stood several yards further upstream.

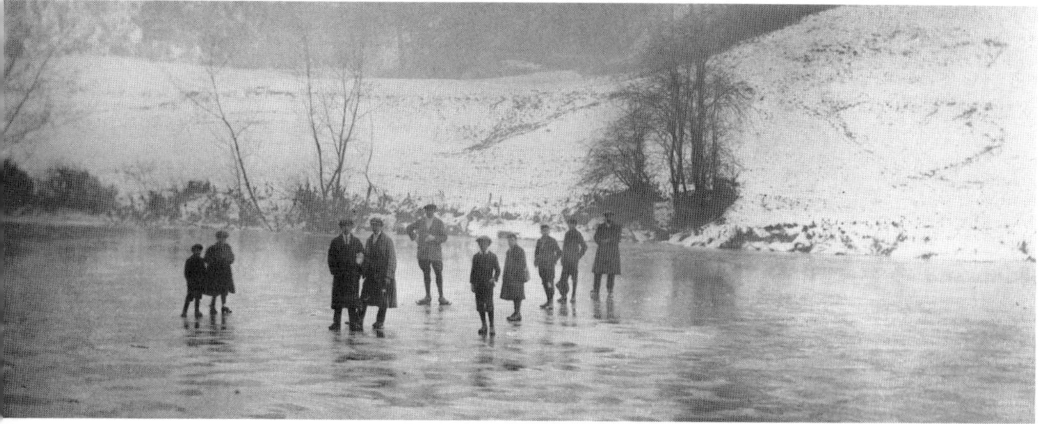

The Severn to Beck's Field, 10 February 1917. Beck's Field in the background should be called the Lower Beck to distinguish it from the Upper Beck on which parts of Shrewsbury School are built. The fields were named after Mr Beck and both were purchased by the school in 1890. The man in the middle wearing skates is Mr De Ruyter who was the manager of Singleton & Cole Ltd, the tobacco manufacturers. He came from Holland, a country known for its colder winters and its love of skating. The Severn has frozen many times in the past. In 1739 the river was icebound for thirteen weeks during which time a tent was erected on the ice, a printing press set up and several sheep were roasted.

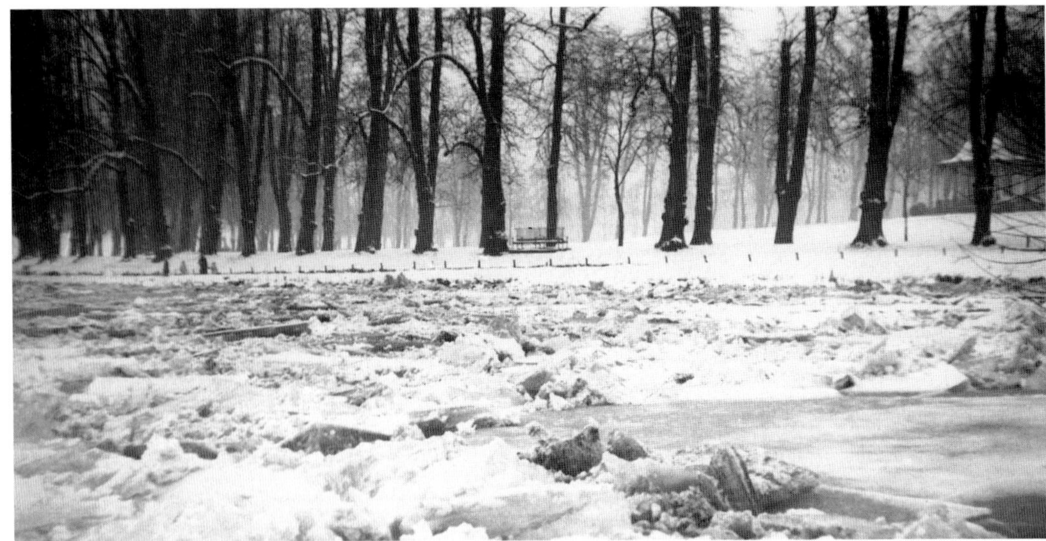

The Quarry, February 1940. Arctic weather hit Shrewsbury early in January with a series of hard frosts which froze all open water and blanketed it with snow. The cold snap lasted throughout the month until the last weekend when the town experienced a variety of unusual weather. A short thaw occurred on the Thursday, which was followed the next morning by a fierce hail storm, a severe blizzard and a hard overnight frost. On the Saturday morning there was another heavy fall of snow followed by rain, which froze before reaching the ground, to cover everything with a layer of ice. On the Sunday another heavy snow storm blocked roads all around the town and skating occurred on a large stretch of the Severn between the Porthill and Greyfriars bridges. When the thaw arrived the snow melted faster than the ice, causing the Severn to rise rapidly, breaking up large sections of ice which floated downstream to jam beneath the arches of the Welsh and English Bridges. As the river rose, ice floes were upended and piled one upon the other creating an amazing sight around the river until the force of water broke them up and sent them crashing downstream.

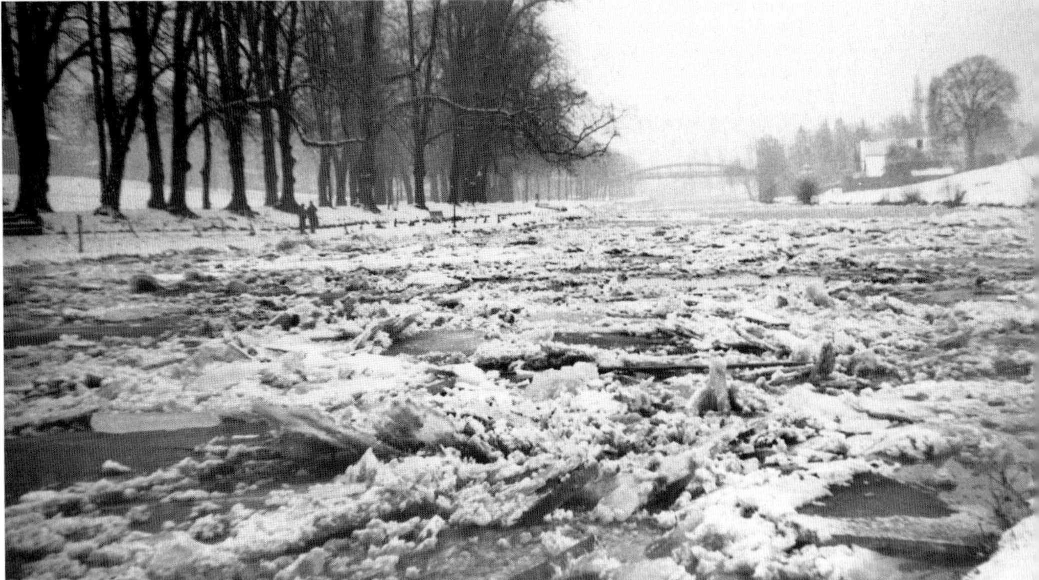

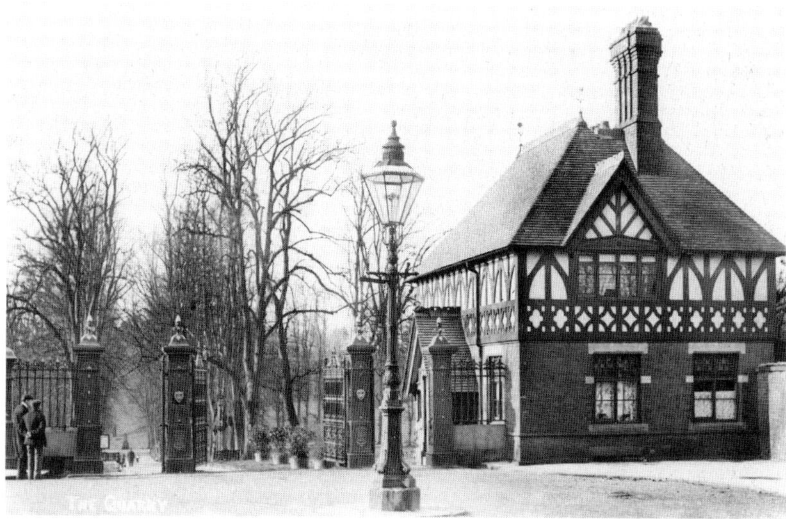

The Quarry, *c.* 1900. For many years Shrewsbury has benefited from the generosity of the Shropshire Horticultural Society who donate part of their profits from the Shrewsbury Flower Show to enhance the county town. One of their first gifts in 1881 were these magnificent gates to the entrance of The Quarry that cost £216.

Five years later they donated £486 6*s* 5*d* to build the Quarry Lodge on the right. For many years it was the home of the park's superintendent, the most famous of these being Percy Thrower who served in that capacity from 1946 until 1974. The narrow gate looks down Gloucester Avenue to the statue of Hercules on the river bank. Note the old lime trees and the absence of the war memorial that was not unveiled until July 1923.

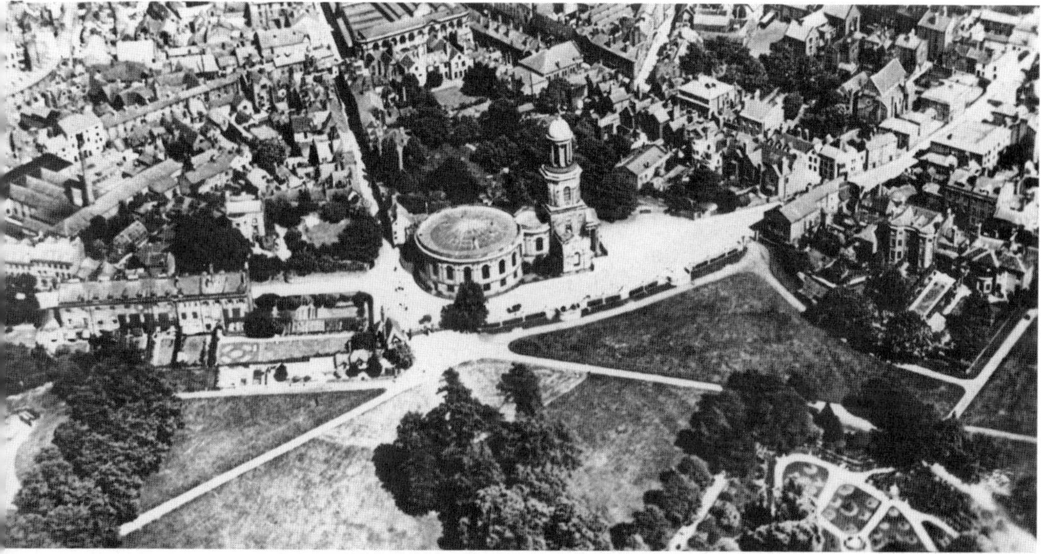

The Quarry and St Chad's Terrace, *c.* 1918. Standing at the top of The Quarry is St Chad's Church. It was built between 1790 and 1793 after the collapse of the old church in the town centre in 1788. It was designed by George Steuart and consists of two intersecting circles, the larger being the nave, the smaller the vestibule. The tower is built in three sections: the lower section is square, the middle section octagonal and the top is round with a dome and cross supported by Corinthian columns. Before the church was built, a narrow lane ran just outside the town wall here, between St John's Hill and Claremont Hill, and was known as Quarry Alley. After the wall was removed and the church built, the road was renamed Quarry Terrace and then St Chad's Terrace

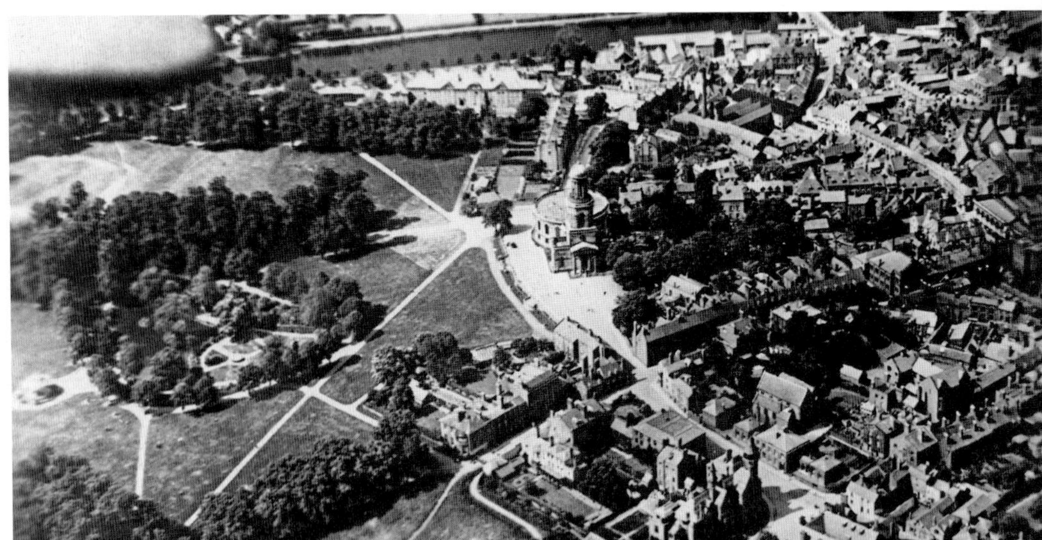

The Quarry, *c.* 1918. This view shows the west end of St Chad's Church with its impressive entrance porch. On the left is The Quarry with the large lime trees that were taken down just after the Second World War. In the centre is The Dingle. Just to the left of that is the bandstand, which was erected in 1879. Moving down from the church is a crossroads with St John's Hill on the right and Quarry Place, which was once known as Duck Lane on the left. Straight ahead is Murivance with the Eye, Ear and Throat Hospital on the corner of the entrance to Kingsland Bridge. Opposite the hospital is Allatt's School, built in about 1800 at a cost of £2,000.

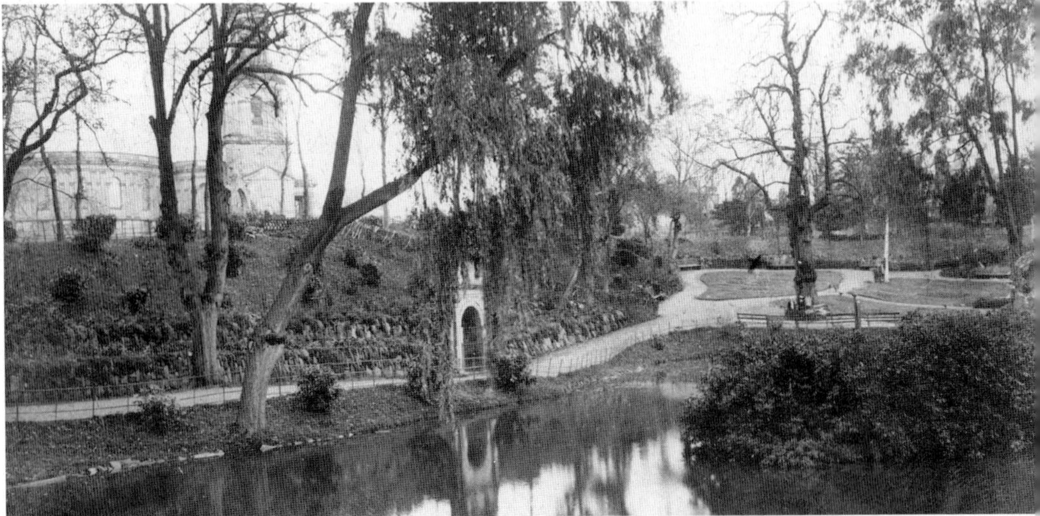

The Quarry, *c.* 1895. The Dingle is where the stone was quarried that gives the park its name. It was first landscaped round this natural pool in 1879 and has evolved over the years into the beautiful forma centrepiece of The Quarry. The Shoemaker's Arbour on the left was moved from Kingsland to The Dingle in June 1880. The horse chestnut tree on the right, with the circular bench around its trunk was one of the favourite spots to sit. Unfortunately it was blown down during a severe gale that created havoc ir the town in April 1947. On the reverse, Ellie writes to Mr Sharpley in Macclesfield, 'One of my favourite spots. I have marked my seat with an X.'

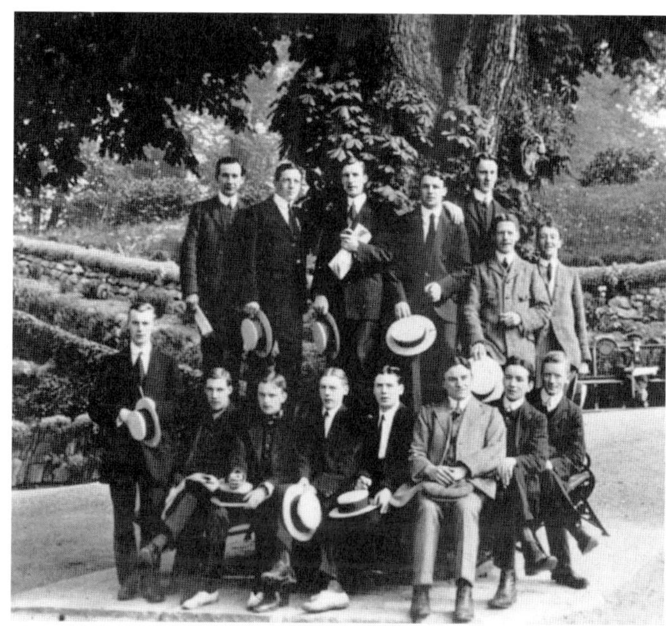

The Quarry, June 1911. A group of boys from Shrewsbury School pose with their master for this photograph in front of the old horse chestnut tree in The Dingle. The tree was the last of several chestnuts that once occupied this area. The others were destroyed after the mud removed from the pond after dredging was piled up around their bases. The message on the back of the card sent to Elsie Jackson in Stafford reads, 'Just a line to wish you a really good time on Monday which day I am sorry to say I cannot be with you. This P.C. is one taken of the fellows of the house, my pals and I being too late to be snapped. The weather is glorious and I hope it will continue to be so over the holidays. Yours sincerely F.R.C.'

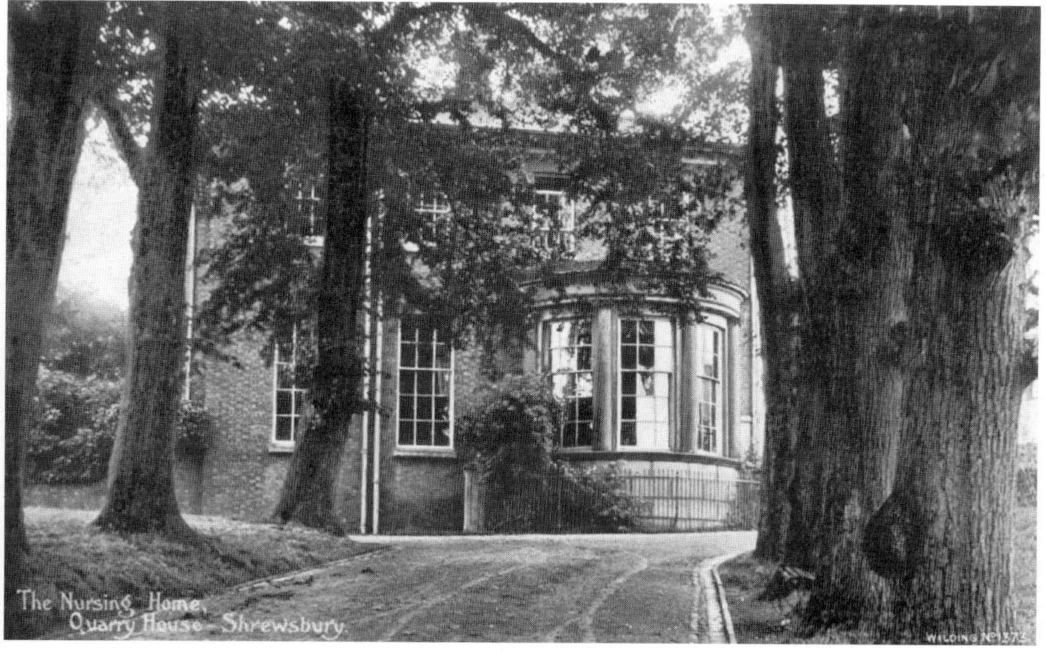

The Quarry, *c.* 1905. This avenue of lime trees leads up to Quarry Place and the nursing home in Quarry House. The house was built in the eighteenth century and was a private home for many years. In 1895 the Right Revd Sir Lovelace Tomlinson Stamer, the Bishop of Shrewsbury, lived there and in 1906 it was occupied by Lady Wilhelmina Brooke. In 1908 it was being used as a nurses' home while the new one was being built next to the Salop Infirmary in St Mary's Place. In 1910 it was converted into a nursing home and during the First World War it became a hospital for officers. By the 1960s the house had been converted back to residential use.

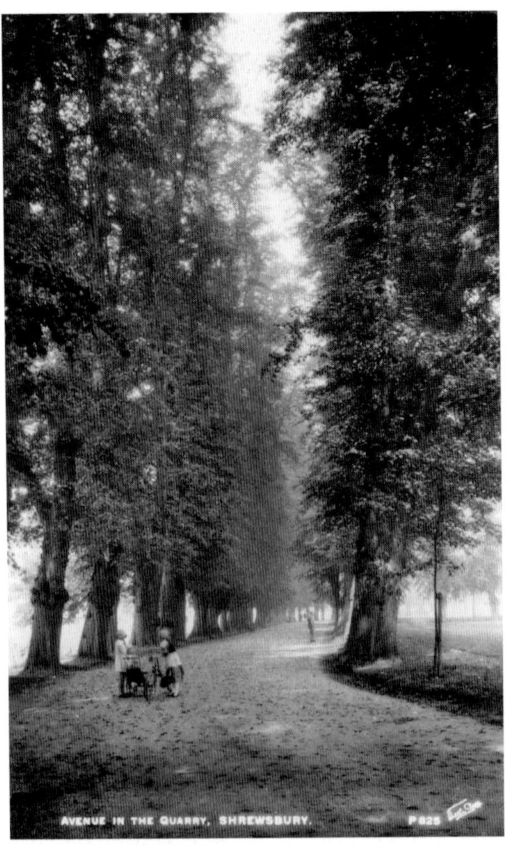

The Quarry, *c.* 1930. Four little girls with a pushchair and bike stand talking between the avenue of lime trees that borders the river on the left. The trees were planted in 1719 by Thomas Wright, a local nurseryman and cost £65 14*s*. In 1923 a young girl was killed while playing under one of the trees. A huge section of branch suddenly broke off and fell on her, smashing her skull – three other children had a narrow escape as they ran away screaming. Soon after the Second World War the old limes were felled and by 1950 replaced by new trees.

The Quarry, *c.* 1905. A large crowd gather around the bandstand to hear a promenade concert performed by a military band. These concerts were very popular on Sundays throughout the summer and usually took place between 2 and 4 p.m. and 7 and 9 p.m. A wide variety of music was played from military marches to classical pieces such as Beethoven's 'Egmont Overture' to lighter operetta pieces by Gilbert and Sullivan. The bandstand was another gift from the Shropshire Horticultural Society in 1879 and cost £233 5*s* 2*d*. They recently paid for it to be restored to its original design, by painting it and removing an ugly 1960s extension. Between 1880 and 1912 the society also donated £557 2*s* toward the running costs of the concerts.

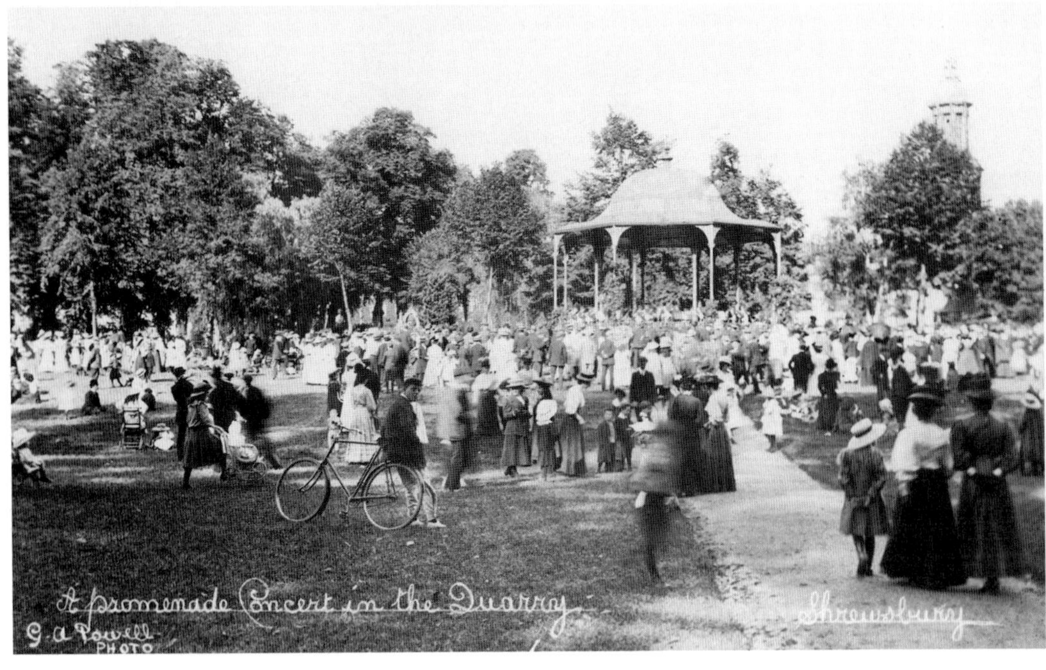

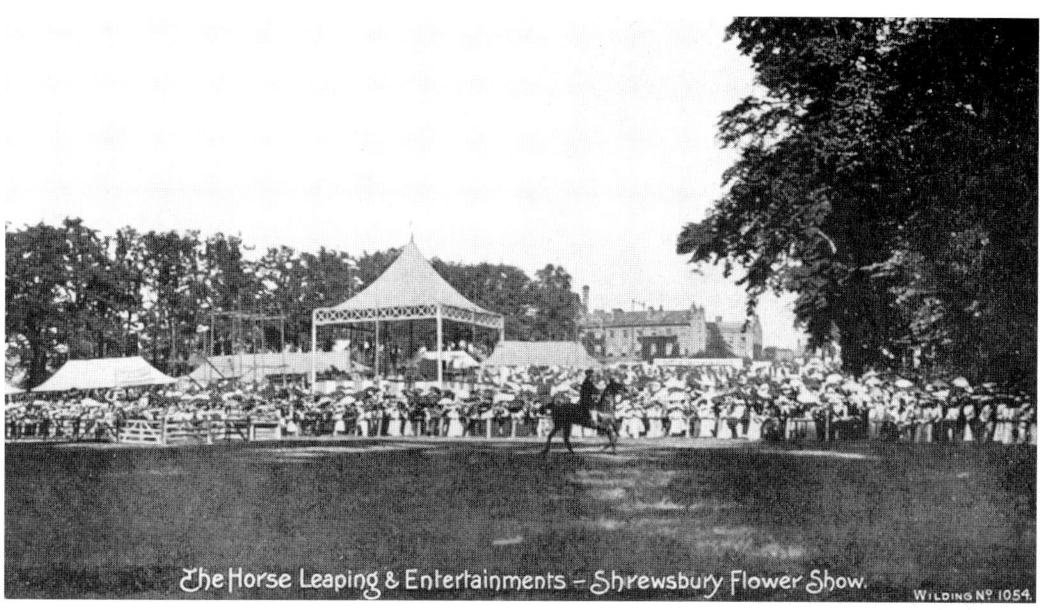

The Quarry and Flower Show, *c.* 1905 and 1955. The large pavilion in the centre of the first view is the stage, which was introduced for the first time in 1880. Over the two days of the show a new act was guaranteed every fifteen minutes. Top class acts were attracted from all over the world as they were paid a full week's fee for just two days of performing. Note the curtain around the rear of the stage in the second view. This was erected to stop people on Beck's Fields from viewing the acts with binoculars after the old lime trees had been cut down! The stage acts were very popular with the crowds but with the advent of variety shows on television and the need for financial restrictions they ended in the 1960s. Show jumping, or 'horse leaping' as it was known in the early days, was introduced in 1889. It is still popular today and over the years has attracted such great competitors as Harry Llewellyn, Pat Smyth, Harvey Smith, David Broome and Liz and Ted Edgar.

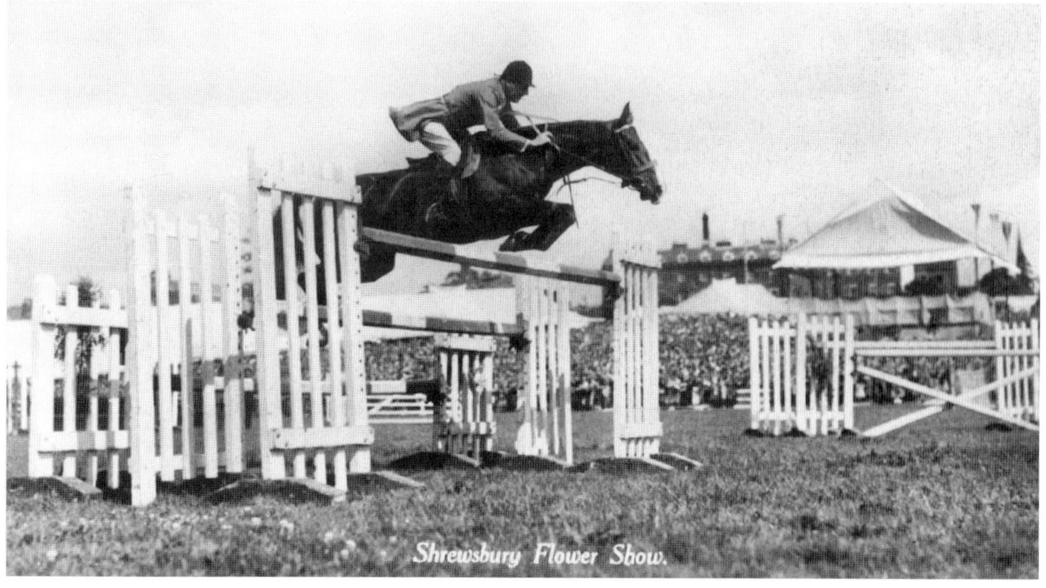

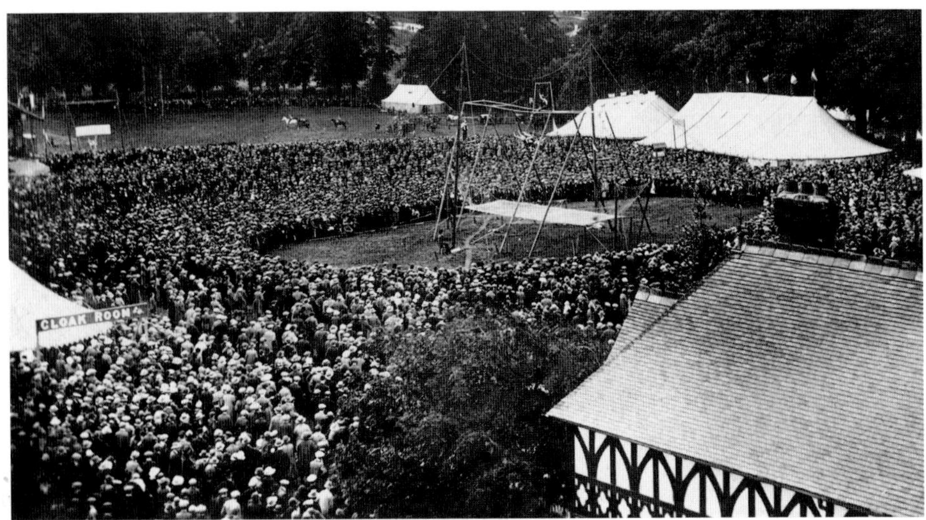

The Quarry and Flower Show, *c.* 1912. This view was taken to the side of Quarry Lodge down to the main arena and the old lime trees on the banks of the Severn. A huge crowd gathered and all eyes were on the trapeze artists. Aerial attractions were first introduced to the show in 1880 and proved a great success bringing gasps of amazement from the audience. In 1901 three aerial performers attended the show, the Luppu Troupe on aerial bars, the Davison Brothers on the high wire with fireworks and the amazing Pedina, a sensational mast performer 100ft above the ground.

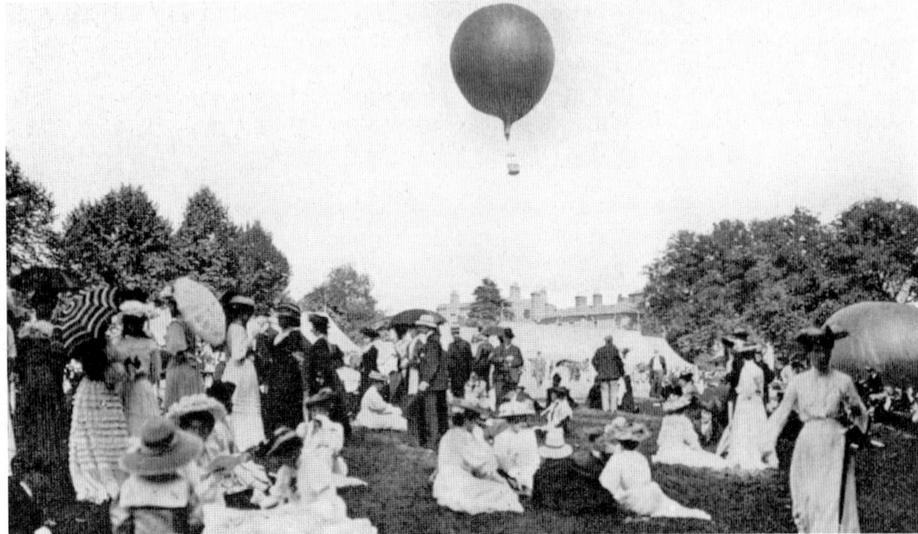

The Quarry and Flower Show, *c.* 1905. The show is also a social occasion where people go to see and be seen and to meet old friends. A good place to meet is by the bandstand where you can enjoy a picnic and listen to the music of a top military band. The Flower Show is also known as Shrewsbury Musical and Floral Fête and music still plays a major part in the two-day event. People picnicking could also watch the balloon ascents. Between 1894 and 1914 Percival and Arthur Spencer from Crystal Palace offered visitors to the show special captive flights for just 5*d*, lifting them up to 500ft into the air at the end of a long rope.

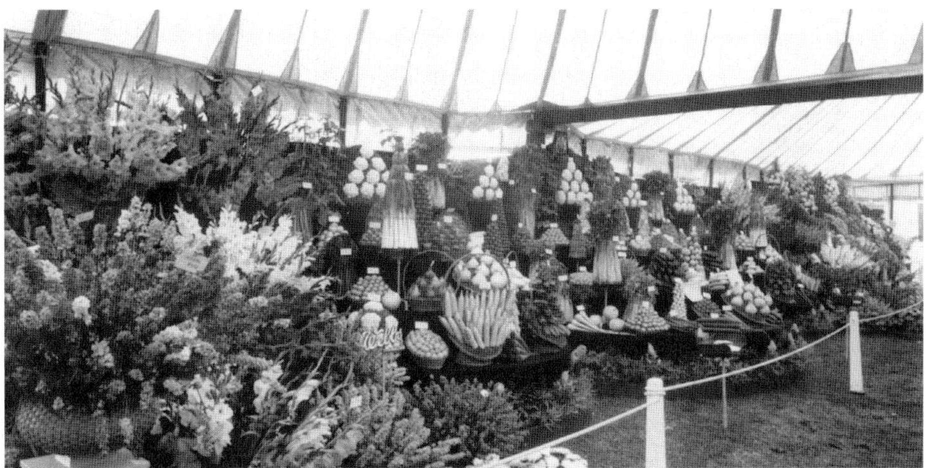

The Quarry and Flower Show, *c.* 1955. This is the main marquee situated at the top of The Quarry by St Chad's Terrace. All the professional exhibitors display their choice plants to the public and the judges in the hope of finding new customers and winning one of the prized gold medals. In the past the coveted gold, silver and bronze medals were made of that substance and are greatly sought after by collectors. Inscribed on each medal is the legend, 'Arte Novas Petimus Natura Educere Formus', which means 'We are always trying to improve on nature'. As well as banks of flowers there are immaculate displays of vegetables.

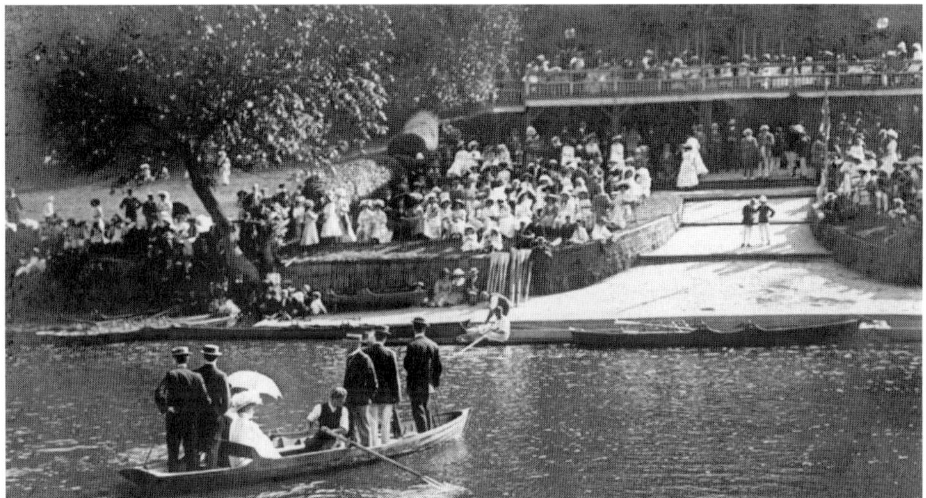

The River Severn, *c.* 1905. Pengwern Boat Club was founded in February 1871 at a protest meeting held at the Lion Hotel against the Shrewsbury Rowing Club and its method of choosing new members. The club took its name from an earlier association formed in 1835, which was reputed to be the first rowing club in the country. It was also known as the Blue Club from the colour of the members' blazers. At first the new club occupied a boathouse on the site of Shrewsbury School's boathouse but moved to these premises in 1881. The architect of the new boathouse was John Laurence Randall of Abbey Foregate. It cost £1,000, which was raised by a special fund. Several other clubs were formed in the nineteenth century including the Amicable Club formed in 1849 by staff from the locomotive works of the Shrewsbury & Hereford Railway and in 1880 the Crusoe Club whose members worked at Maddox Store.

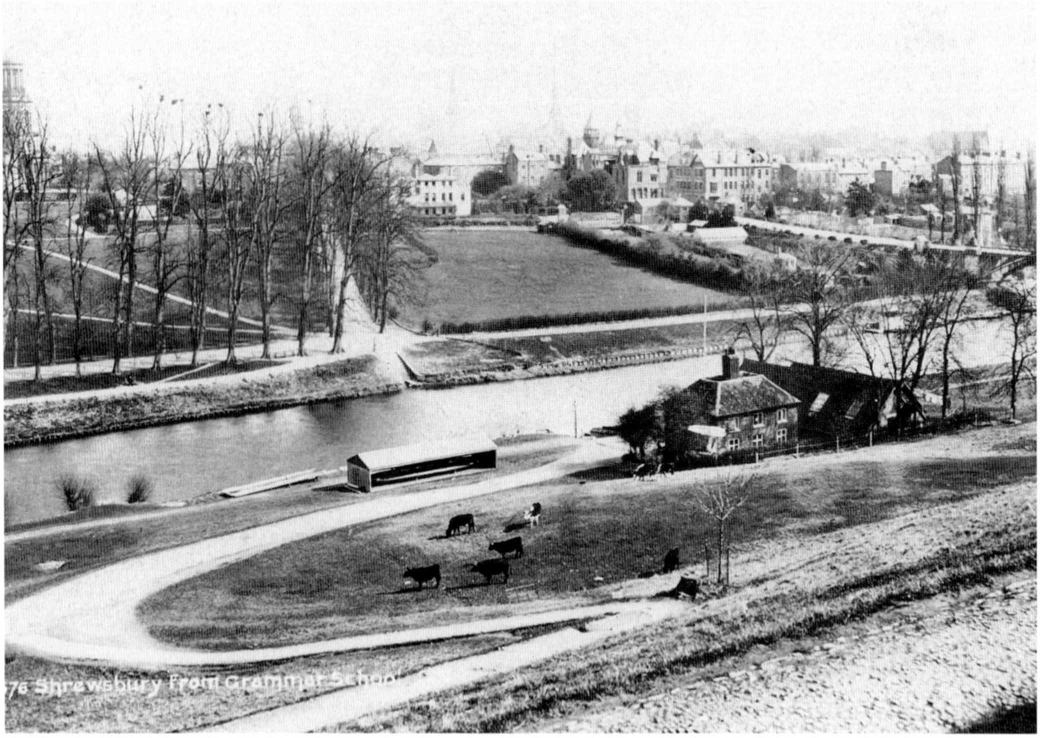

76 Shrewsbury From Grammar School

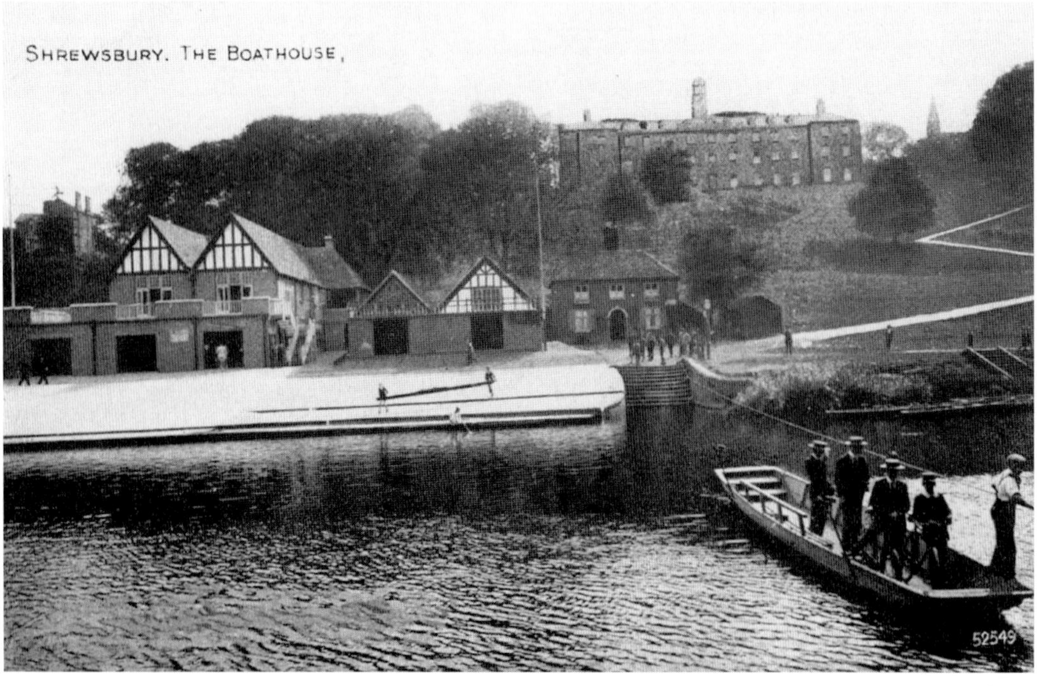

SHREWSBURY. THE BOATHOUSE,
52549

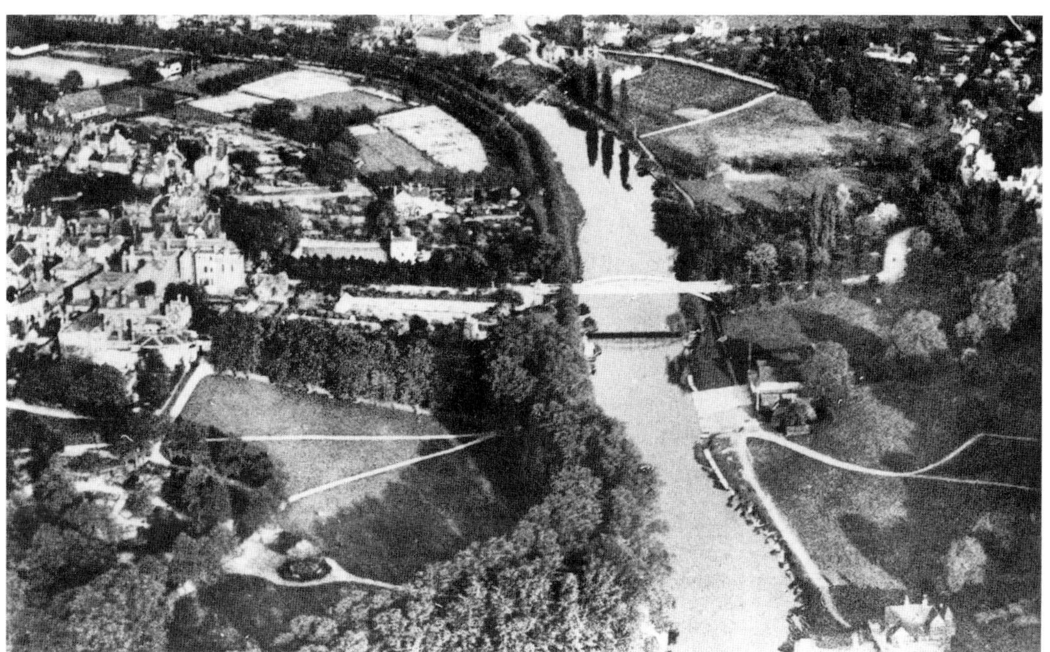

The River Severn, *c.* 1918. Behind the massive lime trees to the left of the river is The Quarry with the bandstand and Dingle. To the right is Beck's Field, perhaps named after John Beck who bought some of the land attached to the foundling hospital in 1826.The riverside path leads from the Pengwern boathouse to the school's boathouse. Straddling the river is the Kingsland Bridge, which was opened in 1882. The lime trees above the bridge on the left were planted in 1897 to commemorate Queen Victoria's Diamond Jubilee. The open area on the opposite bank is Coney Green that was the site of Burr's Lead Works that closed in 1894.

Opposite, top: The River Severn, *c.* 1897. This view was taken from Kingsland towards the town. The old lime trees on the left mark the boundary of The Quarry at that time. The open area between the limes and the Kingsland Bridge was known as Salt's Field and owned by the Salt family who lived in Quarry Place. It became part of The Quarry in 1911 when the Horticultural Society purchased it for £1,842 19*s* 8*d*. After 1897 the river walk from Salt's Field to Greyfriars was widened and planted with lime trees to commemorate Queen Victoria's Diamond Jubilee. The buildings on the river bank are the Prince of Wales Inn and Evans' boathouse, which later became the school boathouse.

Opposite, bottom: The River Severn to Kingsland, *c.* 1910. The building at the top was built as a foundling hospital by Thomas Coram in 1760. After its closure in 1774 it was used as a prison for Dutch soldiers captured during the American War of Independence. In 1784 it became the local workhouse known as the House of Industry until 1871 when it moved to Cross Houses. The building was purchased by Shrewsbury School who moved there in 1882. The Prince of Wales Inn on the right was closed soon after the school moved to Kingsland but the ferry continued to operate until the 1930s. In June 1932 it carried the Prince of Wales over the river after a visit to Shrewsbury School to lay the foundation stone of the Old Wall. To the left are the boathouses. The large one was built in 1920 in memory of J.E. Pugh who was killed during the First World War. It contained a changing room, clubroom and living accommodation for the boatman and his family.

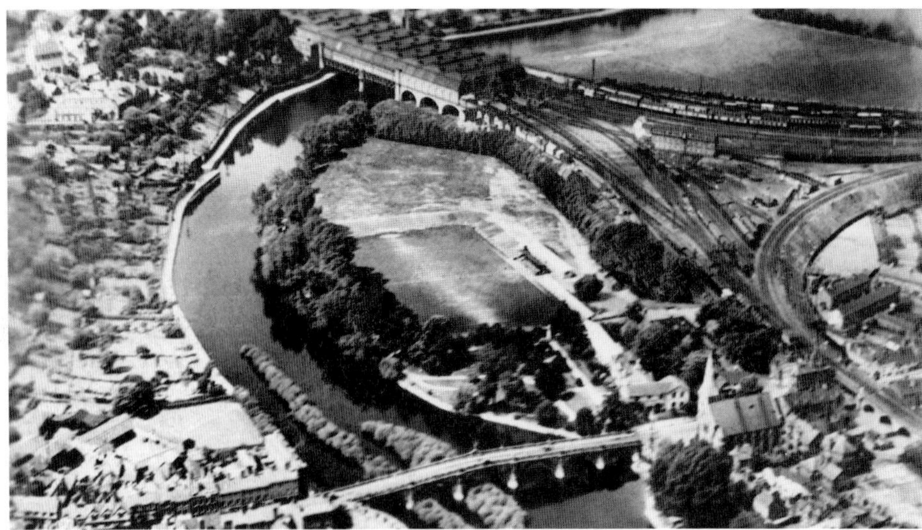

The River Severn, *c.* 1918. At the bottom of this view is the English Bridge before it was rebuilt between 1925 and 1927. It is built over a natural ford created by gravel and silt washed in by the Rea Brook that enters the Severn just upstream of the bridge. The debris also created the impressive islands that were the habitat to a great deal of wildlife, including otters in the first quarter of the last century. To the right of the bridge is the old Technical College, housed in a building erected by stonemason John Carline. Opposite, on the corner of Coleham Head, is the Congregational Church designed by George Bidlake in 1863. The open area in the centre is the Gay Meadow football ground and above that the railway station that spans the river and is covered by an extensive roof. Note the carriages in the siding to the right and the Severn Bridge signal-box just in front.

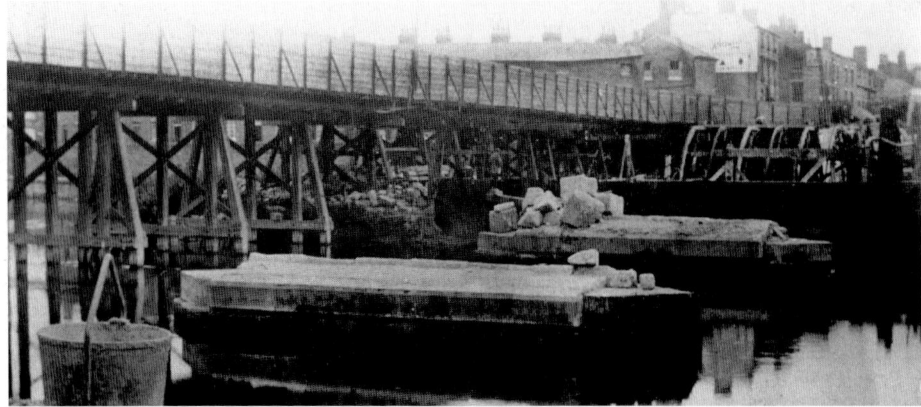

The English Bridge in a view is looking back towards town with Marine Terrace and the Barge Inn just behind, June 1926. Work on the temporary bridge was started on 28 May 1925 and it took two months to build. It was erected on pitch pine trestles spaced 20ft apart. These were spanned by steel girders supporting steel troughs filled with concrete. The road was surfaced with tarmac while the pavement was constructed in wood. Before it was opened the structure was tested by loaded Sentinel wagons weighing up to 12½ tons. In the foreground are the new foundations and the metal girders are in place at the far end over which the stone arches were constructed. The new bridge was opened on Friday 16 September 1927.

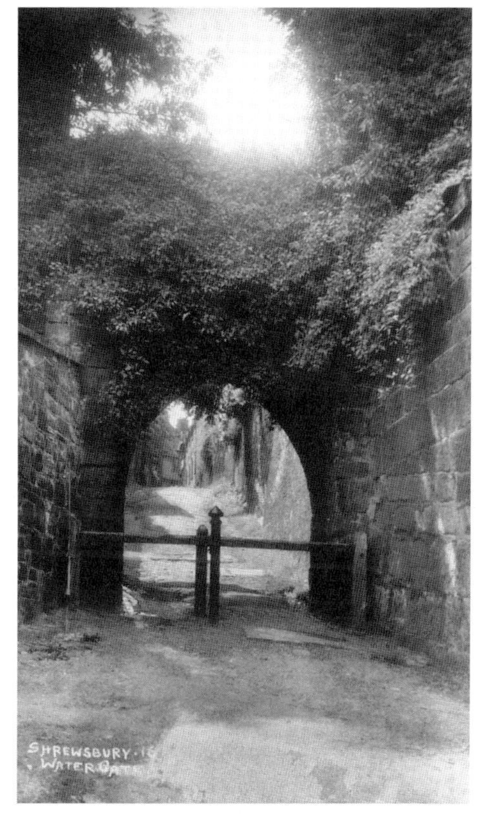

St Mary's Water Lane, *c.* 1925. This steep, narrow hill leads from the banks of the River Severn to Windsor Place and the town centre. The arch is the last remaining gateway into town and dates from the thirteenth century. It was called Water Gate while a second gate, further up the hill where the town wall crossed the lane, was known as St Mary's Gate. Water Gate is also known as Traitor's Gate as during the night of 21 February 1645 Roundhead soldiers were allowed through unopposed and were able to take the castle and the town for the Parliamentary cause.

The River Severn, *c.* 1905. This view looking upstream was taken between 1902 when the extension to the railway viaduct was constructed and 1912 when the weir was completed. On the skyline are the spires of St Alkmund's Church, left, and St Mary's Church, centre. On the right is Laura's Tower. The original stone railway bridge, built between 1847 and 1849, can be seen behind the metal extension. It was sandwiched between two metal extensions built between 1899 and 1902 and covered with a magnificent roof. The arches to the left have a 45ft span and were built out of Broseley bricks with a stone dressing. The extension extended the station over the river, carrying seven platforms and nine lines.

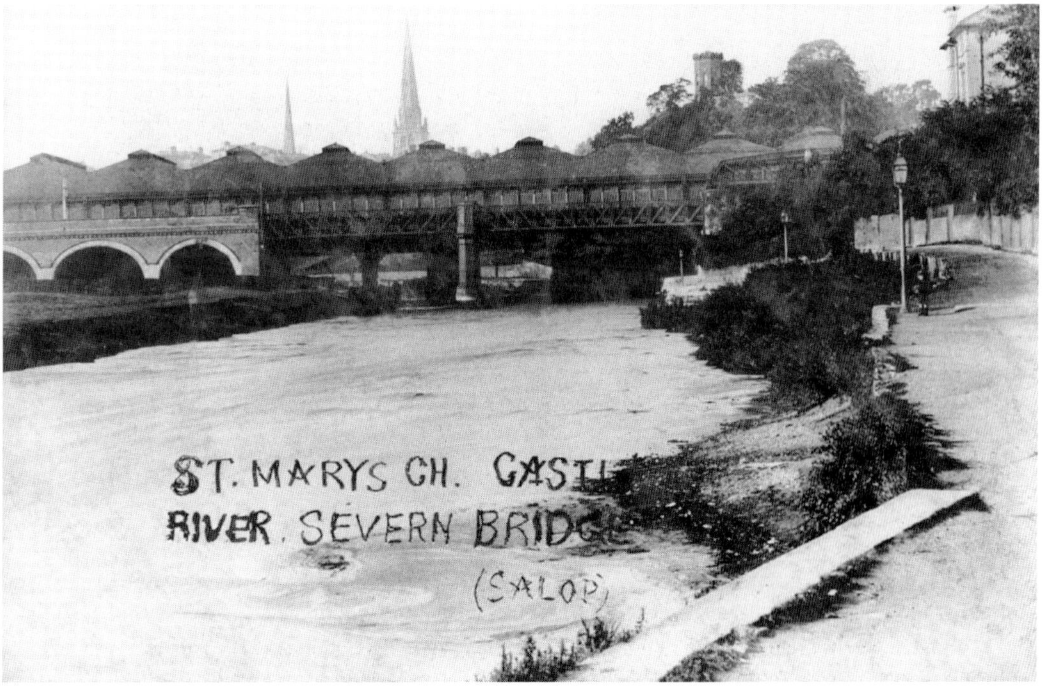

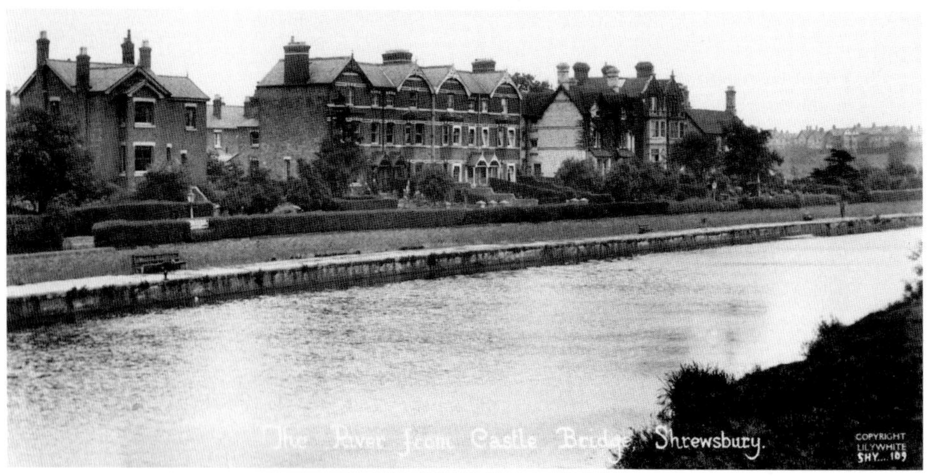

The River Severn to Severn Bank, *c.* 1920. The houses on the Castlefields side of the river between the Castle Walk Bridge and the weir are known as Severn Bank. The impressive building in the centre is split into four houses named, from the left, Hawthorne Villa, South View, Dorset Villa and The Ferns. The Ferns was the home of George Jones Holt, the model of a Victorian self-made man. From a humble railway clerk he built up a thriving beer, wine and spirit business. He retired in 1879 leaving two of his sons to run the firm while he devoted the rest of his life to public service becoming a magistrate, a councillor and then Mayor of Shrewsbury in 1891.

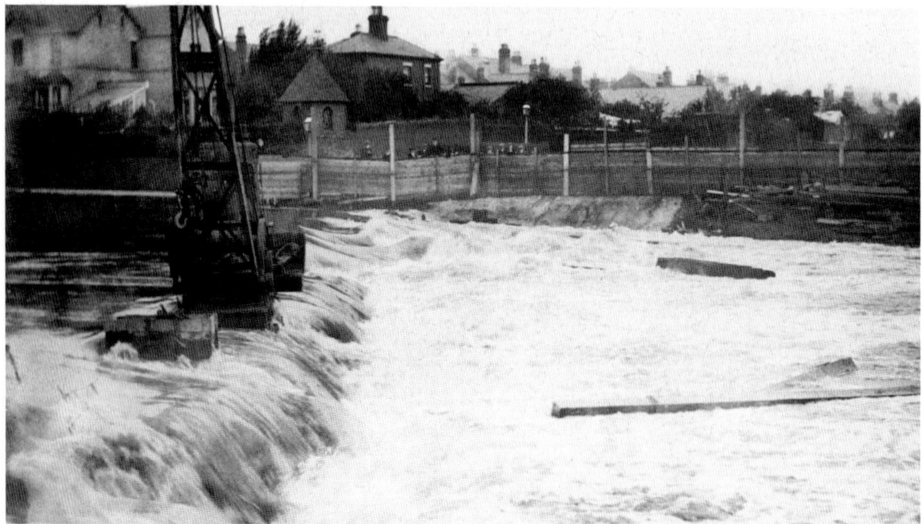

The River Severn and the weir, December 1910. This view is taken from the Underdale side of the river looking towards Castlefields. Note the spectators behind the barricade. When completed, the weir was 195ft in length and attached to the riverbed by green heart wood. It also had a boat ramp to allow smaller craft to move from one level to another. The house on the left is All Saints' vicarage with its brick summer house with the pyramid roof just right of the crane. The flood, which rose to 16ft above summer level, badly disrupted work on the new weir.

9

CASTLE FOREGATE TO THE NORTH

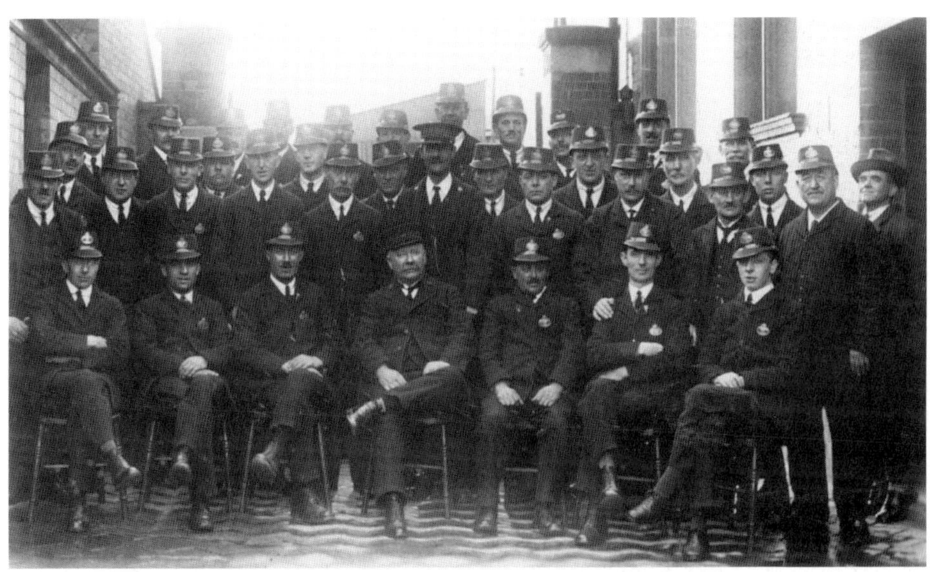

Castle Foregate, *c.* 1915. These are the Shrewsbury postmen, looking very smart in their uniforms with their shako-style hats and highly polished boots. It was taken outside the main gates of the sorting office that faced onto the main road. The sorting office was originally at the rear of the main post office on the corner of Pride Hill and St Mary's Street. Before the sorting office moved here in about 1900 the site was occupied by John Jackson (a tripe dresser), James Nelson (a butcher), Henry Wood (a watchmaker) and Alfred Goodby (a decorator). As well as the sorting office the building also housed the Telegraph Engineer's Department. The man in the front centre could be Thomas James who was postmaster at this time while the man behind in the peaked cap is possibly W.E. Barre, James' superintendent.

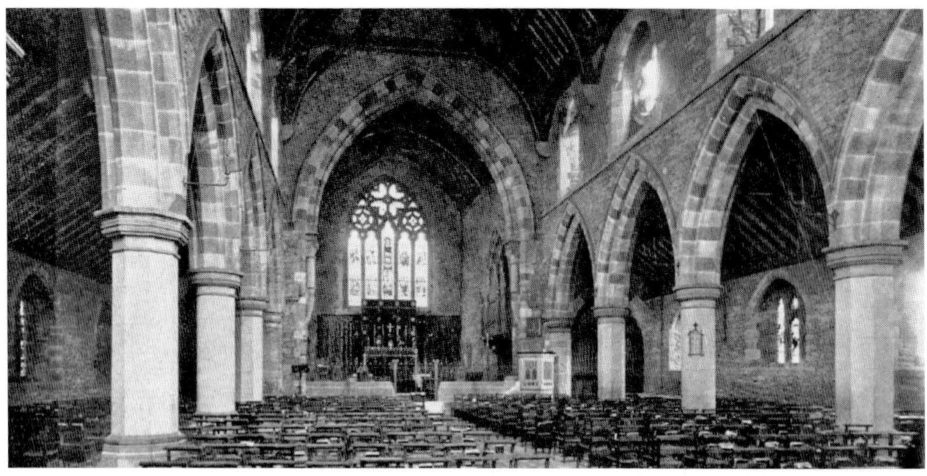

North Street, Castlefields, *c.* 1905. All Saints' Church was designed by Edward Haycock junior and built between 1875 and 1876 on land given by Mr Bulkeley-Owen. A temporary church made out of metal and known locally as the 'Tin Tabernacle' stood on the site and was used for services while the new church was built around it. When the new church was finished it was removed to the top of Argyle Street where it became the Mission Room. All Saints' became a separate parish formed out of St Michael's Church on 28 August 1883. The church consists of a chancel, a nave with a clerestory, side aisles and a south porch. In the north aisle there is a window by Kempe depicting 'Faith, Hope and Charity', while another in the south aisle is from the studio of William Morris.

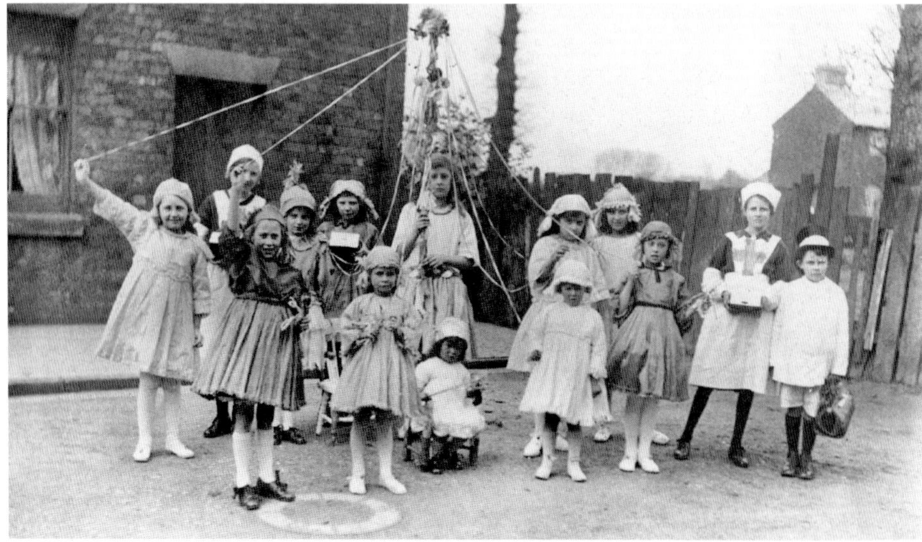

Argyle Street, Castlefields, *c.* 1914. A group of maypole dancers and a boy and a girl dressed as a doctor and nurse pose for the photographer. The occasion is unknown but they could be part of the Cycle Carnival that raised money for local hospitals before 1914 or for fundraising for the VAD hospitals set up in the town to tend wounded soldiers during the First World War. Castlefields is mainly a Victorian suburb and Argyle Street was one of the last streets to be developed, in about 1881. The building in the background is Prospect Cottage.

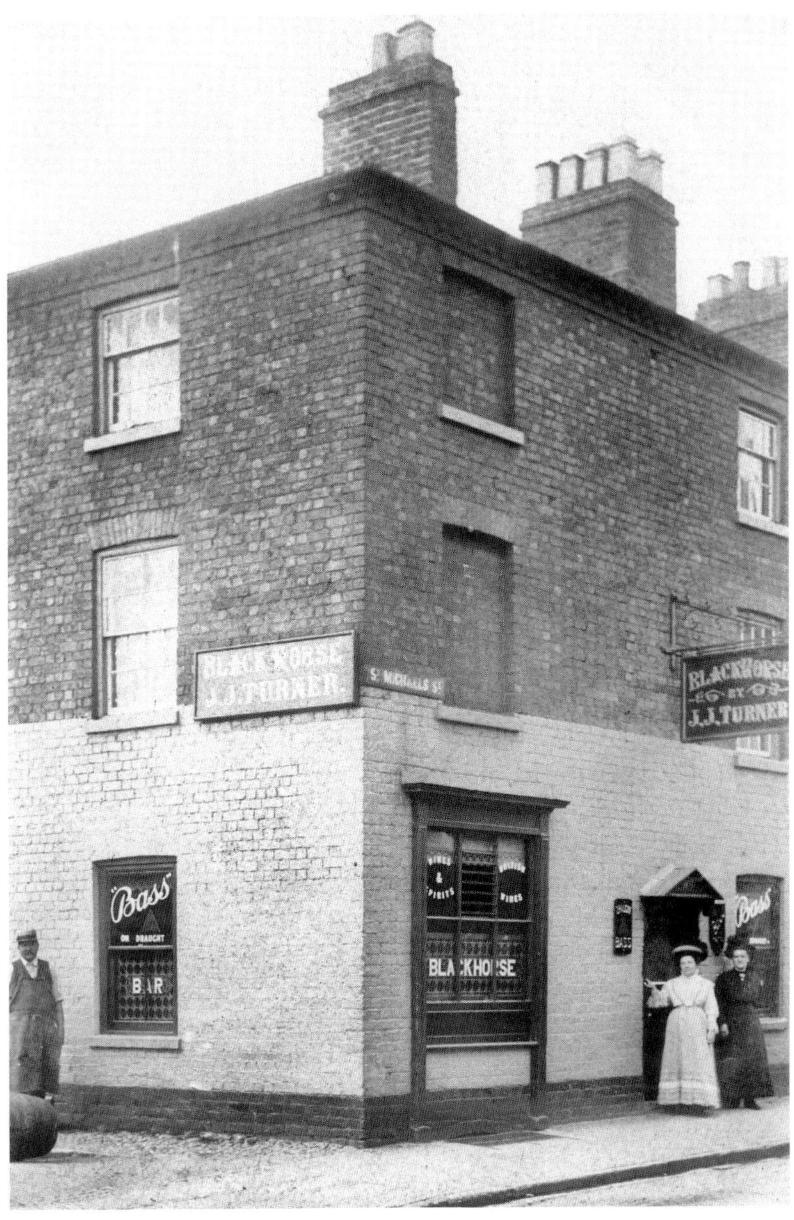

St Michael Street, *c.* 1900. The Black Horse was the first house in St Michael Street. The owner at this time was Mrs Simpson-Newton of Great Malvern, and the landlord was John James Turner, perhaps the man wearing the boater hat on the left. The inn was first recorded at the end of the eighteenth century as the Eagle and was known by that name until 1851. It is believed that an inn known as the Black Horse stood on the opposite side of the road in Castle Foregate on part of the site now occupied by Morris's oil works and when it closed the name was transferred. In 1900 the inn had seven private and two public rooms and could accommodate eight guests overnight. It had two entrances, one in St Michael's Street and one in Simpson's Square. Its customers were mainly working class and a great deal of trade was done through the hatch of the outdoor department.

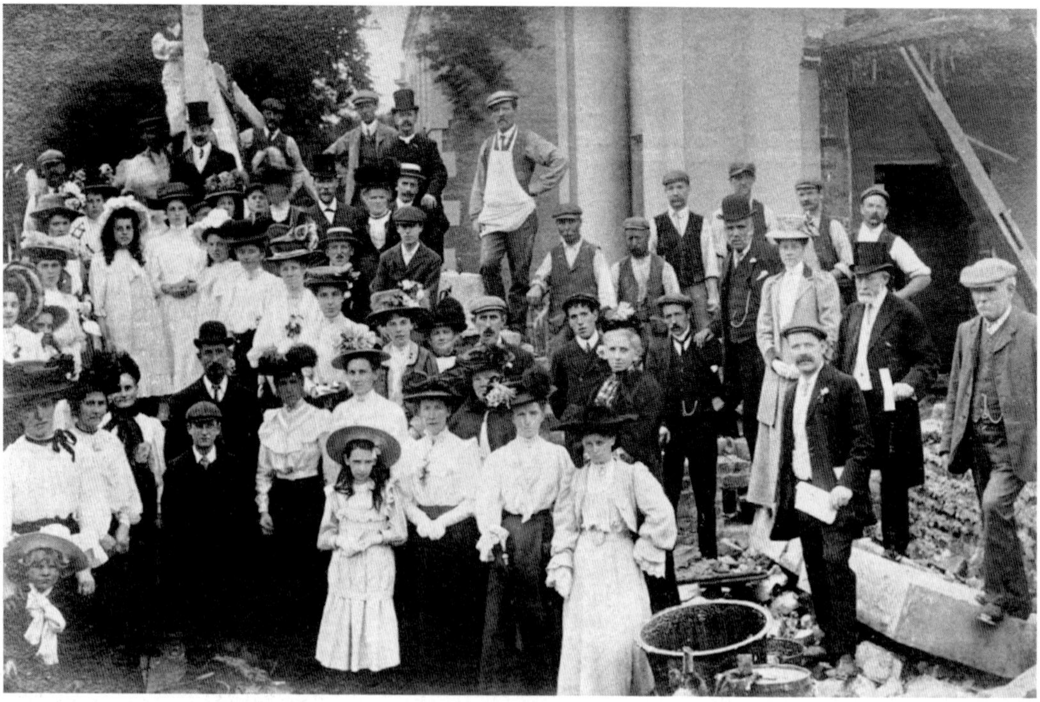

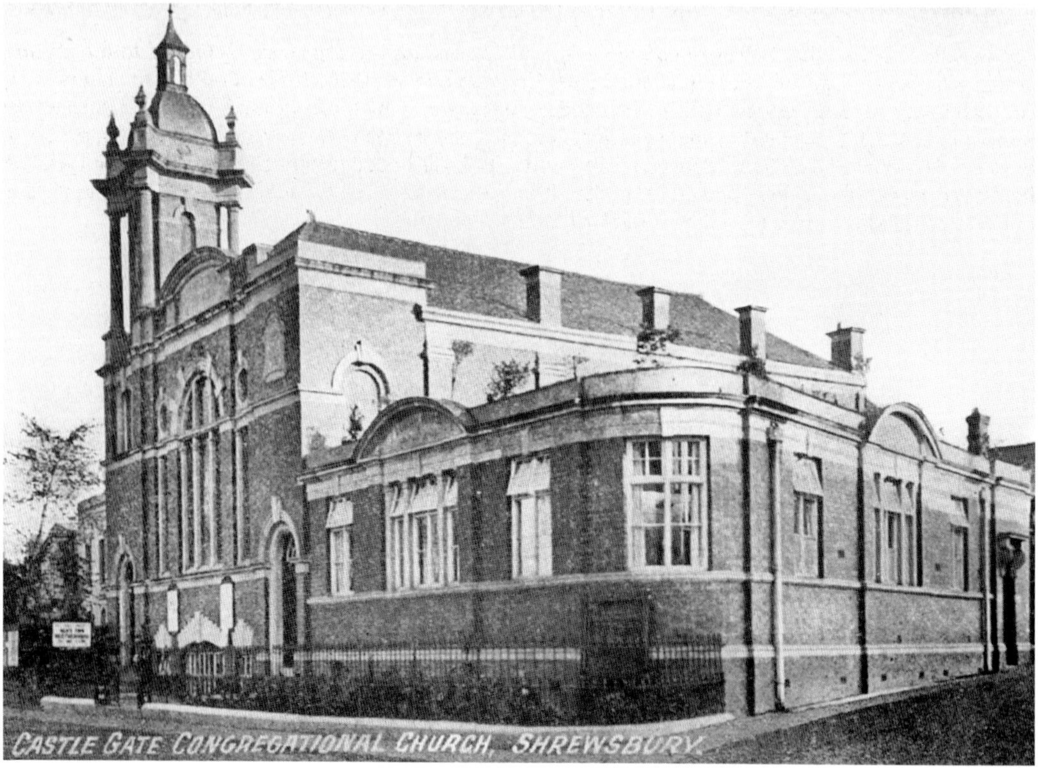

CASTLE GATE CONGREGATIONAL CHURCH, SHREWSBURY.

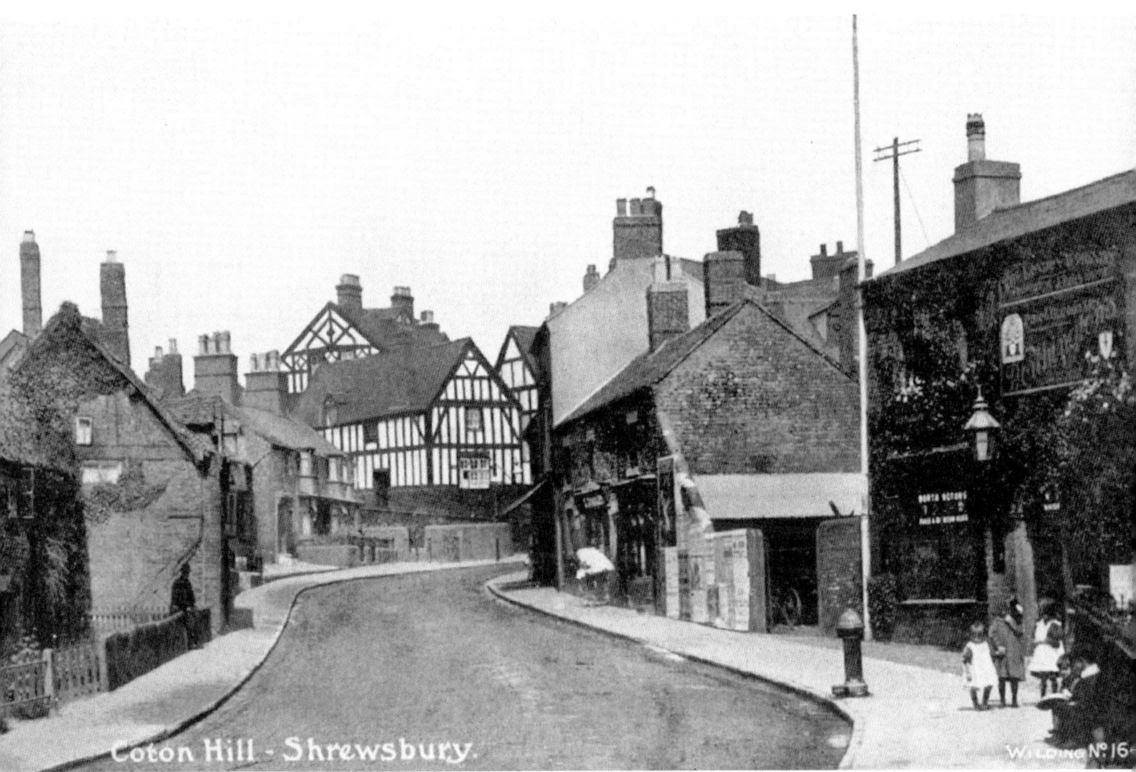

Coton Hill, *c.* 1913. The timber-framed buildings, which included a large barn, belonged to the Mytton family who built a mansion there in about 1500. The mansion was demolished but the outbuildings were converted into cottages. On the right is the London Apprentice, which was formally known as the George Barnwell. It was first licensed in the eighteenth century and by 1900 was owned by Worthington & Co. brewery from Burton-on-Trent. Between 1891 and 1907 Henry Preece was the landlord. Every year he held a Balaclava Dinner there and on his death he was described by the *Chronicle* as a 'Crimean Hero'. The inn was demolished and replaced by a modern building in 1951.

Opposite: Coton Hill, 9 July 1908 and *c.* 1910. The first view shows some of the congregation and workmen at the laying of the foundation stones for the new Congregational Church. The congregation moved to this site in 1909 from their old church opposite Meadow Place on Castle Gates. The building it replaced was the Royal Baths, opened in 1831 by William Onions. The front of the baths was ornamented by a portico supported by two ionic pillars, one of which can be seen next to the workmen. Bagshaw commented in 1851, 'The moderate charges and strict attention to cleanliness and comfort will ensure to them an extensive patronage. The swimming bath is of sufficient dimensions to enable persons to learn or practice the art of swimming. A charge of 21*s* per annum is made for the use of the swimming bath and sixpence for a single bath.' The new church cost over £3,500 and was able to seat 500 people. It was described in 1916 as 'a handsome structure facing the River Severn; it is built of red brick with stone dressings with tower and spacious rooms used for Sunday School.'

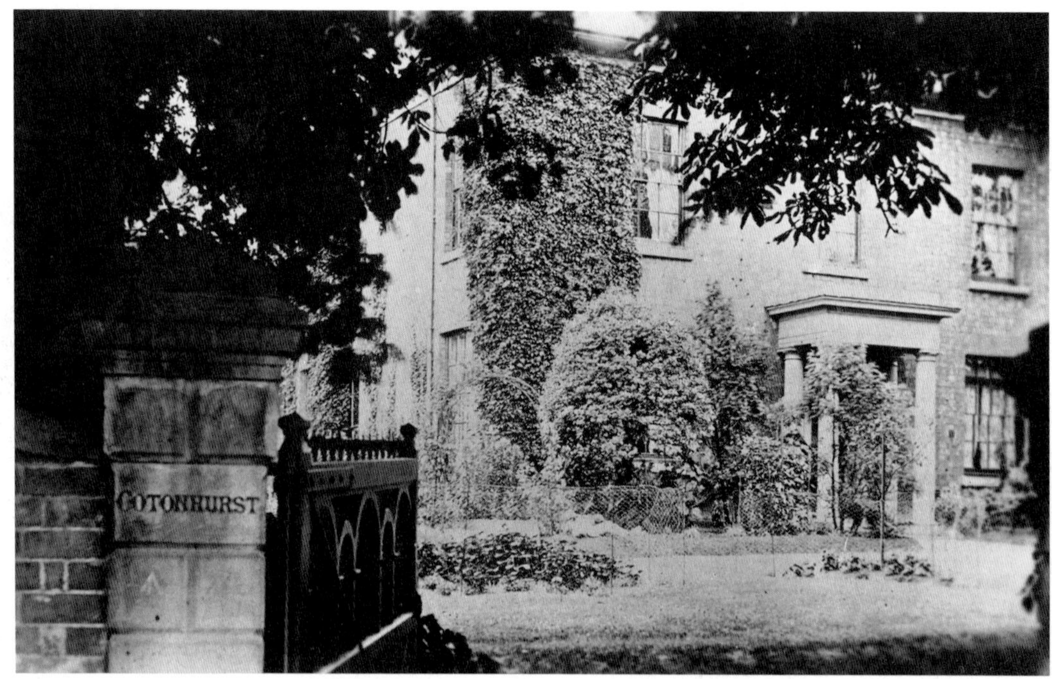

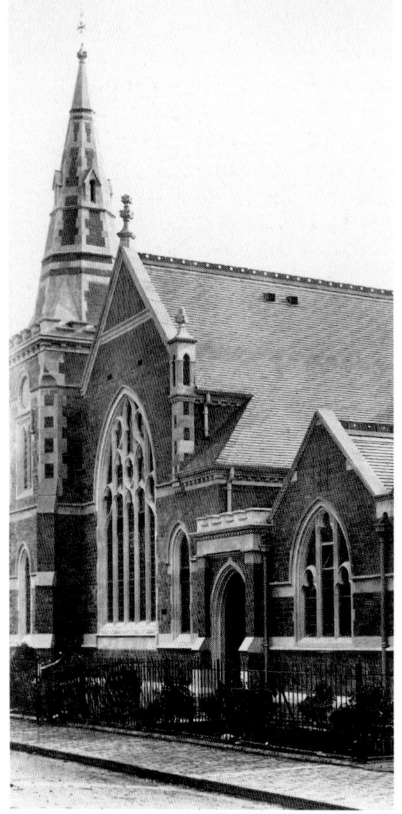

Coton Hill, *c.* 1905. Cotonhurst replaced Coton Villa, the home of Charles Nichols a flannel merchant who was declared bankrupt in 1842. The new house became the home of Thomas Corbett from the mid-1890s until his death in 1917. He was the founder of the Perseverance Iron Works in Castle Foregate and from the garden of Cotonhurst he had a good view of his factory. Previous to this he had lived at 60 Castle Foregate, a house between his factory and the Plough Inn. He was a self-publicist and made several trips around the world to advertise his wares. He was also very involved in local politics and was Mayor of Shrewsbury in 1906/7. His widow continued to live there until the 1930s.

Greenfields, *c.* 1908. The area known as Greenfields was mostly developed in the last twenty years of Queen Victoria's reign. Percy, Hotspur and Falstaff Streets are named after characters made famous by Shakespeare's play *Henry IV*, which depicts the Battle of Shrewsbury in 1405. This Wesleyan Chapel was built on the corner of Greenfield Street and Hotspur Street and opened on 15 October 1908. It was designed by Frederick Davies & Son, architects and surveyors from Avondale, West Hermitage, Belle Vue. It was built out of brick with a stone dressing and had a neat spire and Sunday School room to the right. It cost £2,200 and could seat 250 people. A message on the reverse from A.N. to Mrs Laker of London apologises for not writing sooner but she had been very busy, 'in connection with the opening services of our new church.'

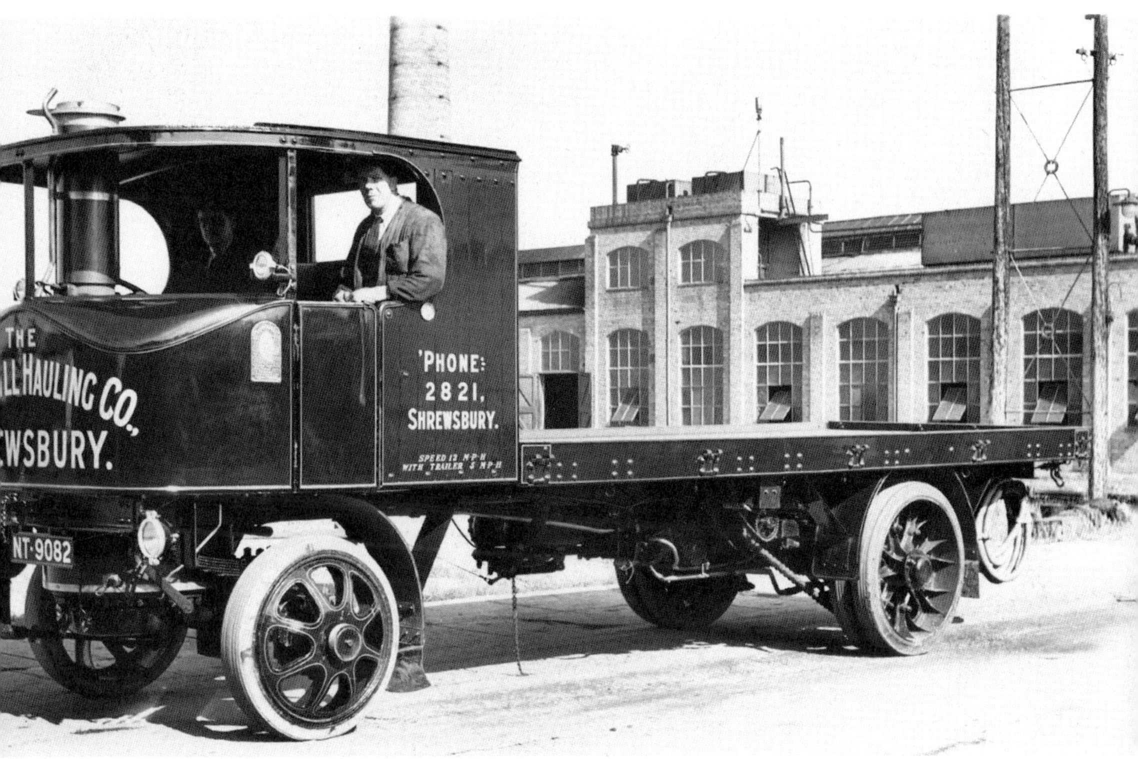

Harlescott, *c.* 1930. This photograph was taken at the rear of the Sentinel Waggon Works. The company always liked to photograph their waggons before they were released to the customers. This model is a D.G.4 and has been sold to the Coton Hill Hauling Co. The speed limit written on the side is 12mph but only 5mph if towing a trailer. The firm of Alley and MacLellan moved to Shrewsbury in 1915. Work began on their new factory in March and by July of that year the first steam waggon had been completed and was ready for testing. The firm traded under the name Sentinel Waggon Works until 1956 when the factory was taken over by Rolls-Royce.

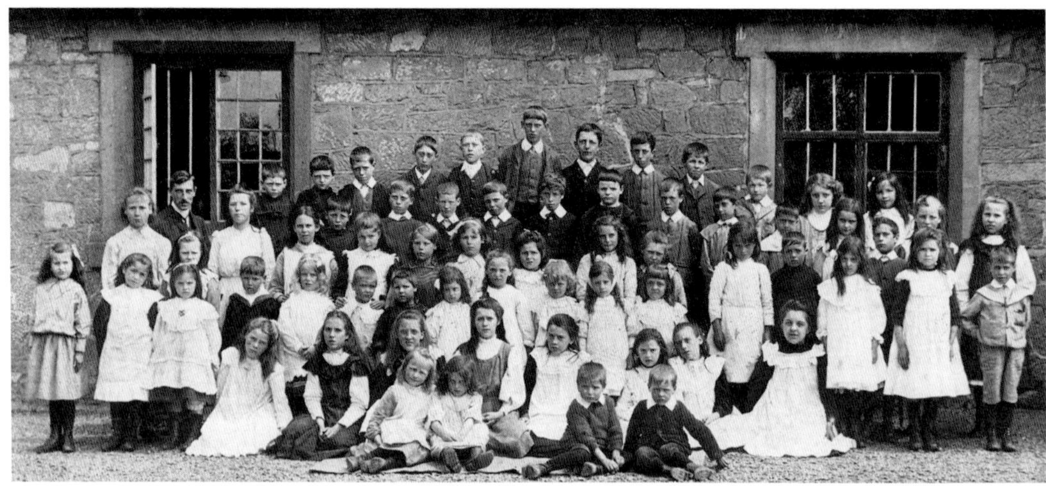

Sundorne School, *c.* 1910. The school was built on the corner of Sundorne Road and Featherbed Lane. *Bagshaw's Directory* of 1851 describes, 'A neat little schoolhouse and residence for the teachers was built in 1849, on the turnpike road leading to Shrewsbury, by A.W. Corbet Esq.; who also munificently supports the institution, which is free to all the children of the tenants upon the Sundorne Estate.' In 1871 the school was still supported by the Corbet family but the children had to pay 1*d* a week. In 1910 the school was capable of accommodating eighty-eight children and the teacher was Mr Isaac Smith. He was followed by Mr Theodore Robinson, the last head teacher of this school. On 2 September 1931 he led the staff and children from the old school to the new Harlescott County School just a few hundred yards up Featherbed Lane.

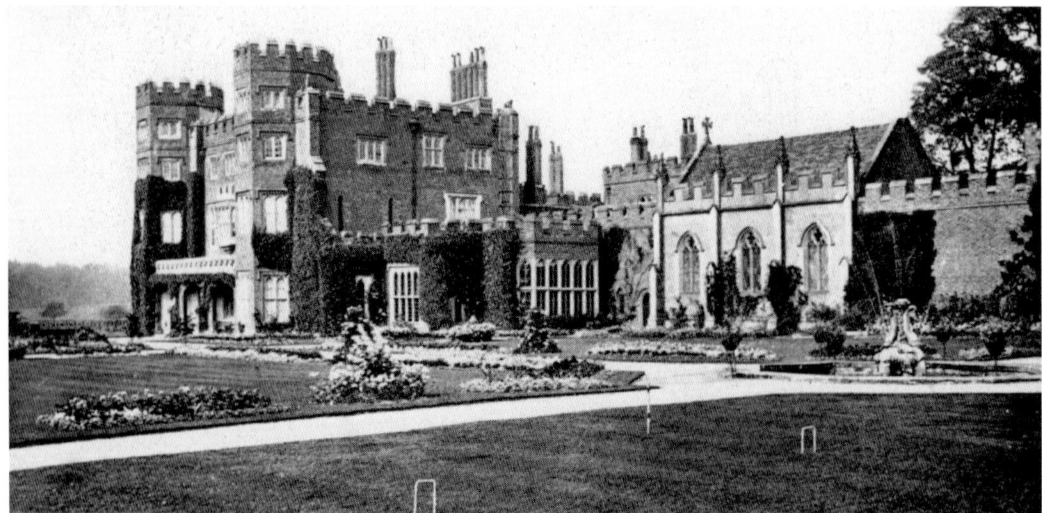

Sundorne Castle, seen here in about 1910, was built at the beginning of the nineteenth century for John Corbet. It was thought to be the work of George Wyatt who created a beautiful mansion of great dimensions with towers, castellated walls, gatehouse and chapel. It stood in parkland of around 80 acres and overlooked a large ornamental lake. In March 1955 the trustees of the castle applied for permission to demolish it and although it was scheduled as being of special architectural and historical interest, there were no objections. The demolition crew moved on to the site in September 1955 and within the month the castle was reduced to rubble. All that remains is the gatehouse, part of a curtain wall and the chapel seen to the right of the main building.

10

ODDS & ENDS

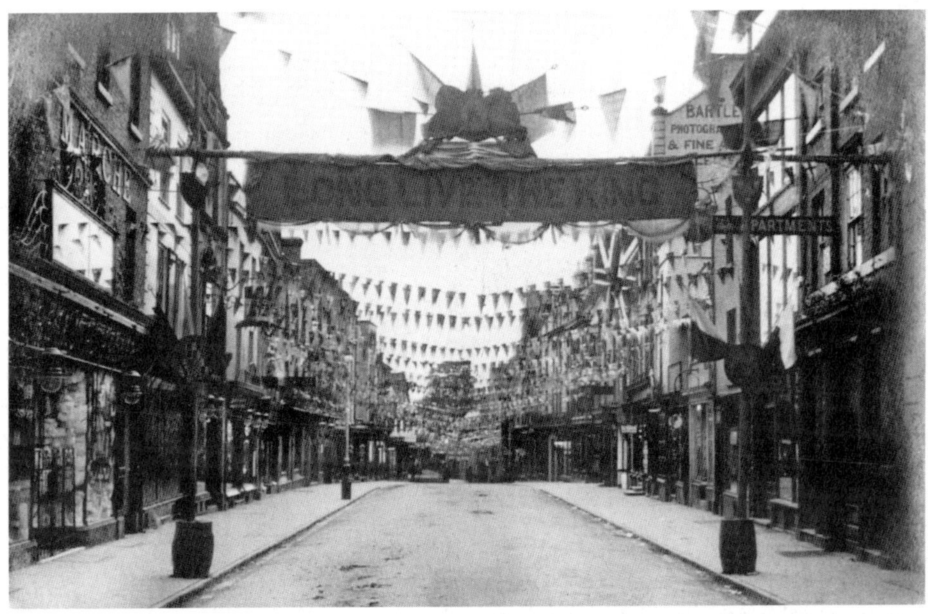

Castle Street, June 1911. This view, probably taken early on a Sunday morning, shows the decorations erected to celebrate the coronation of George V. The legend on the banner reads 'Long Live The King'. The first building on the left houses Bon Marché, a ladies' fancy drapery shop belonging to Arthur Dyer. The shop was later converted into a store for Marks & Spencer. The postcard was sent to Mrs Long in Sussex by her son Arthur. He writes, 'This is a photo of Castle Street as it was decorated for the Coronation. Our shop is marked with an X it has the shutters up.' The shop is just to the right of Bon Marché and is a grocery business belonging to Thomas Bissell Butcher. Next door, slightly hidden by the flags, is Frank Newton's big hat, advertising his gentlemen's outfitters.

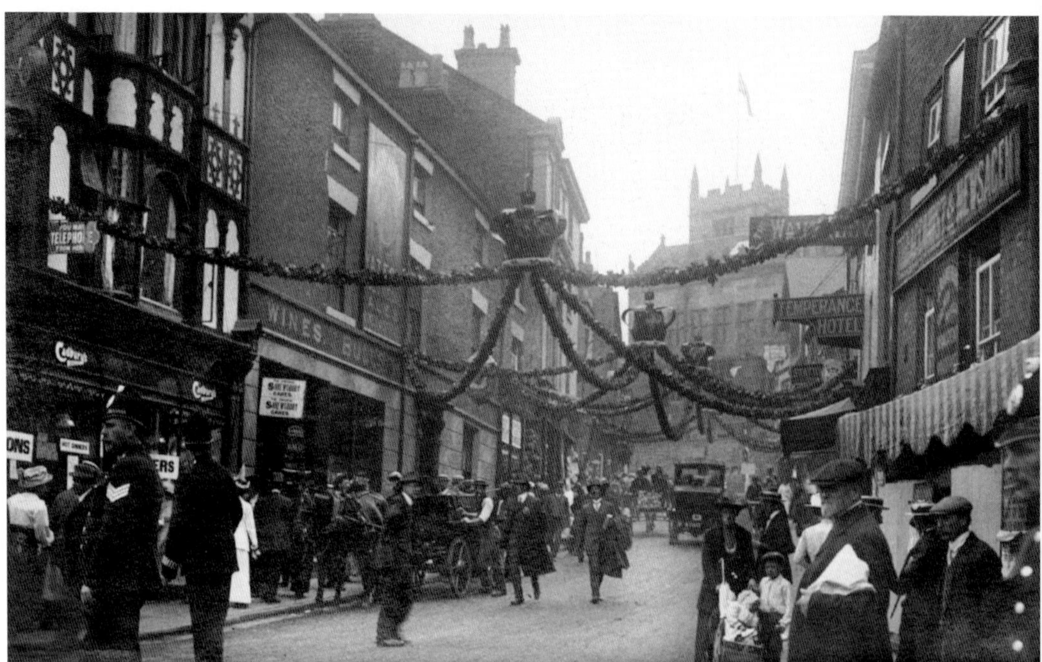

Castle Gates, 3 July 1914. The streets of Shrewsbury were decorated for the arrival of King George V who was visiting the Royal Show on the Racecourse at Monkmoor. This short street was once a drinker's paradise with six pubs within 50 yards of each other. On the left, next to the timber-framed building, is the Bull's Head and just two doors away, the Castle Vaults. Almost opposite is the Station Hotel whose sign can be seen just below the temperance hotel sign. The name was transferred to the Grapes in Castle Foregate just after the Granada cinema was built on the site. The timber-framed building is J.B. Davies' restaurant and confectionery shop. Note the adverts for Shrewsbury Cakes and hot dinners.

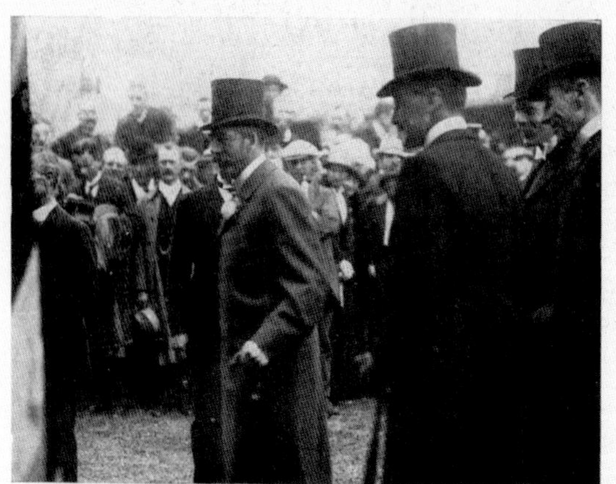

H.M. THE KING

ARRIVING AT OUR STAND — AT THE —

R. A. S. E. SHOW, Shrewsbury 1914.

HARRISON, McGREGOR & Co., Ltd., LEIGH, Lancashire.

GEO. DAVEY, Implement Agent, BAMPTON, Devon.

Monkmoor, 3 July 1914. This is a trade card for George Davey of Bampton, Devon, who was an implement agent for Harrison, McGregor & Co. Ltd of Leigh in Lancashire. The view shows King George V arriving at the Harrison, McGregor stand in Shrewsbury. The Royal Agricultural Society of England was established in May 1838 and incorporated by Royal Charter in March 1840. The king was patron of the show as well as being an exhibitor and he showed a keen interest as he toured the showground. This was the third time the show had visited the town, the two previous occasions being 1845 and 1884. The message on the reverse to Mr Hawkins of Clayhanger reads, 'Dear Sir, Your turnip cutter barrel is now ready for you. Yours Obediently Geo. Davey.'

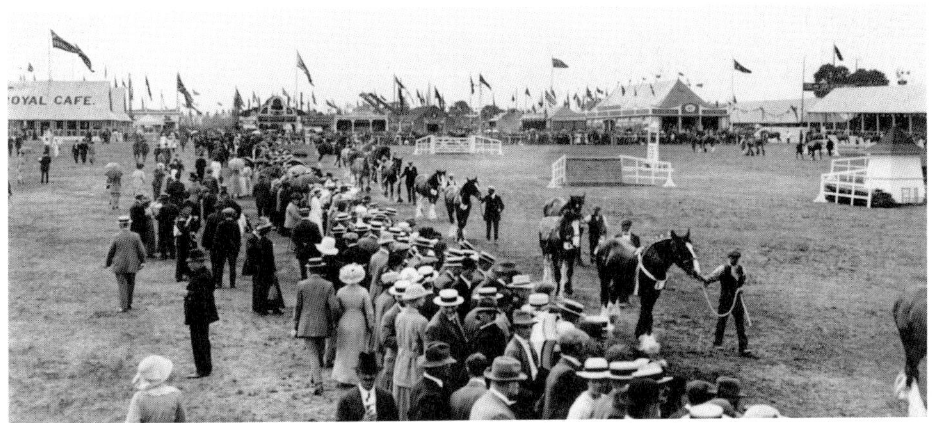

Monkmoor, July 1914. The horse ring at the Royal Show was situated in an area between the old Monkmoor school buildings and Abbots Road. Horses still played a major role in farming in 1914 and 101 classes were being exhibited, from the majestic Shire horses to the small, sturdy Shetland pony. There was also showjumping where competitors were 'required to take the fences at a fair hunting pace'. As well as British agriculture the show also exhibited farming from the Empire and the rest of the world. In the background to the right are marquees displaying goods from Australia and New Zealand. The white stand in the centre was occupied by the Orient Line to Australia who carried the Commonwealth Mail Service. On the extreme left is the Royal Café that catered for the needs of the public along with the Temperance Café on the Monkmoor Road side and the workmen's refreshment tent close to Crowmere Road.

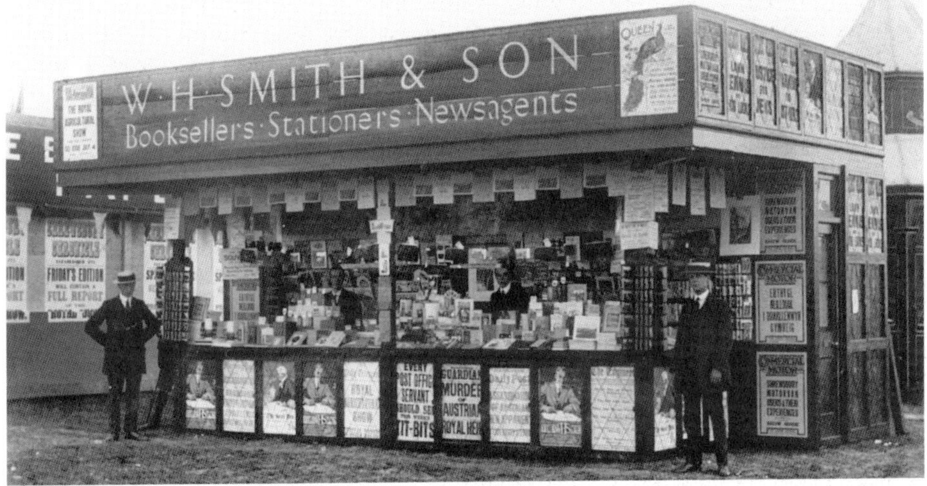

Monkmoor, July 1914. As well as agriculture, other traders attended the show including W.H. Smith & Son. Their stall sold a wide variety of newspapers, books, stationery, handbags and souvenir programmes, as well as postcards of the show. The bumper programme with over 400 pages was priced at sixpence. Many of the posters are printed in Welsh in recognition of the town's close proximity to the Principality. The *Shrewsbury Chronicle* advertises that its Friday edition will 'contain a full report of the Royal Show' while the publication *Tit-bits* urges 'every post office servant' to read their current issue. The *Manchester Guardian*, however, covers a bleaker subject with the headline, 'Murder of Austrian Heir'.

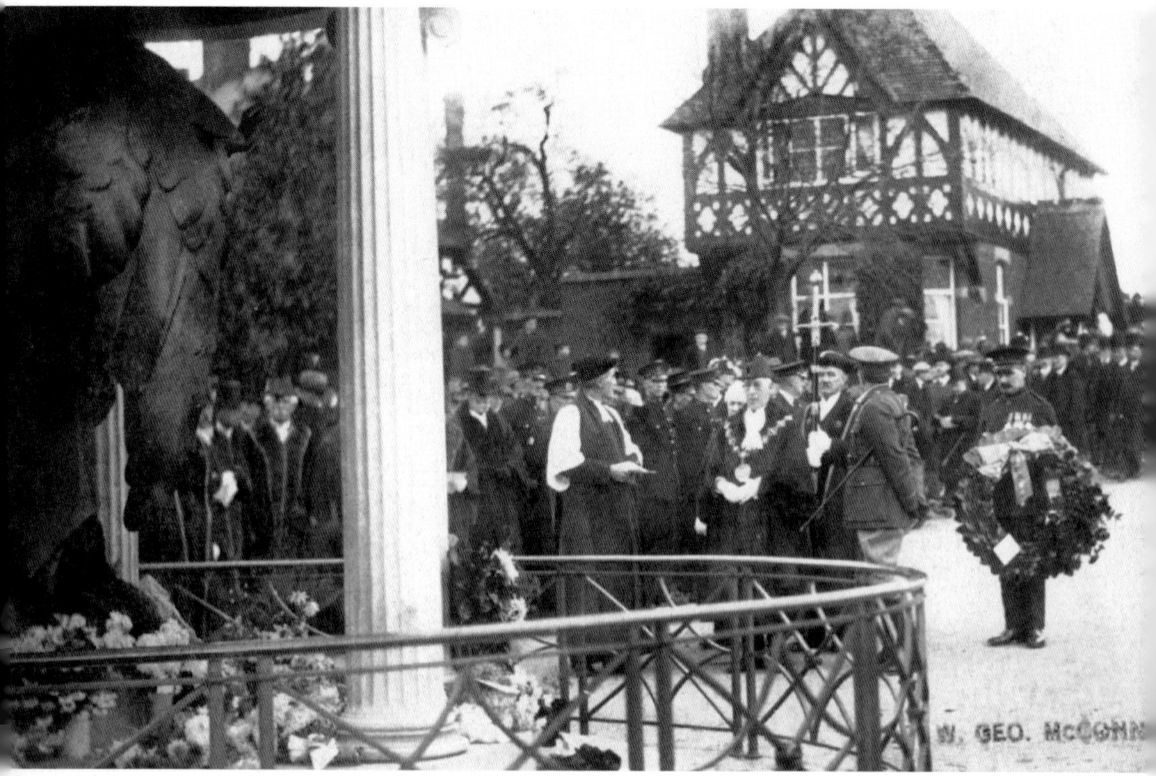

W. GEO. McCONN

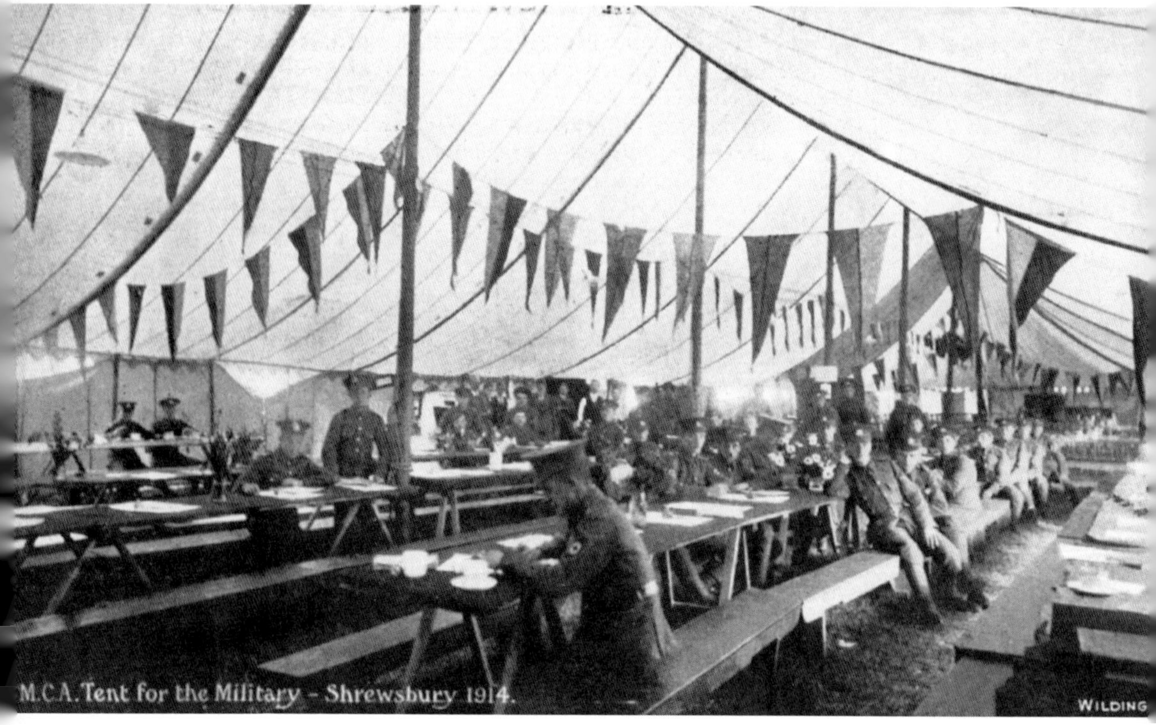

M.C.A. Tent for the Military – Shrewsbury 1914.
WILDING

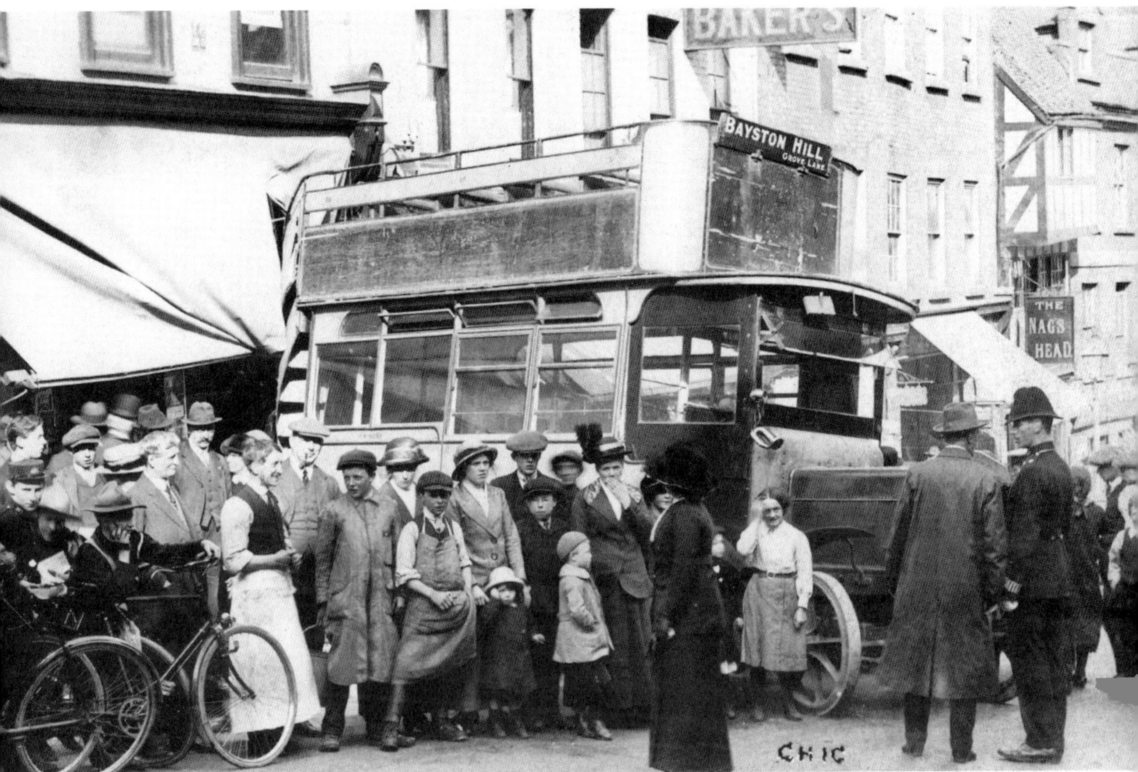

Wyle Cop, 3 May 1915. The double-decker bus belonged to the Allen Omnibus Company that was later taken over by Midland Red. The packed bus was travelling up the Cop with passengers from the Bayston Hill area. Halfway up the steep bank, its drive chain snapped and it began to roll back down the hill until the quick thinking of the driver who mounted the kerb and crashed into Richard Mansell's newspaper and stationery shop. Luckily no-one was passing at the time and his fast response averted a much nastier accident. A crowd of onlookers soon gathered and Chic Photographic Studio situated just below the Nag's Head on the right sent a photographer to record the scene.

Opposite, top: The Quarry, 11 November 1923. This is the first time the Armistice Parade was held around the War Memorial since it was unveiled by the Earl of Powis on 29 July 1923. The mayor, Councillor R. Bates-Maddison, laid a wreath and a brief service was conducted by the Revd Dr Greenway, the mayor's chaplain. The mayor knelt before the memorial and the crowd stood silently as the 'Last Post' was sounded. The service ended with the hymn 'O God Our Help In Ages Past', which was sung by the huge crowd. In the background is Quarry Lodge.

Opposite, bottom: The Quarry, August 1914. This tent was erected by the Shrewsbury branch of the YMCA to cater for the needs of hundreds of soldiers brought to the town at the outbreak of the First World War. It provided reading and writing material, games, music and light refreshments and in the evenings concerts and musical entertainment. A very useful annexe was erected where soldiers could have their clothes mended free of charge by a group of lady volunteers. Chiropody and manicuring was also available, carried out by an experienced nurse. It was estimated that in the first week of the tent opening, over 10,000 letters and postcards had been written.

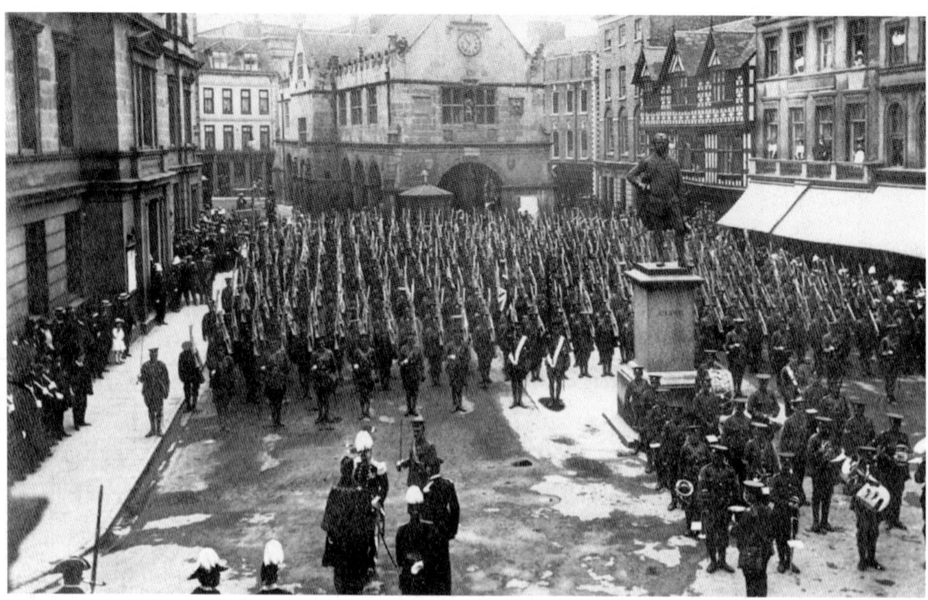

The men of the Third KSLI (Special Reserve) line up in The Square on 14 June 1913 after their return from an annual training camp held at Ross. The regiment had performed well and won great praise from their commanding officer for their discipline and marksmanship. The men arrived back in Shrewsbury looking fit and well and were met by the First Battalion Band and marched to The Square to be received by the mayor and corporation. The troops were then inspected and addressed by the Earl of Powis, the Lord Lieutenant of Shropshire. He praised them for behaving 'in a manner worthy of the great traditions of their regiment.' The men then marched past in columns of four to the Barracks where they were dismissed.

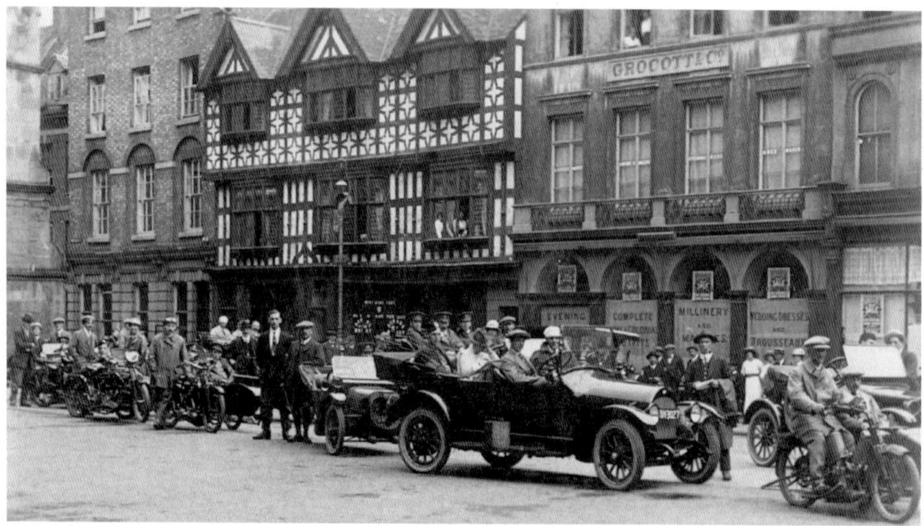

The Square, *c.* 1914. The right-hand side of the timber-framed building is the Plough Inn while the left-hand section was occupied by William Toye, a coal and coke factor. Part of the brick building to the left was used for many years by the Shropshire Country Club whose secretary was H.W. Adnitt, the printer. On the right is Grocott & Co. who were listed as general drapers.

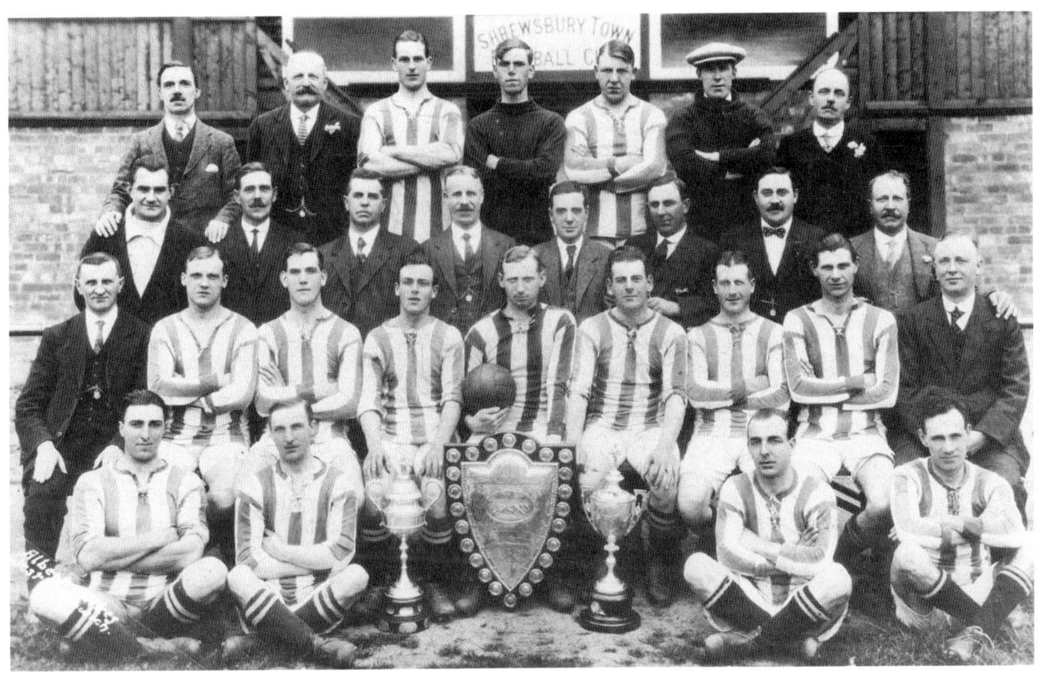

Shrewsbury Town Football Club proudly display their trophies at the end of a very successful season when they became Birmingham League Champions for the first time, April 1923. The team secured the championship with a 2–1 win over their nearest rivals Bilston United in a game that the *Chronicle* described as 'A match outstanding in brilliance.' Goalscorers for Town were Chris Elvidge and Reg Jones. Back row, left to right: Sheldon, Gamble, Crutchley, Causer. Second row: Bowyer, Evans, Gascoigne, Halton, Elvidge, Williams, Whatmore. Front row: Edwards, Jones, Gibson, Taylor. The official without the tie on the extreme left is Sam Powell, the chief masseur and trainer.

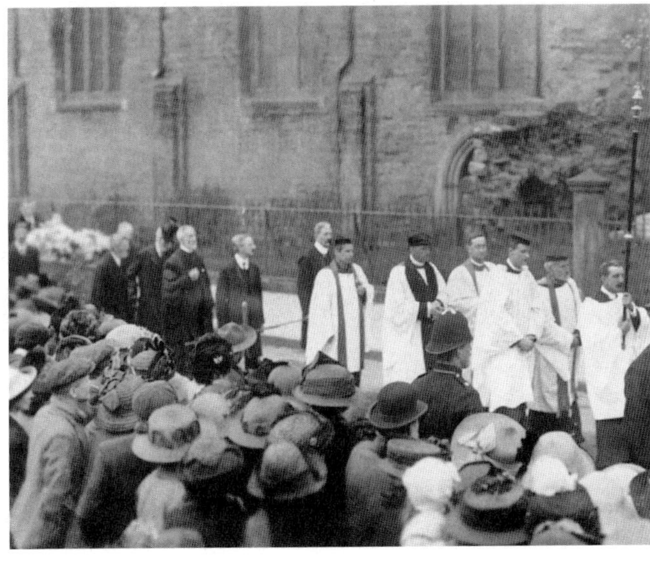

PC Frank Woolham's funeral took place at the Abbey on 24 June 1926. He was killed while on point duty at the Abbey Foregate end of the temporary road bridge. The funeral was described as 'An impressive ceremony', which was attended by the mayor, councillors and police from neighbouring forces. Canon F.A. Hibbert conducted the service and as the coffin entered the church the organist G.W. Tonkiss played Harwood's requiem 'Eternam'. PC Woolham was thirty-eight years old and left a wife and four children. The route of the cortège from his home in Crowmere Road to the Abbey and the cemetery was crowded with mourners.

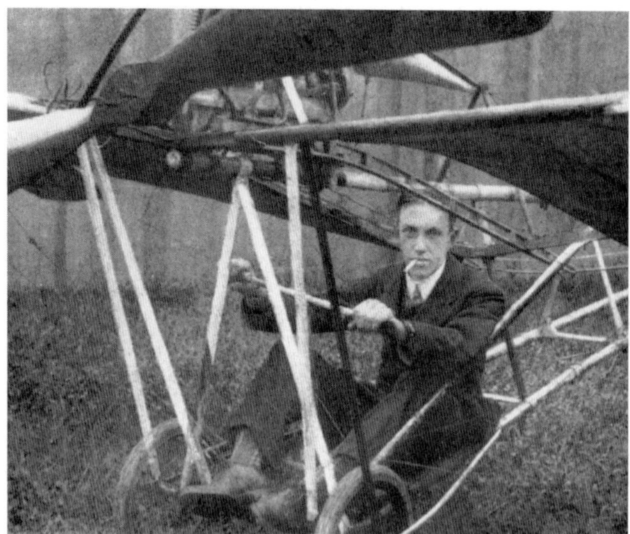

St Mary's Place, Shrewsbury, 1910. This photograph shows seventeen-year-old William Groves sitting in his monoplane. The plane was built from a kit named after the Brazilian aviation pioneer Santos-Dumont and put together in Mr Groves' father's workshop in the Crown Garage. He is reputed to have flown it in Shrewsbury in the summer of 1910 making him the first known aviator in Shropshire. He became a member of the Midland Aero Club and served in the Royal Flying Corps during the First World War, but not as a pilot. The Grove family seem to have been trendsetters in the county as Mr Groves senior is believed to have owned the first car in Shrewsbury, which he used as a taxi.

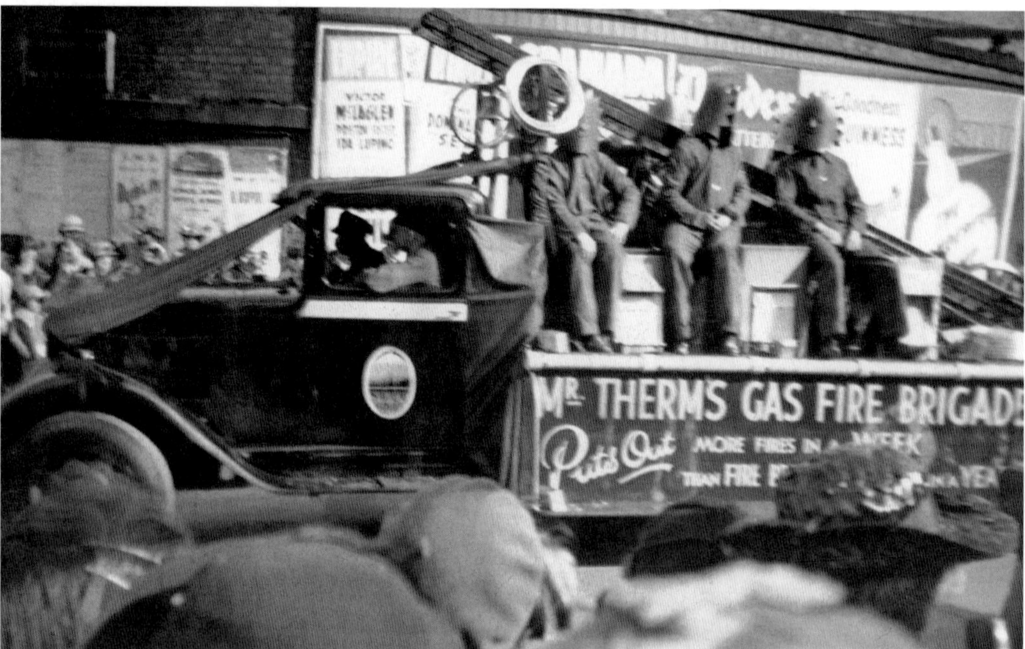

Castle Foregate, 16 September 1930. Mr Therm's Gas Fire Brigade was the Shrewsbury Gas Company's entry in the Shrewsbury Carnival. The *Chronicle* described the vehicle as 'a shiny red fire engine'. It was entered in the local class of trade vehicles, which 'drew some striking exhibits', including Maddox Stores' stately galleon and insurance company Brentnall Beard showing Ann Boleyn making her insurance claim! The photograph is taken on the forecourt of Shrewsbury station. The posters are on the wall of the walk leading up to the Dana. One of the posters advertises the film *Sea Devils* at the Empire. It starred Victor McLaglen, Ida Lupino and Preston Foster and was an 'A' certificate described as, 'A lusty romance, packed with thrills'.

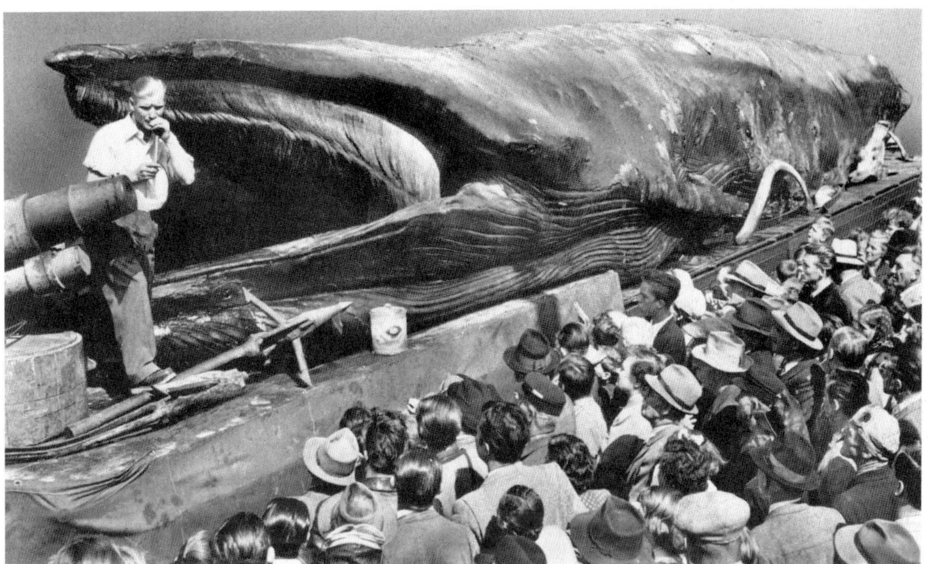

Frankwell, Monday 19 July 1954. An advert in the *Shrewsbury Chronicle* dated 16 July read, 'Attention, One Day Only. Frankwell Recreation Ground. The Norwegian Exhibition Of Jonah The Giant Whale. See The Whale In Its Natural State.' The show was open from 9 a.m. to 9 p.m. and hundreds of people took the opportunity including the three classes from St George's Boys School accompanied by their teachers Mr Thomas, Mr Clarke and Mr Yeomans. The whale was 66ft long and weighed 69 tons. Said to be the weight of 1,000 people, it was exhibited on the world's longest lorry that was parked parallel to the river, close to where the footbridge is now situated.

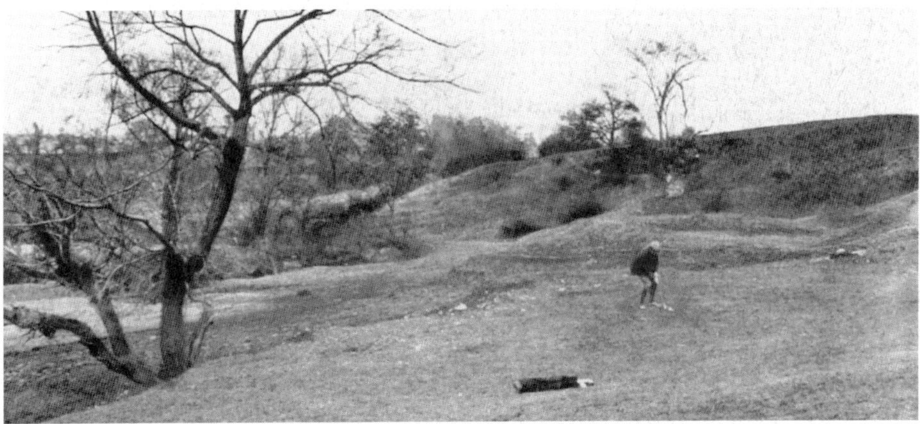

Meole Brace, *c.* 1910. Shrewsbury Golf Club was formed in March 1891 after it moved to Meole from a short and unsuitable course at Hencote, just off the Berwick Road. The course was extended twice in 1903 and 1921. In 1919 an old army hut was purchased as a clubhouse and provided ladies' and gents' changing rooms, a tea room and facilities to cater for the club's social activities. In 1934 the hut was sold for just £20 after a new clubhouse had been erected. The new building catered for all the members' needs and also provided living accommodation for a steward and his family. The club moved to Condover after the size of this course was reduced with the building of the new Column/Meole link road.

ACKNOWLEDGMENTS

In particular I wish to thank all those who have helped me with my research for this new book about our county town. I am once again indebted to the staff at Shropshire Records and Research Centre for their kind and courteous assistance with my enquires. As always, Toby Neal's articles for the nostalgia section of the *Shropshire Star* have proved to be very informative and helpful to me. I am also grateful to Charles Powell and Graham Birch for their encyclopaedic knowledge of the railways, which has helped me with the section on steam engines. I would also like to acknowledge other local authors for the information I have gleaned from their books, which are listed in the bibliography. Last but not least, I would like to thank my wife Wendy for carefully reading through the text and for all her help and support.

BIBLIOGRAPHY

Forrest, H.E., *The Old Houses of Shrewsbury*, Wilding & Son, 1920
——, *The Old Churches of Shrewsbury*, Wilding & Son, 1920
Hobbs, J.L., *Shrewsbury Street Names*, Wilding & Son, 1954
Kelly's Directories of Shropshire, various dates
Lloyd, L.C., *The Inns of Shrewsbury*, Reprint Shropshire Libraries, 1976
Moran, M., *Vernacular Buildings of Shropshire*, Logaston Press, 2003
Morriss, R.K., *Rail Centres: Shrewsbury*, Ian Allan Ltd, 1986
——, *The Buildings of Shrewsbury*, Sutton, 1993
Oldham, J.B., *A History of Shrewsbury School*, Basil Blackwell, 1952
Pidgeon, H., *Memorials of Shrewsbury*, J.H. Leeke, 1851
Rees, H., *Tour of Shrewsbury Sights*, Howell Rees, 2000
Riley, G., *The World's Wonder Show*, Shropshire Horticultural Soc., 1988
Shrewsbury Chronicle, various dates
Trinder, B. (ed), *Victorian Shrewsbury*, Shropshire Libraries, 1984
——, *Beyond The Bridges*, Phillimore & Co. Ltd, 2006
Ward, A.W., *The Bridges of Shrewsbury*, Wilding & Son, 1935
——, *Shrewsbury, A Rich Heritage*, Wilding & Son, 1946